C000067545

WELCOME
TO THE
REVOLUTION

"Finally a manifesto for management that makes sense of the past and takes us beyond the millennium".
Anita Roddick, founder and chief executive of The Body Shop

WELCOME
TO THE
REVOLUTION

◆

Managing Paradox
in the 21st Century

◆

Professor
Tom Cannon

London · Hong Kong · Johannesburg · Melbourne
Singapore · Washington DC

This book is dedicated to
Jean and Bernard

PITMAN PUBLISHING
128 Long Acre, London WC2E 9AN
Tel: +44 (0)171 447 2000
Fax: +44 (0)171 240 5771

A Division of Pearson Professional Limited

First published in Great Britain 1996

© Pearson Professional Limited 1996

The right of Professor Tom Cannon to be identified as author of
this work has been asserted by him in accordance with the
Copyright, Designs, and Patents Act 1988.

ISBN 0 273 62049 5

British Library Cataloguing in Publication Data
A CIP catalogue record for this book can be obtained
from the British Library.

1 3 5 7 9 10 8 6 4 2

Typeset by Pantek Arts, Maidstone, Kent
Printed and bound in Great Britain by
Biddles Ltd, Guildford and King's Lynn

The Publishers' policy is to use paper manufactured from sustainable forests.

About the Author

PROFESSOR TOM CANNON is the Chief Executive of Management Charter Initiative. He is also the Chairman of MDE Services, and the Mercers' School Memorial Professor of Commerce at Gresham College, as well as visiting Professor of Business at Kingston University. He holds non-executive directorships in a number of UK companies. Earlier in his career, he was Director of Manchester Business School and was founding Professor and Head of Business Management at Stirling University. Earlier appointments included the Universities of Durham, Middlesex and Warwick, and marketing management posts in consumer and industrial goods companies. He was the Founding Director of the Scottish Enterprise Foundation and the International Institute for Corporate Responsibility.

He has strong links with policy makers in government and industry in the UK and the EU as well as Australia, New Zealand, the USA, CIS, India and Pakistan. His consultancy includes work in Britain, Europe and the USA for firms such as Virgin, IBM, Shell, ICI, Mirror Group Newspapers, Burson-Marsteller and Hong Kong & Shanghai Banking Corporation. He was joint Chair of the Institute of Management's Management Development to the Millennium study in 1994.

He makes regular contributions in all areas of the media. This includes the best selling *Guinness Book of Business Records,* and *How to Get Ahead in Business* for Virgin Publishing, 14 other books notably *Women as Entrepreneurs* and *Corporate Responsibility: Issues in Business Ethics, Governance and the Environment,* besides almost a hundred academic and professional papers largely in the fields of marketing, enterprise development and innovation. He broadcasts on TV and radio and also writes for national and international newspapers and magazines.

CONTENTS

◆

Part II
ENTERING THE PARADOX

Contents

Part III
THE MILLENNIUM MANAGER

◆

Industry and commerce face the same challenge today – they can resist the revolution or adapt. The price of resistance is high but the returns from adaptation are vast.

◆

Preface

◆

WELCOME TO THE REVOLUTION

"The [production] system Ford created [on the River Rouge] boggles the mind. ... Ships and rail cars delivered steady streams of iron ore, coal and limestone continuously to blast furnaces from which iron went directly to a casting foundry where engine blocks and other parts were made in a continuous flow."[1] Henry Ford claimed[2] that in 1926 "our production cycle is about eighty one hours from the mine to the finished machines in the freight car, or three days and nine hours (from ore to car)". In his book, *Today and tomorrow,*[3] Ford went beyond a catalog of his achievements to a clear vision that he had created the production system of the future. It expressed his confidence that industrialization had reached its peak in scale and form. The production system created by Ford was a true wonder of its age. Its impact is still seen today.

At the heart of this book, however, lies a challenge to the systems, structures and thinking of Ford and his contemporaries. They created systems of production, organizational structures and ways of thinking that are increasingly irrelevant to modern technologies and market conditions. Attempts to hold onto these approaches are barriers to success to the individual, the enterprise and the community. Managers who want to prosper, build successful enterprises and contribute to the health of their society have not only to redesign their systems of production, challenge existing assumptions about the best ways to organize work, they must also rethink their assumptions and ways of managing.

Many will find the challenge uncomfortable, even inimical, to their established assumptions. After all, our old ways of working are not so bad really. The failure of old style managers to hold on to their position in markets as diverse as vehicles, white goods, electronics, textiles, ship building, construction, toys and steel can be blamed on government, unions, workers and even customers. The fundamentals of good management are right, have always been right and always will be right. This comfortable belief is rejected in the following pages. The central tenet of this book is that the right way to manage changes with economic, technological, market and social conditions. The first industrial revolution at the end of the 18th century produced a way of managing people and resources that was, perhaps, the most important determinant of long-term success. Proprietor capitalism depended on the ability of owner–managers to exercise effective control of local, medium sized multi functional enterprises that were largely dedicated to the production of a single product. At the end of the last century, a new kind of enterprise emerged. This was the giant, multifunctional, multiproduct firm. It required a new kind of professional manager with specialist, functional skills and production knowledge. Managerial capitalism depends and has depended for most of this century on these professional or technical experts.

the right way to manage changes with economic, technological, market and social conditions.

The achievements of managerial capitalism are vast. In its most confident form, it played a vital role in providing the resources to win World War II. It produced goods and services in vast numbers to meet the needs of expanding world markets. Its limitations are, however, increasingly evident. Ford's factory at Highland Park symbolized a change from the way of thinking about organization and operations that characterized the 19th century. In the same way, General Motors' problem development at Hamtramck represents the current transition. It took Fordism – the dominance of scale and machine to its logical conclusion – at the wrong time. New approaches to management were emerging which reflected new needs and new circumstances. In this book, these ideas and the challenges they present to individual managers, their enterprises, educators and communities are outlined.

The ways forward are already emerging. They can be seen in the success of those firms that have faced up to the risks involved in change and built responses based on current reality not habit, wishful thinking or easy options. Change is endemic today. Technologies, markets and organizations are more dynamic than at any time in history. Products based on an innovative technology can emerge, gain global prominence and virtually disappear in a few years. This is as true for Cabbage Patch Dolls as it is for laser disks, integrated software systems like Lotus Symphony and semi manipulable, robotic arms.

Technology life cycles are shrinking in response to the push of innovation and the pull of market demand. Radio and film took 40 years to move from innovations to mature products, the portable telephone took 4 years to shift from being an exciting novelty to a public nuisance. Technology push increases as the science base expands with more PhD students, larger research establishments and growth in Research and Development expenditure.

Technology life cycles are shrinking in response to the push of innovation and the pull of market demand.

Markets show no sign of being satiated. Consumers, especially those with disposable incomes, expect a constant flow of new products and services. Surveys of industrial and retail buyers consistently show that they expect to be more innovative. They anticipate more innovation from their suppliers with shorter lead times and more features. The same demands and pressures exist in the public sector with constant demands for new products or services in sectors as diverse as defense and education.

Organizations are obliged to adapt to these changes or fail to meet the needs of their shareholders, clients, employees or communities. The fierce debate about the ways to manage successfully in the contemporary environment reflects the wider environmental turbulence. The focus on core competences or the pressure to reengineer are symptoms of the effort to get control of the business in the face of turbulence in the wider environment.

Organizations and their managers are expected to reinvent themselves to cope with change while holding onto their core competences and capabilities to sustain themselves and keep ahead of their rivals.[4] In this environment, successful innovators do not merely adopt new technologies, they adapt their business and work practices to new technologies. They seek technologies which allow them to jump generation gaps in products, processes and services.[5]

The combination of these technological, environmental, economic and organizational changes transforms the nature of the changes facing modern management. The increase in the quantity of change which characterized the post World War II era has been transformed into a qualitative shift in the nature of change. This shift is partly a result of the convergence of different types of change. Equally, it reflects the failure of established explanations for economic or business

> *Hardly a month goes by without some new approach to transforming business performance.*

performance effectively to describe, explain or predict the changes being experienced. Talk of the need for a "new economics"[6] or the "death of economics"[7] dominates economic thinking. Business faces the same turbulence in ideas. Hardly a month goes by without some new approach to transforming business performance.

This book explores the nature of the economic revolution and examines the emerging technologies and markets. Changes in the wider environment require shifts in management thinking and assumptions about the best ways to produce results. Often, the "right way" seems to conflict with the old way. This produces the type of paradox that causes so many problems to firms and their leaders. The anguish expressed by many people and the variety of explanations for failure highlights the difficulties posed by change in this form and of this scale. The relative economic decline of an economic superpower like the USA is the focus for much of this debate. Over the last few years, explanations for the difficulties of US industry have ranged from too much government interference in the workings of markets to too little. Alongside these, too much education is as frequently criticized as too little. More recently, commentators have asked whether the mystique of management[8] was not, in part, part of a myth of success that is now exposed by new economic demands.

These ideas help frame the argument of the book but are tempered by evidence of the remarkable ability of managers and enterprises to adapt to new and changing conditions. After the last industrial revolution much attention was paid to the failures of UK firms, managers and industries to sustain their economic lead. For great swathes of British industry, the analysis was valid. This was only part of the picture. Companies like Unilever, ICI and Glaxo adjusted to the demands on the new managerialism. They built up cadres of expert and professional managers that matched and sometimes overtook their rivals in Procter & Gamble, Du Pont and Bayer. The ways that they succeeded in adjusting are as important in framing answers to today's challenges as the failures of their contemporaries. That managers can cope with change in organizational form, resolve paradoxes and change their ways to fit new conditions is as clear a message as the difficulties they face in making these adjustments. The way forward provides the central theme of the following pages.

Established thinking no longer seems to satisfy contemporary concerns. The wider publics in the USA, Europe and Asia express the same worries in different ways. In North America, French Canadians seek security in a stronger sense of national identify. In Europe, the French are among the greatest advocates of increased European integration. In the USA, underlying dissatisfaction with the economic and social remedies of Republicans and Democrats is demonstrated by volatile shifts in voter preferences and support for "outsider" or third party candidates. Germany struggles to contain nationalism while the separate countries of the UK seek increasing autonomy. In Asia, Hindu nationalism is partly an expression of the fear of change while Chinese Communism battles to accommodate diverse economic systems. Even a gradualist like Fukuyama argues that contemporary change "affects the overall structure of national economies, the sectoral distribution of industries, the role that the state can play and the day-to-day conditions under which workers related to managers and to each other."[9]

That managers can cope with change in organizational form, resolve paradoxes and change their ways to fit new conditions is as clear a message as the difficulties they face in making these adjustments.

The scale and nature of contemporary change has immediate parallels with two earlier periods in modern history: the first between the late 1770s and the early 1820s, sometimes called the first industrial revolution; the second was between the early 1880s and the 1920s. Both periods were characterized by features still seen today. Technological change transformed economies, industries and work. Earlier scientific developments made older technologies uncompetitive while creating opportunities for innovation and market development. Economic turbulence went alongside social and political upheaval.

Established ideas no longer fitted the world experience of people. Groups that saw themselves as "protected" from economic difficulties were threatened by the new conditions. Just as the protected tenant or farm laborer lost their security during the first industrial revolution, and the craftsman was overtaken by the second, the office worker and middle manager are threatened today. The implicit contract between corporate man and large firms or public agencies is disappearing. Instead of lifelong employment in return for lifelong loyalty,[10] they must engage in lifelong learning to retain their lifelong employability to different employers.

Alongside these threats came opportunities for individuals, enterprises and communities. In the first industrial revolution, entrepreneurs in Britain, Europe and the USA grasped the opportunities created in the new textile, iron making and shipping industries. In the process, India's handloom textile industry was shattered, Japan's 2000-year-old ceramics industry was undermined, and traditional producers of iron and ships across the world were forced to adapt or be destroyed. The UK achieved an economic dominance that survived for almost a century. Communities like those in Lowell, Massachusetts were at the hub of a new and growing prosperity.

A century later, new entrepreneurs in chemicals, electricals and vehicles wrested economic power from those who ignored or failed to respond to change. The USA and Germany, in particular, developed approaches to economic and business development that provided a century of global leadership. The challenge to business leaders, managers, enterprises and communities is to decide on the way to respond to today's revolution. Britain's textile, coal and iron industries started on a century of decline when they ignored the opportunities created in new European and North American markets and failed to tap into the new technologies emerging from innovations in chemistry and engineering. They did not change their ways of working so they could not realize the full potential of these opportunities. Industry and commerce face the same challenge today – they can resist the revolution or adapt. The price of resistance is high but the returns from adaptation are vast.

Throughout the program of research and development associated with this book two themes interact. First, the challenges facing managers today are qualitatively different from those faced in the past. They involve a fundamental rethink of their assumptions and ways of operating. Second, there are practical ways to overcome the dilemmas posed by the requirement to adapt behaviors while meeting current responsibilities. Some aspects of the changes that are taking place are well publicized. Rapid shifts in work practice put jobs at risk. Managers have learned that job security is increasingly rare. There is less appreciation of the greater importance of employability, i.e. the creation of a portfolio of skills and competences to cover different career opportunities.

The characteristics of successful organizations has evolved from the giant, multiproduct, multifunctional organization to more tightly focussed but flexible ventures that built themselves around the capabilities of their people. In these organizations hierarchies, authority and control are less important than involvement, ownership and creativity. The fit or, more often, the failure to fit between the organizational form, management expectations and market needs creates many of the paradoxes that dominate business life today. The major paradoxes are identified and the ways they can be tackled and have been, are examined in depth. Throughout the book there is a strong emphasis on change and innovation. The notion of continuous discontinuity has a special role in the analysis and conclusion. This describes the environment created in many of the most effective companies by their more successful leaders and managers.

The challenges facing managers today are qualitatively different from those faced in the past. They involve a fundamental rethink of their assumptions and ways of operating.

The notion encompasses the principle of continuity that underlies the assumptions of many highly effective organizations. They establish and maintain an ongoing partnership with all their employees, the community and the wider society. According to the Frankfurter Allgemeine, Germany's Miele, a medium sized but profitable producer of premium washing machines "manufactures as many components as possible, preferably within a small region with firmly rooted workers." They share this desire for continuity with the UK's Marks and Spencer, which establishes long-term relations with its major clothing suppliers. Some go back to the origins of the stores group early this century when manufacturers like the Dewhurst Group supported Marks and Spencer's early development. These relationships have parallels with the Japanese *Keiretsu* and the Korean *chaebol* systems of commercial relationships, networks that are an integral part of the successful development of global giants like Mitsubishi and Samsung.

Continuity is not enough to explain the success of these firms. They avoid the sterility and rigidity often linked with continuity by building in innovation and its associated discontinuities. Innovation might be technical: smaller German companies like Miele have an outstanding record for technological innovation despite placing a premium on continuity. They achieve this by adopting an integrated approach to innovation that weds their expertise with that of their suppliers and customers through partnership development. At Marks and Spencer, the trust created between the firm and its suppliers encourages them to initiate new developments which open new market opportunities for Marks and Spencer. In Japan, large customers like Toyota support their suppliers in their search for innovative ideas in production, processing and even sourcing.

The solutions described in this book are firmly rooted in the success of organizations and their managers. The results highlight the ways managers learn to adapt to conditions. The central importance of learning is a theme which recurs in the analysis and its conclusions. Managers have special responsibilities in learning organizations. They have to learn to learn, while creating learning organizations in which all members collaborate in joint learning and development. In the current revolution, failure to learn is the expressway to failure.

In writing this book, I've had the help of a host of committed and dedicated entrepreneurs, managers and professionals. My insights into the nature of the revolution were shaped by people like Anita Roddick, Richard Branson, Derek Wanless, Sir Len Peach, Sir Bob Reid and others who showed, in a host of different ways, the fundamental changes that are occurring. Others like David Wheeler, David Miles, Shelagh Avery, Malcolm Allen, Tony Goulbourn, Alan Maltpress, Fabrizio Pini, Tony Tighe, Nick Jaspon, Rod Toomey, Tom Edge, Alan Beswick and Janet Boulding provided opportunities and platforms to explore the thinking behind the book. I've also been lucky enough to work with colleagues at MCI, managers from across the world and managers from agencies like Training and Enterprise Councils who constantly add to my understanding of the changes taking place. I have been especially lucky with my publisher, Richard Stagg, who has constantly guided, enthused, criticized and supported the efforts to get the book completed. The rest of the team notably Mark Allin, Linda Dhondy and Helen Baxter added an extra dimension of expertise and professionalism. The patience of my wife Fran and my children Robin and Rowan was sorely tested and they, at least, came through with flying colours. My thanks go to all these and many others, the responsibility is mine – I can't even blame the blues (Everton, that is).

> *In the current revolution, failure to learn is the expressway to failure.*

Introduction

◆

THE CHALLENGE OF THE MILLENNIUM FOR MANAGERS

This book is the result of a research program that has lasted over 15 years. It has involved close observation and detailed discussion with some of the world's most successful corporations and corporate leaders. These include entrepreneurial businesses driven by the new kinds of adventure capitalists who are shaping and reshaping the world of work and the skills managers need to succeed.

The range of firms extends to established firms that have been transformed by merchant venturers who deploy the resources of their corporations to grow and prosper while others flounder. The sample includes organizations from the public sector that have adapted and responded to the fundamental shifts in the role of government and public agencies over the last 15 years. The lessons of survival, growth, achievement and success are tempered by the lessons of decline and failure.

The achievements of these corporate leaders show a willingness to adapt to new conditions. They are able to ask deep-rooted questions about their businesses and produce answers that reflect both the capability of their firms to respond and the needs of their environment. The most successful achieve deep-rooted changes in their organization – extending the capabilities of their businesses and the people involved – while maintaining the integrity of the enterprise and the commitment and loyalty of all those with a stake in the organization.

Most start with a willingness to ask deep and fundamental questions. They move on to accept the implications of their answers, even if they are uncomfortable. Along the line most have realized that the world of the late 1990s and early 21st century is different to the world most grew up in. There is a new economic, industrial and business paradigm in which the conditions and requirements of success are fundamentally different from those of the past.

The kinds of questions asked by managers and business leaders from Akron, Ohio to Zjerjiang in China and Birmingham, England to Yokohama in Japan show surprising similarities. They ask:

- How do I keep delivering improved products and services at lower prices?
- How can I build on my core strengths while constantly reengineering my business?
- Can I keep producing solutions for short-term problems while building strategies for the long term?
- How do I manage to consolidate what I have achieved in the past while continuing to grow my business?
- How do I think global and act local?
- Why is it that, whatever I achieve, I remain dissatisfied and under stress?
- Can I satisfy the financial expectations of my stockholders while meeting my social responsibilities?

These and other questions come up in conversations with managers across the world. They know that solutions exist. They see the successes that have been achieved. They even sense the similarities that allow adventure capitalists like Richard Branson at Virgin and Paul Fulton at Sara Lee to redefine their industries to their advantage and others, merchant venturers like Jack Welch at General Electric and Allan Sheppard at GrandMed, redefine their corporations to get ahead. Managers across the globe sense that fundamental changes are occurring in the business world. Typically, they feel a mixture of dissatisfaction and anticipation.

Their dissatisfaction comes from an awareness that the old solutions do not work any more. IBM, ICI, GM, Shell are typical of the giants that learned to dance only to find that the music had changed. They are struggling to fit the old steps into the new tune. IBM failed to understand how quickly the catch-phrase "no one was ever sacked for buying IBM" could turn against them. CEOs started asking whether IBMs were being bought because they were the safest machines or the best.

ICI found that its committee structure changed from being a source of stability and strength into a barrier to change. General Motors had built 50 years of success on the dedication of its cohorts of organizational men, organized into a managerial bureaucracy that could mobilize massive resources against known goals. Unfortunately when the goals were unknown or misread problems proliferated. Shell lost share in global markets because it did not understand or respond to the expectations of environmentally aware consumer groups.

The anticipation comes from the ferment of opportunities and ideas in the business world. This is vividly illustrated in the speed with which fashions in thinking about business change. Sticking to your last is no sooner understood than it is overtaken by the search for competitive advantage. Time based competition soon gets dated in the battle for reengineering. The focus on core competences and capabilities struggles to answer the question "is it possible to shrink to greatness?"

This turmoil in ideas, markets and technologies has parallels in the history of business and in other fields of human endeavor. Turmoil of this kind characterizes revolutionary change when one set of ideas and certainties are overtaken by a new set. In effect, one paradigm or way of thinking and working is giving way to another. It occurred at the end of the 19th century when the British industrial paradigm of the small, personal, manufacturer/trader was overwhelmed by the corporatist, managerial revolution that emerged in the USA and Germany. British corporations and the British management system could not compete in world markets against the ability of US firms like Standard Oil, Armco and later General Motors or their German equivalents like Bayer and Mercedes Benz.

British industries and firms that entered the late 1880s as world leaders failed to appreciate the depth of the change in the industrial world that was caused by the new industrial revolution. They adopted new technologies but did not recognize the need to change their thinking to tap the real potential of the new machines and ways of working. These British managers were steeped in the batch production that characterized industries like textiles. They lacked proper qualifications and believed managers were born not made. This fitted conveniently into a deferential culture. New ideas equated to new threats.

Little wonder then that they could not compete with the new highly qualified US and German managers who saw properly organized science and technology as an opportunity rather than a threat. Education, training and development in the USA and Germany reflected the needs of the new managers and the new industries. The business schools in the USA and the *Fachhochschulen* in Germany symbolized this link between training and performance. The new corporation men might be grey but they knew their subject. The new corporations adopted the new ideas about markets, research and development and business organizations. This allowed them to develop global positions in the richest markets.

At the heart of the managerial paradigm of the 20th century lay the search for control. Managers and corporations wanted to bend technologies, markets, thinking and even communities to their will. The secret of General Motors' success lay in the superb management control systems designed and developed by Alfred P. Sloan. In the vast corporate empires, people knew where they stood. They could find themselves somewhere on an organization chart. They spoke a common language developed at Wharton or some other business school. They shared values that they knew were superior to those available anywhere else. Once they knew their goals they could mobilize vast resources to achieve them.

They reached the zenith of their achievements in projects like delivering the vast arsenal required to win World War II or putting a man on the moon. The solutions were known – more tanks, aircraft and ships, getting enough thrust into the Apollo rocket to get the payload to the moon and back – and the 20th century manager could manage the resources to deliver the goods. Its greatest failure occurred when the problem was recognized but the answer was not known. President Nixon tried to match Kennedy's promise about manned space flight when he promised a cure for cancer, but all the resources in the world cannot get you to a destination if you do not know where it is.

Now this managerial paradigm is collapsing under the same kinds of pressures that destroyed the 19th century systems of management. The rise and fall of IBM symbolizes both the strength of the old system and its inherent weakness. IBM successfully fitted the new information technologies into the old production systems and used the systems and structures of mass production and the Fordist age to build its success. It succeeded – to a point.

It failed, however, to see the logic of its own situation by ignoring the implications of the software revolution and the

All the resources in the world cannot get you to a destination if you do not know where it is.

changes in the marketplace. It had the chance to be the first virtual organization, capable of using its technologies and market power to break down the barriers between organization and strategy, between its internal and external operations and its acquisition of information and expertise and the creation of a learning organization.

These are some of the challenges facing organizations which strive to succeed during this revolution and the managers who are determined to switch their thinking from catching up with their rivals to coming out of this turbulent era ahead of the game. The book addresses the ways this new generation of managers and businesses recreate their businesses and reshape their relationship with the environment.

These managers know that they can only shape their own destinies if they learn to shape the destinies of their markets. The architecture of their organizations, the systems, structures and values that hold them together, will need to be conceived in novel ways. This requires managers to reexamine their role, and their contribution. At the heart of their task lies the challenge of generating new ways to direct and shape their businesses. Innovativeness in key areas like:

- building the skills portfolio in the firm;
- shaping the product and service mix;
- designing process which achieve a true symbiosis between the firm and its environment;
- directing resources in ways which reflect needs not structures;
- sustaining the energy level of the enterprise and its members;
- learning to manage talent.

Entering the paradox moves beyond an examination of the environment of change to a substantive exposition of what the revolution means for business leaders, managers, business educators and the wider community. The argument draws on the experience of people as diverse as Richard Branson, Anita Roddick and Jerry Cohen to Jack Welch, Jeff Steifler and Allan Sheppard. Firms like Microsoft and Virgin are examined and we show how their experiences are related to those of giants like GE, SmithKline Beecham and successful middle sized companies.

There are important similarities between the first, the second and, now, the third industrial revolutions. Some centre on the reasons why some communities and businesses managed to survive the change. Other similarities highlight the scale of the change taking place. Survival and achieving prosperity will not be easy. That is why entering the paradox with an understanding of its implications and the skills and abilities needed to prosper is so important.

Each chapter explores different aspects of the transformation. Part I of the book focusses on the nature of the revolution with the opening Chapter examining the characteristics of the revolution, while others explore the lessons from different eras. The nature of the paradox created by the revolution is examined in Part II. The modern management paradox itself is explored initially, while specific paradoxes and their implications are examined in subsequent chapters. In each case, the paradox is related to ways in which managers and organizations can respond.

The heart of the book lies in the analysis of the millennium manager in Part III. This identifies the key characteristics of this new generation of managers: their distinct characteristics and the way these will transform our views of the nature of management. It is not just the skills and competencies of the new managers that will change. The managers themselves are being drawn from new groups. Women, ethnic and cultural minorities and younger age groups will be far more prominent among both the adventure capitalists and the merchant venturers.

These chapters will look beyond the challenges posed to individuals to the ways in which corporations and educators will need to evolve. The emerging crisis in the business schools is linked with their habit of developing yesterday's managers for tomorrow's businesses. Radical change is needed if the close identification they achieved with corporate man during the 20th century is not to prove fatal.

The first and second industrial revolutions saw winners and losers. During the first industrial revolution Britain achieved global power and unrivalled prosperity. France, Spain and Portugal saw a century of economic decline. British companies like Swires and Jardine Matheson created worldwide trading entities.

Their French and Dutch rivals could not keep up. This was the price of success and failure. The second industrial revolution was similar, but this time Britain failed to change. Her share of world trade declined from 29% in the 1890s to 7% in the 1990s. The new vehicle, engineering and chemicals industries were dominated by US, German and eventually Japanese firms. They developed the managers and tapped these markets.

The USA and US corporations and their managers are at the heart of this analysis. Their struggles show remarkable similarities with the experience of the UK at the end of the last century. Even the recent improvements in US performance and productivity mirror the short-term successes of British corporations during the "golden age" of the 1890s. They improved their short-term performance by cutbacks on resources and reemphasising their traditional strengths in traditional markets.

Unfortunately, it was not enough. The challenge to US firms is to learn the real lessons of the revolution they created. Very few dominant groups in history have survived a revolution. The core question of *Welcome to the Revolution* is whether today's dominant groups can learn and adapt fast enough and deeply enough to succeed beyond the millennium.

The challenge facing individuals, firms and communities is whether they want to be winners or losers during this revolution. *Welcome to the Revolution* lays down the challenge and provides powerful insights and guidelines to action for those who decide they want to be the winners.

Tom Cannon
July, 1996

Part I

◆

DIFFERENT DAYS, DIFFERENT WAYS

◆

At the end of the Vietnam War the US Military Academy was forced to conclude that "the determined effort to fight the new war by the rules and with the techniques of the last war is the surest explanation of defeat." Firms and managers that do not change face the same fate.

◆

◆

Businesses made progress by
learning to control their
environments, concentrating on
incremental improvements,
minimizing risk and specializing.
Bigger was better because it gave
more control to the corporation and
greater opportunities for the new
managerial bureaucracies.

◆

Chapter 1

THE THIRD INDUSTRIAL REVOLUTION

MASSACRE OF THE ARISTOCRATS

The most dramatic symbol of revolutionary change is the destruction of old aristocracies and the elimination of some of the most glorious leaders of the old regime – the French Revolution saw the end of the Bourbon aristocracy, the Russian revolution destroyed the Romanoffs. There are distinct echos of the proliferation of redundant posts and the indulgences of the old aristocracies in the lifestyles of the corporate aristocrats. Louis the XVI had 406 officers whose only task was to attend to the ceremonials at Versailles. When they were abolished "away went 13 chefs and 5 assistants of the Grand Pantry; away went the 20 royal cup bearers (not to be confused with the 4 carriers of the royal wine), the 16 'hasteners' of the royal roast, platoons of tasters, battalions of candle snuffers, brigades of salt passers and (most regrettably) the 10 aides speciaux for the fruits de provence".[11] Ross Peterson of RJR Nabisco seemed to be trying to match this with his fleet of company jets and the sports stars on call. "The top thirty one executives were paid $14.2 million ... no expense was spared in decorating the new headquarters ...

the top floor's backdrop was an eighteenth century $100,000 lacquered Chinese screen, complemented by a $16,000 pair of powder blue Chinese vases from a slightly later dynasty. Visitors could settle into a set of French Empire mahogany chairs ($30,000) and ogle the two matching bibliotheque cabinets ($30,000)".[12] Even the royal tradition of giving gold livres to the poor was matched by Peterson's habit of dispensing $100 tips.

The victims of industrial and business revolutions do not pay the same price as French or Russian aristocrats but their fall from grace can be just as dramatic. Just days before John Aakers was toppled at IBM he talked confidently of the backing he expected from his fellow directors. "This IBM board supports this management. The board supports me. And I do not plan to stand aside." After Aakers was sacked, a board member said "There is going to be change. This is a tough board. This is not American Express." Louis XVI of France and Czar Nicholas of Russia were just as confident of the support of their people – until it was too late.

The dismissal of one chief executive might be a dramatic event but it hardly symbolizes a revolution on its own. It is the number, seniority and range of the dismissals that shows that the greatest centers of power and privilege are affected. General Motors is the largest corporation in the world. This did not save Robert Stempel when a series of failures to understand the way technologies and markets were evolving cost him his job. He had reached the top because he was a skilled and capable manager of the old regime. He failed largely because the thinking, policies and skills acquired during his earlier career were inappropriate. The Hamtramck robot factory was the logical extension of the traditional GM approach of throwing resources at problems but the nature of the problem and the character of the solution had changed. Without fundamental changes in thinking the plant was almost certainly doomed to failure.

In the UK, British Petroleum has similar status to General Motors. It is almost the establishment company. The notion that its chief executive could be sacked was almost laughable – until it happened to Bob Horton. James Ross had served a long apprenticeship at British Petroleum. His track record, training and skills seemed to fit Cable and Wireless's needs perfectly. He failed, however, to cope with the new political economy of modern business and was toppled. The list seems endless. Kay Whitmore at Kodak, James Robinson at American Express, Rocco Forte at Forte Group and John Nevin at Firestone are just some of the more prestigious names that have fallen from grace.

> "a roll call of the largest computer companies – DG, IBM, Unisys, Bull, DEC, Olivetti, Siemens, Prime – reads like the waiting list in the emergency room."

Even former stars are not protected by their reputation. John Scully had no sooner written the story of his triumphs at Apple[13] than his plans started unravelling, and he was following his mentor, Steven Jobs, out of the door. Past entrepreneurial success is no guarantee of security as Ken Olsen at Digital found out. Boards, institutional investors and shareholders are casting about so anxiously for solutions to seemingly intractable problems that *Fortune* magazine was obliged to comment in 1995 that "a roll call of the largest computer companies – DG, IBM, Unisys, Bull, DEC, Olivetti, Siemens, Prime – reads like the waiting list in the emergency room."

The safest job in town

Nothing in the experience or training of these corporate leaders or their armies of subordinates prepared them for the kind of changes that have occurred over the last decade. Mary-Francis Mitchell, a former IBM staffer in marketing services, spoke for thousands like her when she commented: "In January, I was told that my job was the safest in the nation. In February we were told that half the jobs would be gone. People can't handle this stress: a lot have given up." Antony Sampson, the British social commentator, summed up the process:[14]

> **The assumption of a lifetime job had long been the pattern of professional and public service careers, at the heart of the middle class. The unemployment of the thirties had made security still more valued in the post war decades, while war had encouraged quasi-military attitudes and loyalty, making public and private service seem more alike. ... But by the nineties many people had little choice about their destinies as global competition stepped up, boom was followed by recession, and the state felt little responsibility for employment. Even accountants and lawyers no longer felt confident of their jobs.**

The patterns of managerial behavior, the skills and attitudes which served people and businesses well during times of relative stability were a disadvantage when turbulence was the dominant feature of business life. From the second quarter of this century to the last quarter, technological change was broadly linear and markets shifted in broadly predictable ways. Managers who thought in straight lines and were as predictable as their markets were right for their times. Their times were coming to an end by the late 1980s. Boeing, one of the success stories of the later era, cultivated a different kind of manager. Larry McLean, Boeing's Director of Human Resources, described the change.

"As a young man I'd stood in line to work overtime. I'd often work seven days a week. Suddenly, the new employees are challenging authority, complaining about the eight layers of management and wanting empowerment. They had new values."

Managers who thought in straight lines and were as predictable as their markets were right for their times. Their times were coming to an end by the late 1980s.

These new values are a better reflection of the current environment than the old straight line, search for stability and security that characterized the old style manager. The most vivid illustration of this point of view is the constant call by traditional managers for "time to consolidate." They want to slow or stop change so that they can consolidate their gains before moving on. It is the mentality of the military leaders of World War II – move your army forward, consolidate your position and at a time of your choosing move on.

> *While you are trying to consolidate, they are changing the rules. So you find that you have consolidated your position on quicksand.*

Modern business competition, like modern warfare, is not like this. Change is so quick, the rules change so fast and rivals attack from all sides. While you are trying to consolidate, they are changing the rules. So you find that you have consolidated your position on quicksand. At the end of the Vietnam War the US Military Academy was forced to conclude that "the determined effort to fight the new war by the rules and with the techniques of the last war is the surest explanation of defeat." Firms and managers that do not change face the same fate.

AN AMERICAN TALE

Anglo-US corporations from both sides of the Atlantic remained locked into old style almost adversarial ways of thinking and managing. These had a role when demand generally exceeded supply, products were homogeneous and technological solutions outweighed human inputs in determining price/output relations. This contrasts with the needs of the new environment in which supply exceeds demand, product differential is the key to success and adding value through people is the key source of production advantage. Anglo-US firms face serious difficulties competing with a Japanese system in which "actual consumer demand 'pulled' the product through the factory. Therefore, instead of long standardized production runs, on the final assembly line, wagons, two door hatchbacks and four door sedans with red, beige and white bodies, with left hand and right hand steering wheels, with a variety of transmissions, engines and options rolled one after the other along the line 'seemingly at random' in response to customer orders flowing on computer printout into the factory from dealers."[15]

The division of labour to produce homogeneous products was the great US contribution to mass production. In 1900, Litterer described how it gave US producers massive advantages over their European rivals:

The skill and knowledge of the Europeans ... was the equal and sometimes the superior of that of the Americans. The difference was in how this technical knowledge and skill was used. The European manufacturer used it to make a product. The American manufacturer used it to make a process for making a product.[16]

Scientific management was at the heart of the American approach. Job analysis, work measurement, time and motion were all developed to enhance this process of making products, which they achieved by breaking down work into its component parts and reallocating the work among workers who stopped being skilled operatives and became machine minders.

In this way, a fundamental change took place in the contract between workers and management during the second industrial revolution in North America. During the first industrial revolution the direct control by management of the industrial workforce was very limited. In key sectors like railway construction, ship building, mining and even textile production, management's direct role in the production process was very limited. Controls were largely exercised through internal or external subcontractors. Sometimes their relationship was indirectly with the employer through contractor. Elsewhere, the relationship was mediated through craft unions or guilds. They retained their position through "a jungle of restrictive practices" which did nothing to improve output but did sustain the worker's sense of control over his job. The Taylorite revolution transformed this.

It is no coincidence that Taylor's works soon overtook those of Samuel Smiles in popularity among the new factory owners and managers. Samuel Smiles emphasized the importance of Self Help for an industrial workforce that still retained some control over its work practice. Taylor sought to eradicate this control and transfer authority over the means, form and volume of output to managers and owners. It is intriguing to read of the sustained popularity of Smiles' work in Japan well into this century, after its translation by Masanao Natkamura. His ideas have a greater consonance with the Japanese faith in a highly integrated and motivated workforce which retains considerable control over its work.

The Japanese pattern of management has many parallels with the approach adopted in Germany, where the notion of codetermination is well established. Codetermination in its broadest sense expresses the belief that workers and management share in determining the direction of the enterprise and its operations. The commitment has two parallel effects which together sustain the commitment to integrated working practices. First, codetermination makes firms reluctant to engage in large-scale reductions in labor. As it is hard to dispose of labor, the incentive is to focus the company's activities in those areas of business which are less vulnerable to competition. For much of German industry this means lower volume, higher value, technically complex products and services where quality of labor is more important than price. The second effect of codetermination is that it reinforces the importance of technical expertise (*Fachkompetenz*) at the expense of administrative expertise. Managers gain status from a technical expertise that can be aligned against the worker's expertise rather than a separated administrative expertise. Simon[17] describes how successful German companies rate "industry specific qualifications highly. ... Of the 250 member workforce at Aqua Signal, world leader in ship-lighting systems, 50 are engineers. At Hauni/Korber the more than 1500 engineers on its payroll represent almost one in four employees."

In a sense this emphasis on integration harks back to the previous industrial revolution with its notions of craft and technical skill. Its key relevance for the current revolution lies in the bridge it offers to new technologies and markets. The new technologies provide flexibility and adaptability and are built around customer expectations of value and fit to their needs. The integrated company, dedicated to tapping these technologies and satisfying these needs, provides the way forward during this revolution.

FROM PUZZLES TO PARADOXES

Tom Kuhn, the philosopher of science, draws an important distinction between normal science and revolutionary science.[18] Normal science occurs when there is general acceptance of a set of beliefs and assumptions about the way the world works, either generally or in a specific field of endeavor. Scientists feel no need to question their core beliefs or assumptions and concentrate their efforts on "puzzle solving" and refining their professional skills and techniques. Kuhn comments that "perhaps the most striking feature of the normal science problems ... is how little they aim to produce major novelties, conceptual or phenomenal." Change is cumulative, gradual and conforms to accepted rules. Scientific revolutions occur when these rules and beliefs are rejected and replaced by a new set of beliefs.

> *Change is cumulative, gradual and conforms to accepted rules. Scientific revolutions occur when these rules and beliefs are rejected and replaced by a new set of beliefs.*

The revolution usually occurs in three stages. First there is the emergence of anomalies. These are phenomena or research findings that do not fit into the old set of beliefs. One classic example of this was the "discovery" of oxygen and the subsequent revolution in chemistry. The first stage in this revolution occurred when scientists like Priestley, Lavoisier and Scheele produced effects in their experiments that could not occur according to the old phlogiston theory of gases. The accumulation of these anomalies makes it progressively harder for people to accept the status quo.

This eventually produces a crisis in which the defenders of the status quo and the advocates of change, may clash. The defenders either attack the advocates of change as in the case of Galileo, or they assert that the difficulties reflect some failures on the parts of the innovators. Innovators produce a wide variety of claims, theories or beliefs to explain or justify their position. Many of these provide partial but unsatisfactory explanations. Eventually, the crisis is resolved when the profession has "changed its view of the field, its methods and its goals." In virtually every major corporation studied as part of this investigation there were managers who identified the emerging problems and proposed alternative ways forward. They were not blinded like Galileo for seeing too clearly, but they seldom survived to see the predicted crisis emerge or to have their ideas implemented.

Management by panacea[19]

The same stages can be seen in the development of business and industry. For most of this century there was broad agreement about the best way forward for management and business. Managers became better educated, more professionalized and more specialized. In the Anglo-American world business education was separated from other areas of education in business schools or dedicated faculties of business or commerce. These, in turn, became preoccupied with increased specialization.

Businesses made progress by learning to control their environments, concentrating on incremental improvements, minimizing risk and specializing. Bigger was better because it gave more control to the corporation and greater opportunities for the new managerial bureaucracies. Anomalies like shareholders – especially those who believed they owned the firm – could be marginalized and controlled. Even customer dissatisfaction could be contained because the customers had nowhere else to go. This mindset was underpinned by a combination of technological, market and economic forces.

The dominant technologies of mass production produced huge advantages for scale especially in the major industries of vehicle, chemical and raw materials production. Massive corporations like Standard Oil (Exxon) and General Motors tapped into these technologies and developed management systems to exploit their capabilities.[20] The new consumer, retail and corporate markets grew rapidly. They accepted the mixture of incremental change and employment security the giants offered. Dissent became a threat instead of a source of insight into real threats.

The first anomalies probably emerged in the 1960s, and the number grew during the 1970s. The UK and US motor cycle industries virtually disappeared under a flood of Japanese imports. Neither size nor highly sophisticated, traditional management systems were a defense. Similarly with a RCA that had dominated TV production in the USA since the introduction of color television. Its management cadres were full of MBAs, while its labs were full of PhDs but this could not stop the erosion of its US television market. The process was even faster in the UK. Lacking either the MBAs or the PhDs, the giants of UK television and domestic appliance production soon disappeared as significant players. Many UK companies were still locked in the even older 19th century management paradigm of family and social network preference. This proved totally unable to resist Japanese competition. By the 1980s the old style managerialism was in crisis.

Different views symbolized this crisis. At his lecture to the White House Conference on Small Firms in 1988 Tom Peters attacked the growing pressure for protectionism in the USA. He highlighted the Japanese commitment to quality with the comment: "The Japanese produced the first cars that did not require a built in mechanic." The Japanese challenge goes far beyond the specifics of technical superiority in particular goods and services and its success undermined the separated, managerialist consensus of the second industrial revolution. The division of labor and its management from outside by specialist, managerial bureaucrats justified the US reward system which was skewed heavily in favor of management. Management was the main source of high output, low costs and added value. It became obvious that management's rewards should reflect this disproportionate contribution.

An enterprise based on group leadership struggles to justify the disproportionate distribution of rewards to one group of specialists.

The Japanese experience suggests a more equal partnership in creating wealth. "The essence of the Japanese company is in the people who compose it. It does not, as in the American firm, belong to the stockholders and the managers they employ to control it, but it is under the control of the people who work in it."[21] An enterprise based on group leadership struggles to justify the disproportionate distribution of rewards to one group of specialists. The economic justification of old style managerialism was undermined by its limited role in the two most successful economies in the world – Japan and Germany.

In the greatest bastion of managerialism the criticism took an additional form. The legitimacy of managers as servants of the owners was under attack. In his fictional attack on the old corporatism, Oliver Stone has Gordon Gekko comment at a shareholders' meeting:

Now in the old days of the free market when our country was the top industrial power, there was accountability. The Carnegies, the Mellons, the men that built this great industrial empire made sure that it was – because it was their money that was at stake.

Today, management has no stake in the company. All together, these men sitting up there own less than three per cent of the company. And where does Mr. Cromwell put his $million salary? Not in Teldar stock. He owns less than one per cent.

You own the company, that's right, you the stockholders and you are being royally screwed over by these bureaucrats with their stock lunches, their hunting and fishing trips, their corporate jets and their golden parachutes.

Teldar Papers, Teldar Papers has 33 Vice Presidents each earning over $200,000 per year. I have spent the last two months analysing what these guys do and I still can't figure it out. One thing I do know is that our paper company lost $110 million last year and I'll bet that half of that was spent on the paperwork going between all these Vice Presidents.

The debate on the managerial revolution has widened to a sustained critique of the changes introduced into the priorities and preoccupations of top management. Their focus shifted during this century from an engineering, whole firm perspective to a financial, partial view. Top managers became dependent on tiers of managers to deliver the information and control while providing access to the operations of the enterprise. Locke describes this process as a fundamental shift in priorities:

Because top managers concentrated on the dynamics of money rather than product management, they required staff that could deal with corporate finance and marketing. They required managerial accountants who could oversee money flows through the various corporate divisions because this information was much more vital to decision making in multifaceted strategic setting. Moreover, emphasis on Return on Investment (ROI) at headquarters required financial reporting from the engineers below, accounting information that, if it satisfied the money men upstairs,

did not serve the needs of the technocratic-minded shop floor. They needed physical measures more than monetary measures. And so we entered the era when comptroller, financial experts and accountants dominated the firm. While in the workshop skilled workers had lost control to the system's managers of Taylorism, in the big corporation the owner-manager lost control to the professional money managers at the top. Since engineers' influence waned outside the factory proper, the money managers at corporate headquarters set the new managerial tone.[22]

This was predominantly an Anglo-US phenomenon. Engineering retains a leadership role in German corporation. This is vividly illustrated by the high technical standards of German firms and their continuing investment in technical development. Siemens, for example, can claim to be the most innovative large company in the world. It currently holds about 40,000 patents across a workforce of 400,000. Germany holds a powerful position in world rankings of patents, with 264 held per capita as against the USA's 117 and the UK's 140. The holistic view of the enterprise is well expressed by Klaus Grohmann, founder CEO of Grohmann Engineering,[23] a leading supplier of electrical components. "We consciously employ no salespeople. Our managers have total responsibility for their projects: they sell, make the offer, develop the solution and execute the project ... everyone takes a holistic view of the project." Japanese firms take this holistic approach to the enterprise even further with widely distributed power, cross employment with unions and extensive networks beyond the enterprise into supplier and client networks.

The old managerial system was in crisis because successful rivals used new methods, and traditional approaches could not respond. The search for solutions degenerated in many instances into the search for panaceas. Some managers expected instant answers to changes that were reshaping the world of business. *The 110% solution*[24] competed with *The one minute manager*[25] in airport bookstores. Zapping,[26] Chaos,[27] Zen[28] and a host of similar nostrums were proposed as solutions. Even when the conventional thinking of great business schools was challenged[29] the solutions were often returns to earlier answers[30] or untestable ideas. Prerevolutionary France and Russia showed the same search for panaceas or easy solutions. Serious reformers like Necker in France and De Witte in Russia were rejected and soft options adopted temporarily but even they were discarded. Failure was inevitable because serious reform challenged vested interests while less threatening alternatives failed to meet the needs of the new environment.

Giant bureaucracies and elaborate systems of checking and counter checking produced bloated overheads and shoddy goods.

The real cues to the nature of the new environment lay in the most striking anomalies and greatest concerns. The quality challenge was central. US, UK and many European companies could not match the quality standards reached by their Japanese rivals. Giant bureaucracies and elaborate systems of checking and counter checking produced bloated overheads and shoddy goods. Three related changes exposed this gap with devastating implications for old style corporations and their managers. First, there were changes in the dominant technologies. As in previous revolutions, these shifts went beyond production to logistics and communication. Second, markets were transformed by a mixture of technological change, greater wealth, increased access and rising expectations. Third, new competitors were able to exploit gaps in the offerings of established suppliers, challenge their assumptions and cut prices.

ROW, ROW, ROW THE BOAT

Technological changes made it much easier to reach markets. The combination of roll on–roll off (Ro-Ro) shipping and containerization made it far easier to ship relatively large and bulky goods overseas. Ro-Ro ships moved cars from the point of production to the point of consumption overseas cheaply, reliably and safely. Old style docks and cargo handling systems had been major barriers to entry for complex consumer goods. These barriers shrank just when the gap between the quality of Japanese cars, electricals etc and that of their US and North European rivals was greatest.

Markets were already changing. Consumer expectations were shifting as markets based on diversity gradually overtook mass markets. Their dissatisfaction with the existing offering was increased when critics like Ralph Nader exposed the flaws in corporate thinking. Increased travel and better communications increased customers' awareness of the alternatives. Perhaps the final element in this transformation occurred with the success of free market economics under Ronald Reagan in the USA and Margaret Thatcher in the UK. Both endorsed the view that reduced tariffs and more open markets created more dynamic economic conditions as cheaper imports forced domestic producers to increase efficiency and cut costs.

Price anomalies were equally striking. Japanese workers could produce equivalent or superior products for far less than their US and European rivals. General Motors' CEO, Roger Smith, found this out when he asked Isuzu, a Japanese producer in which GM held a major stake, how much it would cost to produce a small car that GM were developing. He found that Isuzu could produce the car for $2857. This was less than half the $5731 it would cost GM. Technological and market change forced the pace faster than the older giants could respond: IBM failed to spot the importance of either the personal computing revolution or the inherent value of the operating systems; even an innovator like Ken Olsen failed to introduce the kind of changes that would enable Digital to keep up with the market.

CONCLUSION

The clearest lesson of the first and second industrial revolution is that there are winners and losers. Some corporations and their leaders will understand and adapt to new conditions. They will survive and prosper. They have the capacity to grow. Others will strive to retain their old ways of operating in the face of new conditions. These efforts to "buck the market" involve massive costs and high risks. Some will survive by affirming distinct core strengths and concentrating their efforts around a specialism. The role of management is to establish a framework within which the options are understood and decision made. For managers, the options are clear (see Table 1.1).

Table 1.1

Management Choices	
Pre-revolution	*Post revolution*
Lifelong employment	Lifelong employability
Minimize risks from change	Maximize opportunities from change
Adversarial management	Collaborative management
Narrow view of main stakeholders	Extensive view of main stakeholders
Concentrate rewards	Distribute rewards
Emphasize administrative expertise	Emphasize technical expertise
Focus on continuity	Focus on continuous discontinuity
Separation and specialization key to success	Holistic approach to organization
Fragmented view of work and enterprise	Integrated view of work and enterprise
Stick by old rules	Search out new rules

Innovative businesses and business leaders have absorbed these choices and opted for change. At Perot Systems, Mort Meyerson used development programs, reward systems and his leadership to provoke change. On adversarial management he comments:

"We identified people who were abusive. We coached them and took them through a personal reinvention process to show them new ways of leading. These were high ranking company officials who had generated significant business, met or exceeded their financial goals – but simply mistreated their people. Not all of them could convert. Those who couldn't change, we asked to leave." He extended this approach to rewards. "We still tell people we'll give them anything we can in the way of rewards. In fact, more than 60 per cent of the company is owned by the people who run the company ... [but we offer] them another dimension that they can't get in other high performance companies: a human organization."

Meyerson places a premium on his own accessibility; "I'm accessible to anyone in our company, in real time, anywhere."

The integrated and integrating approach to management that works in a high tech, highly competitive firm like Perot Systems also works in more traditional product fields. Whole Foods in the largest natural foods retailer in the USA. Cofounder and Chief Executive, John Mackey makes clear that "the team, not the hierarchy, is the defining unit of activity. Referenda among team members extends to crucial decisions like recruitment. It takes,

> "I'm accessible to anyone in our company, in real time, anywhere."

for example, a two thirds vote of the team an applicant hopes to join for a candidate to get a permanent job." Openness extends to areas like salaries. "Every Whole Foods store has a book that lists the previous year's salary for all 6500 employees by name."[31] The consistent message from these and other successes is that major changes are occurring in the optimum organizational form and the best way to manage. Consistent success requires a shift in approach to adapt to change and build new management approaches and systems. The best firms evolved a new approach to internal dissent and external challenge. Leadership groups learned to listen to dissent and hear the voices of those that questioned old assumptions and comfortable beliefs. External challenges created opportunities for change, development and innovation.

◆

The first industrial revolution was driven by coal, the second by oil – the third will be driven by knowledge. The key to the effectiveness of managers and their business lies in their ability to access, use and enhance their knowledge.

◆

Chapter 2

◆

REFORMERS AND REVOLUTIONARIES

"In the land of the blind, the one eyed man is king" according to the proverb. The search for security implicit in this statement partly explains the proliferation of attempts to fit current changes in the business environment into established frameworks. The same search for security underpins many of the recent efforts to define the best ways to manage the future in terms of established approaches. US and UK companies, for example, have tried to tackle fundamental external change by tightening their financial controls. Many of the same firms acknowledge their lack of engineering, technical and other production expertise. Faced with these gaps, they choose to restrict their operations within their existing capabilities instead of looking for ways to extend their capabilities to meet emerging or new needs.

This restrictive approach to change is not unique to economic conditions. The second industrial revolution posed the same challenge to the UK and other successful economies. The options for British firms were clear: concentrate on current capabilities or devise ways to compete for future capabilities. Many of the leading companies adopted the former route. They focussed their attention on Imperial markets, that were defended by Imperial preferences. They avoided the investment needed to develop the large, multiproduct firms which fitted the requirements on the new richer markets of North America and Europe. These firms were reluctant to build up the large professional, managerial, engineering and research teams established by US and German companies. The result was the long decline of the UK's economic strength. There was nothing inevitable in this decline. The best UK companies in consumer and industrial goods, in foods, chemicals and pharmaceuticals made the necessary changes which meant that firms like ICI, Glaxo, Cadbury, Beechams continued to prosper. Some of the clearest successes grew from the international partnership that produced Unilever and Shell confounding the easy excuse that some external forces – government, geo-economic shifts or even sunk investments – inevitably produce failure. As the saying goes success has many parents but failure is an orphan. In business, the leadership and the managerial group produce both outcomes.

New conditions require new thinking. From the 1880s to the 1920s a revolution in ideas coincided with the economic revolution. Writers like Weber, Taylor, Follett, Gilbreth, Mayo and Dale Carnegie and practitioners like Ford, Woolworth, Edison and Andrew Carnegie described, classified and even theorized about business and organizational form. Their works became best sellers in a world anxious to understand and exploit the opportunities produced by the new economic conditions. There are many parallels today. New theories are emerging to describe, analyze and understand the new business environment and the ways entrepreneurs, leaders and managers can adapt themselves and their organizations to these conditions.

ROOTS OF THE NEW REVOLUTION[32, 33]

New thinking has emerged in response to changes across the business system. Total quality management drew on the lessons of Japanese thinking to focus the attention of the entire firm and its suppliers on quality. Business process reengineering highlights the extent to which the way the organization works can be reengineered to respond to change. Time based competition identified new imperatives and opportunities. In their different ways the advocates of these approaches were playing the part ascribed to trailblazers in any revolution.

Their focus on specific solutions differs from the thinking of those writers who see an understanding of the architecture, capabilities and competences of the organization as the key to adapting to new circumstances. The architecture of the enterprise is the set of relationships within the firm or between the firm and its suppliers or customers that determines the character or nature of the enterprise. Its capabilities are those attributes of the firm that allow it to perform specific tasks or achieve its goals. The organization's competences are those skills that determine how well it uses its capabilities. "The distinctive competence of a firm is more than what it can do; it is what it can do particularly well."[34] These distinctive competences generally reflect the adaptation of the firm to its past environment.

These past strengths can become future weakness if the enterprise, its leaders and managers fail to appreciate the extent of change and the scale of response needed. Successful firms have the dangerous habit of trying to repeat their past successes. Kodak's greatest success in the camera in Britain market was the Brownie, which established Kodak as a global company. In the second half of this century, new camera makers emerged to threaten Kodak (UK) by offering more sophisticated cameras, notably single lens reflex cameras. Kodak's response was to go back to the tried and trusted. In the 1960s it launched the Instamatic camera in Britain, the Brownie in all but name. Its partial success did little to stem the growth and increasing success of SLRs, Auto Focus and other products. Kodak (UK) responded with the disk camera – another rerun of the Brownie. The market had moved on but the firm was responding by repeating past successes – only this time it failed. Successful chief executives and leaders learn to ask is this the right thing to do or the easy thing to do.

VISIONS, DIRECTIONS AND UNDERSTANDING

Revolutionary change in the external environment requires fundamental change in the internal environment of the enterprise. Robert D. Haas, the CEO of Levi Strauss, accepts the need for fundamental change. He argues that "the most visible differences between the corporations of tomorrow and its present day counterparts will not be the products they make or the equipment they use – but who will be working, why they will be working and what work will mean to them ... organizations [must] create the common vision, sense of direction and understanding of values that binds the enterprise together."[35]

Revolutionary change in the external environment requires fundamental change in the internal environment of the enterprise.

The forces which the bind the organizations vary widely. Some are reinforced by wider national or cultural forces. In Germany notions of industrial codetermination date back to the first half of the 19th century, proposals for codetermination winning support from the interventionist Prussian state. Only during the Nazi era was there widespread opposition from business and political leaders. The greater integration of German firms is well rooted in the national, industrial tradition. Integration is further reinforced by the emphasis on on-the-job training. Anglo-US corporations place greater emphasis on off-the-job training which is often rigidly heirarchical and divisive. Managers being groomed for leadership are sent to an international business school such as Harvard, senior managers are sent to leading national business schools such as Cranfield or Kellogg, middle or junior managers go to schools like Manchester in the UK or US state universities while supervisors receive on-the-job training.

The integration of Japanese firms is reinforced by deep rooted cultural and social forces. There is a strong sense of group in Japan-

24

ese society with, for example, "a relative absence in the Japanese language of anything remotely resembling the personal pronoun."[36] Notions of duty, group and social responsibility permeate language, literature and social interaction. Robert Locke contrasts these values with the US approach which "during its great industrial boom (1880-1929) adopted a low-dependency strategy, one where management carefully spelled out job descriptions, without much worker input and implemented control techniques that permitted management to measure performance." The US approach suited the needs of a fragmented workforce, the low levels of technology and mass markets. The strengths of more integrated, better educated and cohesive workforces had limited impact on these market conditions. Techno-

> *The environment determines the appropriate organizational form.*

logical changes which placed a premium on products and services differentiated by quality, with high rates of change and market fragmentation shifting the balance of advantage, which in turn shifted in favor of the cohesive, flexible and more involved workforce. The environment determines the appropriate organizational form.

Four features of the new environment dominate the new industrial revolution:

- globalization;
- diversity;
- computers and telecommunications;
- information and knowledge.

Each affects the nature of the enterprise and its management and the kind of management structures most likely to produce success.

Globalization

Globalization goes beyond the growth of markets outside the rich Northern industrial markets. East Asia's share of world economic output grew from 4 % to 25 % between 1960 and 1990. The same region is expected to account for 40 % of world economic growth during the 1990s. The sphere of growth is extending beyond Japan, South Korea, Hong Kong, Singapore and Taiwan to include Malaysia, India, China and Indonesia. North American and European corporations cannot afford to ignore these markets. The UK's failure to compete effecïively in North America, Germany and other growth markets at the start of this century was a key point in its decline as a major industrïal power. Imperial markets were more easily accessible and required a minimum of change, but the action was happening elsewhere.

Learning to compete where it matters is one of the most important and difficult challenges facing organizations striving to use globalization as a means of strengthening the enterprise. The main characteristics of organizations that have established capability are:

- awareness of emerging opportunities;
- understanding of the organization's capabilities;
- organizational flex;
- the ability to deploy capabilities against opportunities.

Most firms and managers have the capacity to scan the environment and identify opportunities. The difficulties lie in filtering out the noise and turbulence that cloud assessments while avoiding the easy route of interpreting opportunities in terms of preconceived beliefs or assumptions. IBM were not ignorant of the personal computing revolution. Their problems were caused by the assumption that this revolution would produce few real changes, and that the computer market would change in ways IBM hoped it would.

Entrepreneurs succeed because they take a minimum of assumptions into an environment, and the ratio of start ups to successes is so high that the odds shift in favour of some successes. Competing where it matters requires that managers select markets on the basis of real and substantial potential. In effect, if you want to be the best you have to compete with the best. Success in this type of competitive environment goes to firms that understand the real language used by the bureaucrats who operate wish driven marketing (see Table 2.1).

Table 2.1

The Ten Assumptions of Wish Driven Marketing	
Comment	*Meaning*
It's a virgin market	There are no customers
We don't think there will be any local resistance	We don't know
The market's too crowded	We can't compete
Everyone will buy it	No one will buy it
We are so advanced technically that buyers will flock to buy	Its so complicated that we hope our customers will explain it to us
It will sell itself	It better had, because we can't
There's a big gap in the market	Everyone is avoiding this part of the market
We'll soon overcome price resistance	It's too expensive
We're selling on our reputation	We're copying a successful rival
It satisfies a universal need	We don't know who will buy it

Selectivity is crucial. It lies at the heart of globalization strategies. There is a considerable literature on the questions faced by managers and organizations in choosing these strategies. Issues like competitive superiority have received considerable attention as organizations have tried to concentrate their resources in markets in which they have a distinct or unique fit of capabilities to opportunity. Marks and Spencer have set competitive advantages that confirm their leadership position in the UK market. Some of these, notably close supplier links, distinct reputation, outstanding locations and reputations with important market segments, do not translate easily into non-UK markets, and are not easily duplicated. Rivals are obliged to rely on more generic capabilities like management skills, operating systems or product development.

Successful globalization goes to the heart of the organization's values and mission. The policies, skills and attitudes of managers in a global corporation show an inclusive world view not the exclusive world view that characterizes many executives today. An inclusive world view recognizes the distinctive nature and value of different world views. North American and European firms tend to adopt a Judeo-Christian world view. Increasingly this needs to be tempered by an appreciation of the Shintoist, Hindu, Confucian beliefs and other ways of viewing the world. The pressure imposed by many companies for homogeneity and conformity is gradually being replaced by an acceptance of the positive features of heterogeneity and diversity.

Sanrio, the Japanese toys and entertainment group, faced a major difficulty in its US operations because of its insensitivity to the US market. In 1988 there was a crisis in US–Japanese relations when a Japanese government official criticized African–Americans. The backlash hit Sanrio who sold a range of "Little Black Sambo" dolls. The image these dolls presented was deeply offensive to African–Americans who were already angry at the comments of the government officials. The wave of protest forced Sanrio to withdraw its entire range of products and had a deeply harmful effect on its trade in North America.

Sanrio's problems occurred because they did not build up the intensive market knowledge they required for effective market penetration. Some firms succeed globally because they identify distinct and often highly specialized global markets. Piranha Mouldings in the UK specialize in competition quality white water canoes. They chose their name because they were going to "eat up the opposition." They concentrate on the top end of the quality market, where fractions of seconds make the difference between success and failure. They have over 60 % of this market and at a recent world championship 14 out of 16 national teams used their canoes. Koenig and Bauer showed the same dedication to their niche in building a 90 % market share of the global market for money printing presses. These companies succeed because they effectively integrate their vision, strategy and capability from a global perspective.

Diversity

This shift to a global view affects every aspect of the organization – from its view of markets to the kind of control systems it operates. It is linked with a renewed awareness of the diversity of the business environment and a wish to recognize this diversity in the firm's culture and operations. Management control systems where all members of the management team speak the same language, expect the same rewards and punishments, and share the same values are different from those in firms in which none of these assumptions holds true.

An important feature of the failure of the UK to respond to the last industrial revolution was the rigid mindset of so many UK business executives in the first half of this century. They were a closed group who had been to the same schools and shared the same cozy beliefs – especially of their own superiority. The diverse origins of US and Germany business leaders made them far more responsive to the different expectations of the new consumer and industrial markets. The Japanese pioneers of industrialization recognized the importance of a society which was well integrated with a unity of vision. Schoppa highlights the policy makers' call, following the Meiji

> *Management control systems where all members of the management team speak the same language, expect the same rewards and punishments, and share the same values are different from those in firms in which none of these assumptions holds true.*

restoration, to "mobilise the talents of the whole nation, regardless of class." British observers were surprised to see that "children of all classes attended the same school." This emphasis on integration was translated into both work practices and individual behavior. The pattern is being repeated in Korea, Taiwan and Malaysia, where it is reinforced by a mixture of a sense of external threat (Korea and Taiwan), group consciousness (Bumiputra in Malaysia) and state policy.

In the Economist Intelligence Unit's study of the *Successful Corporation of the Year 2000* almost 40 % of business leaders identified "increasing diversity" as a major feature in the developing business environment. Culture, gender and ethnicity are just the most visible aspects of the increasingly diverse, external environment that is reshaping the internal and operational environment of firms that seek to prosper. There is growing evidence that enterprises that try to ignore this diversity are cutting themselves off from talent, missing major market opportunities and creating resistance to their development in both domestic and overseas markets.

Computers and telecommunications

The computing and telecommunications revolution makes it practically easier and conceptually harder for managers to design, develop and implement the changes required in the new global, heterogeneous and diverse environment. Advanced computer systems provide corporations with the capacity to manipulate far more data and variables than in the past. This often produces manipulation myopia or a sense that manipulating vast quantities of data is the same as managing useful information or knowledge. Computing power is dropping in price while systems are becoming more accessible. The integration of computing and telecommunications systems allows providers, users and intermediaries to open up new ways to communicate, manage operations and innovate.

These changes give managers access to information on the different aspects of the firm's operations and the ways the enterprise interacts with markets and others. IT enhances management's ability to understand, control and direct resources. It is easy to concentrate on the superficial aspects of computing power and ignore its scope for improving information systems, enhancing knowledge and understanding, and changing the nature of management. Novel developments in information systems will move the technologies out of the routine and the repetitive into areas that enhance the abilities of managers to develop and innovate. Korendo Shiotsuke, Fujitsu's director of public relations believes that "most systems in the past were used to replace human beings. In the future, we see the role of systems as supporting the creative work done by human beings."

The Anglo-US approach to business is dominated by a much more impersonal reductionist approach. Work and tasks are reduced as much as possible to their component parts. The role of workers is prescribed and controlled with efforts concentrated in avoiding human error, minimizing risk and replacing human systems with machine based ones. The different economic and social traditions of Japan and Germany produced a pattern of work that was far less reductionist than the UK and USA. The focus on added value in Japanese factories, novelties like quality circles, codeterminism in Germany and employee representation on supervisory boards created a much more integrated set of working relationships. This is reinforced by the smaller gaps in remuneration, the high proportion of technically qualified staff on the shop floor and the lower social barriers between workers. Technical and technological competence create a level of credibility that the highly mobile, professional manager with an administrative background cannot match.

This lack of credibility of management levels raises questions about the current emphasis on human relations skills, coaching and mentoring in Anglo-American management writing and advice. Many firms are drawing the superficial lesson from the "integrated people focus" of Japanese and German industry and successful firms like Asea Brown Boverie (ABB). Christopher Bartlett[37] describes how Goran Lindahl an executive vice president of ABB "spends 50 to 60 per cent of his time communicating directly with his people in a process he calls 'human engineering'." This prompts the notion in some firms that a greater emphasis on communication and more time spent walking and talking by the managerial bureaucrats will transform their separated, adverserial, low trust firms into integrated, value adding enterprises.The sunk investment of the managerial groups in firms like ABB is wished away.

Closer analysis highlights the strong links within the labor force, managerial and operational. Many managers have engineering and technical backgrounds and serve long periods in the heartland of the business, in operations or production. This establishes their credibility and provides a platform for trust building. Trust is reinforced by open lines of communication, greater sharing of benefits and more secure employment. The confidence goes both ways. Lindahl asserts that "people want to learn and are greatly motivated and satisfied when they do. Top management's challenge is not only to help people develop but to ensure that they do so in ways that support and reinforce the company's objectives."

A virtuous circle of interlocking elements can be identified which shaped modern Japanese, integrated, value focussed management (see Figure 2.1). Initially, lack of capital, skills and other resources precluded the type of resource intensive, machine driven systems adopted in the UK and North America. Cultural and social imperatives encouraged firms to link a people oriented approach to management with the search for continuous improvement, *kaizan*. These shortages allied with government leadership encouraged collaborative relationships and partnerships across the supplier–customer chain. The initial gains from these approaches encouraged further shop floor experiments with, for example, quality circles. Lack of indigenous local resources and expertise prompted Japanese firms to welcome external inputs. Before World War II Japanese leaders frequently visited UK and US industrial centers, and even the Emperor's sons went on "fact finding tours." After the war the work of the US military mission reinforced this pattern of search and adoption. The relatively high cost of market entry faced by Japanese firms and their reputation for low quality and weak distribution systems forced them to look for ways to cut costs (Just-In-Time Production), add value (Lean Production) and improve quality (Total Quality Management). This was achieved by channelling energy, skill and commitment into integrated work systems.

Figure 2.1

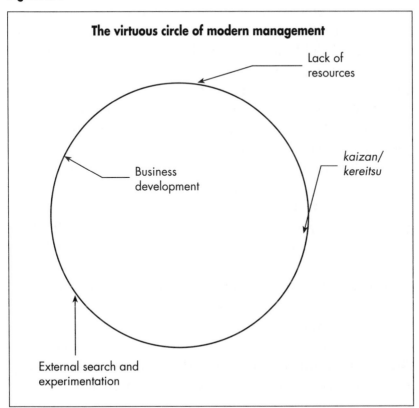

The virtuous circle of modern management

Lack of resources

kaizan/ kereitsu

Business development

External search and experimentation

Information and knowledge

In part this shift in emphasis towards channelling the energy, commitment and skill of people marks a wider move in the dominant influences on business performance. The first industrial revolution was driven by coal, the second by oil – the third will be driven by knowledge. The key to the effectiveness of managers and their business lies in their ability to access, use and enhance their knowledge. This is evident in the key unifying theme of the better, contemporary writing. Michael Porter's analysis of the roots to competitive advance places an emphasis on analytical skills of a high order. Porter comments that "implementing the generic strategies successfully requires different resources and skills. The generic strategies, also, imply differing organizational arrangements, control systems and inventive systems."[38] He is implicitly calling for the knowledge to identify, mobilize and analyze this material to produce effective strategies. Tom Peters uses action imagery when he talks of "liberation" and "chaos" but behind these are persistent references to the need to "understand the power of our smallest actions"[39] or "it's the dumb question followed up by a dozen even more elementary questions, that yield the pay dirt."

The search for, distribution and use of coal and oil shaped the previous industrial and economic revolutions. The same will be true for knowledge during this revolution. Those firms that get closest to the primary source, that learn to use it and that manage the distribution of knowledge are those best placed to prosper. Management systems in successful firms will reflect this. Tomorrow's manager/ leader will not adopt a casual, fragmented approach to the search for, use and exploitation of knowledge. Manager/leaders will seek knowledge with the same determination and systematic effort that oil, gas and raw materials companies now use to explore for those products. They will want to manage its distribution as much as Rockefeller wanted to control oil distribution. We are already seeing knowledge wars in, for example, the struggle to gain control of the Internet. Novell and Microsoft are not unlike Standard Oil and Shell in their determination to win and control new supplies, and there are more similarities. Some knowledge corporations and manager/leaders will set up large, established enterprises while "wildcatters" will look for speculative gains such as those occurring in Biotech companies

CONCLUSION

In a knowledge based industrial revolution, reductionist approaches are especially inappropriate. Innovations based on knowledge frequently come from the successful integration of two separate elements into a new unity. This form of creative development requires open and integrated organizations and management systems. The effective use of knowledge is essential if organizations hope to tap the opportunities created by globalization, diversity, computers and telecommunications and information while minimizing the associated risks. People or stakeholder focussed organizations seem more able to absorb the longer term shifts associated with radical change in the primary sources of competitive advantage described above than machine or money focussed enterprises.

This emphasis on people or knowledge has wider implications for business practice than is generally assumed. It is not enough for old style bureaucratic managers to add a little mentoring, counselling or walking about to their portfolio of skills. They will need to regain the trust of the workforce. This might involve a greater involvement in the negative as well as the positive features of corporate life. It is hard to establish trust and credibility on the back of low levels of loyalty, limited technical skills and disproportionate reward systems.

Knowledge is neither a passive nor a neutral factor in business. McKinsey & Company emphasize the importance for corporations to see knowledge as a strategic asset. The knowledge audit is a powerful tool in assessing the role, value and strategic contribution to the organization (see Table 2.2).

Table 2.2

The Knowledge Audit			
Do we have a clear picture of:	Yes	No	DK
The current key knowledge assets of the company	☐	☐	☐
The distinctive knowledge assets that give us a competitive edge today	☐	☐	☐
The knowledge assets of our major rivals	☐	☐	☐
The main sources of distinct knowledge assets that will affect our future competitive position	☐	☐	☐
The quality of our access to future knowledge assets	☐	☐	☐
The distribution of knowledge assets in the organization	☐	☐	☐
The effectiveness with which knowledge assets are deployed	☐	☐	☐
The current holders of competitively important knowledge inside and outside the enterprise	☐	☐	☐
The effectiveness of the knowledge transfer process inside, outside and at the point of exchange, e.g. through knowledge gatekeepers	☐	☐	☐
Effective ways to audit knowledge assets on a recurrent basis	☐	☐	☐

McKinsey argued that knowledge based strategies start with the strategy to be achieved, not with the knowledge. The strategy provides the focus and purpose for the knowledge resource. Focus and purpose are needed if knowledge strategies and assets are to be linked with the more traditional measures of assets and performance. Knowledge strategies are fundamentally people based. This is important, not only for the search and distribution of knowledge, but to provide the key integration elements between knowledge and more general aspects of business development. People and the networks they build, manage and engage in provide the key source of leverage for knowledge assets. This pushes power out from the center, headquarters or top of the enterprise across the enterprise to the users of knowledge. The combination of these forces shifts the center of gravity from the center onto the individual members and operations of the organization.

◆

The management structures can
now reflect more fully a more
natural organic structure freed
from the limitations of established
mechanistic structures

◆

Chapter 3

◆

STRUCTURES AND STRATEGIES FOR SURVIVAL AND PROSPERITY

MANAGEMENT STRUCTURES

Management structures generally reflect the mixture of technology and culture that shapes the industry or enterprise. Communication, control and information technologies are especially important in shaping management structures. In the 19th century, communication was generally personal, hand-written and slow. Management structures reflected this. Manufacturing plants were concentrated and their owners lived locally. This provided direct personal supervision and control. Distant operations required a different form of control system or structure. Poor and slow access meant that local managers required a great deal of autonomy, which, in turn, posed special problems for the great international trading concerns like Swires, Jardines, The Hudson Bay Company and others. They resolved this by placing particular emphasis in recruiting their agents from groups they trusted, especially family members. Trustworthiness was even more important than competence. There were, also, very few levels of hierarchy between the agent or local manager and the proprietor. They were neither needed, because of the infrequent contact, nor appropriate, because of the wide and distant relationship.

Technological and market change transformed these structures. Many of the new oil, chemicals, electronics, vehicles or engineering sectors provided opportunities for significant economies of scale. New communications technologies and sharp increases in the speed and reliability of existing technologies made it possible to extend the direct span of control of managers. The autonomy of managers was reduced while information systems became more impersonal and relatively fast. The local agent of the Conrad novel gave way to the corporate man. Changing technologies had altered structures which went on to change the culture of businesses. The growth of mass production techniques especially in the type of multiproduct, multifunction firm that dominated the middle part of the 20th century was closely linked with a sharp increase in the numbers and levels of supervisory management. "Between 1948 and 1966 ... the ratio of supervisory to non-supervisory employees in the private business sector increased by nearly 75 per cent – from roughly thirteen supervisory employees per hundred non-supervisory employees to more than twenty two."[40] Although UK industry seldom matched the scale and structure of US corporations, a similar transformation took place. Alister Mant[41] argues that this was partly a result of the "massive, dependence" on the USA "to the point where it is hardly an exaggeration to suggest that the leadership function in the collective mind of British industry was vested in America." These shifts in industrial practice were mirrored by the increasing specialization and fragmentation of education and training for managers and businesses.

> *The local agent of the Conrad novel gave way to the corporate man. Changing technologies had altered structures which went on to change the culture of businesses.*

The end of hierarchy

The most immediate effect of the new information technologies that dominate modern industries is the move away from rigid, hierarchical structures. Traditional technologies worked best when workers and managers were concentrated in a single location. Their workflows reflected the hierarchical flow production of electromechanical systems. Alfred P. Sloan had built on Henry Ford's transformation of the factory to revolutionize the office. Complex managerial bureaucracies were created at General Motors around committee systems that were invaluable in creating cohesion and system throughout the enterprise. The approach was replicated throughout the Anglo-US industrial world at firms like IBM, ICI and BP.

Sophisticated management tools were introduced which reinforced the separate, professional role of managers. These tools frequently reflected past best practice, but seldom produced the long-term gains anticipated. Several commentators[42] have considered the contrasting fortunes of 3M and The Norton Company, who over the last 20 years have engaged in head to head competition in the US abrasives market. 3M has sustained a strong internal, entrepreneurial and people oriented approach over this period. The firm's philosophy is well summarized by Livio D. De Simone, Chairman and CEO. "Senior management's primary role is to create an internal environment in which people understand and value our way of operating ... our job is one of creation and destruction – supporting individual initiative while breaking down bureaucracy and cynicism. It all depends on a person trust relationship between those at the top and those at the lower levels of the business." In contrast, Norton were pioneers in the use of analytic techniques ranging from the Profit Impact of Market Share (PIMS) developed by The Boston Consulting Group through the Nine Block Grid to matching resources to opportunities. In the late 1960s the firms were roughly the same size. By the end of the 1980s 3M was eight times the size of Norton. In 1990 Norton was absorbed into the French company, Compagnie de Saint-Cobain.

41

Robert Hall, author of *The soul of the enterprise,* would define 3M as a firm with a new type "soul" while Norton has an old type "soul" (see Figure 3.1).

Figure 3.1

Hall's new and old soul of enterprise						
Mode A					*Mode Z*	
Profit first priority					Customer satisfaction first priority	
Assets are things					Assets are people	
Thinkers are separated from doers					Doers and thinkers the same	
Traditional mass production					Lean production	
Separated marketing with suppliers and customers at arm's length					Integrated marketing with partnership based relationships with suppliers and customers	
Performance measurement for control					Performance measurement for improvement and adding value	
Strong hierarchies					Weak hierarchies	
Scale economies important					Time economies important	

Source: Locke, R. (1996) *The Collapse of the American Management Mystique.* Oxford: Oxford University Press

Notes:
Company A's profile indicated by the solid line is that of a traditional "old soul" business
Company B's profile indicated by the dotted line is that of a "new soul" business

New information and control technologies are best when they are organized on a nonhierarchical, user–need basis. Hierarchies give way to hub based structures. This means that information flows where it is needed rather than where tradition or authority expect it to flow. The multiple layers of traditional structures reflected limited personal, spans of control. Information technologies extend these spans of control. The capabilities and "reach" of those closest to policy and operations extend, reducing the need for multiple levels of intermediary managers. The role of the intermediary or middle manager changes from being one of controlling and supervising to one of enabling and developing. They become managers of the company's heartland. This is easier in an organization which accepts the notion of codetermination, joint decision making, empowerment or ownership of tasks than in an environment which emphasizes authority, control and the separation of tasks.

The management structures can now reflect more fully a more natural organic structure freed from the limitations of established mechanistic structures. Dr Yoshito Maruta of Japan's successful Kao Group has his own version of this when he talks of building the business around a system of

Shifts in the capabilities of and relationships between suppliers, employees, operating systems and customers mean that the locus of authority moves closer to the point of action.

"biological self-control." Multiple layers of management become redundant as improved information flows reduce the need for personal scrutiny and supervision. New technologies can flow on a "need to know" basis further limiting the need for successive levels of the managerial hierarchy to act as filters or funnels. Shifts in the capabilities of and relationships between suppliers, employees, operating systems and customers mean that the locus of authority moves closer to the point of action. None of these groups expect to battle through layers of bureaucracy for either decisions or delivery.

The chief executive of one successful German company quoted by Herman Simon highlights this approach. He comments that "if people are not challenged by hard work, they resort to unproductive activities like writing memos, holding meetings, occupying themselves. Most of the intrigue and bureaucratic hassle that plagues large companies is avoidable...." Percy Barnevik of ABB takes this approach further by asserting the importance of using the total capability of people. "We have to be able to recognize and employ that untapped ability that each individual brings to work every day." For most of the new generation of successful business leaders the cutting edge of this approach is improved customer satisfaction and competitive advantage. Josef Kratz, the CEO of JK Ergoline, links the twin issues of commitment and customer satisfaction in his views. "Wherever the opportunities lie, we will be fast enough and flexible enough to grasp them. And we will strive for market leadership, there's no question about that. We have proven our flexibility ... [we were] determined to become number one in the world. That was our goal, and here we are." Komatsu's "Growth, Global, Groupwide" strategy is based on the same determination to grow through people and customer satisfaction, to win global leadership and extend this across all the firm's activities. These approaches are especially important in knowledge based industries and companies because "unlike capital, knowledge is most valuable when those on the front line control and use it."[43]

The reluctance of many Anglo-US corporations to accept and internalize this perspective leads some people to doubt their long-term competitiveness. Konosuke Matsushita, founder of the Matsushita Electrical Industrial Corporation (total sales 1994, $61Bn) takes a clear view on these prospects.

We are going to win and the industrial West is going to lose out; there's not much you can do about it because the reasons for your failure are within yourselves. Your firms are built on the Taylor model, and even worse, so are your heads. With your bosses doing the thinking while the workers wield screwdrivers, you're convinced deep down that this is the right way to run a business. For you the essence of management is getting ideas out of the heads of managers and into the hands of labour.

We have gone beyond the Taylor model. We realise that business has become so complex, the survival of firms so precarious, and our environment increasingly unpredictable, competitive, and dangerous that firms' continuing existence depends on their day to day mobilisation of every ounce of intelligence.

This organic, integrated, mobilized approach lies at the heart of successful management in the new business environment. Hammer and Champy[44] describe the ways in which management structures must change to reflect new circumstances. They open *Reengineering the corporation* with the injunction that:

A set of principles laid down more than two centuries ago has shaped the structure, management and performance of American businesses throughout the nineteenth and twentieth centuries ... the time has come to retire those principles and to adopt a new set. The alternative is for corporate America to close its doors and go out of business.

Although their comments oversimplify the nature and the form of change, their essential argument holds true. The challenge is not just to corporate America. It extends to UK and other businesses that are locked into traditional management structures. The challenge is equally great for those public and voluntary enterprises that have adopted managerialism without recognizing the needs to change that are recognized by the best firms.

DIVIDED WE FALL

At the heart of these changes lie fundamental shifts in the nature of work. Success in the first industrial revolution was founded on the effective application of the notion of the division of labor to the work of

The challenge is not just to corporate America. It extends to UK and other businesses that are locked into traditional management structures.

45

operatives. As early as 1798 Eli Whitney was using the notion of the division of labor to fill an order from the US government for 10,000 muskets. His use of interchangeable parts was duplicated with increasing frequency as the century progressed. Machines gradually replaced manual labor in factories across North America making clocks, watches, agricultural machinery, sewing machines, typewriters, and bicycles.

Process production was employed in making shoes, textiles, hammers and wrenches as well as foodstuffs such as meats and canned fruits and vegetables. The system was sufficiently well established by the middle of the 19th century to be called "the American System." Henry Ford drew all these ideas together when he linked interchangeable parts and process production with the moving conveyor belt originally employed in the UK in the Liverpool docks. The first industrial revolution had transformed the integrated labor force of agricultural society into one fragmented and shaped by the division of labor.

Fordism took this to its logical conclusion. It took one of Ford's peers, Alfred P. Sloan of General Motors, to introduce many of the changes that marked the move from the first to the second industrial revolution. During the 19th century the separated labor force was led by an integrated managerial group. This integration took many forms. Social integration was an important characteristic of 19th century managers. Their management systems were integrated with little separation of the marketing, production and financial systems. Management structures in large companies were characterized by relatively little departmentalization or divisionalization. In a sense, Ford was probably the last best example of 19th century industrial organization while General Motors were one of the pioneers of the new business paradigm.

Sloan spelt out his problems. "There was a lack of control and of any means of control in operations and finance, and a lack of adequate information about anything."[45] His solutions centered on the application of the division of labor onto management.

He created "a highly rational and objective mode of operation" in which roles and responsibilities were decentralized and closely specified. The dominant management paradigm of this century is a separated labor force directed by a separated management group.

Yesterday's managers for tomorrow's businesses

Competitive success today and tomorrow depends on undertaking the same type of fundamental review of the suitability of existing management and business systems as Sloan undertook in the 1920s. The key question is: do we have yesterday's management for tomorrow's businesses? It is evident that neither the fragmented workforce nor the separated management is required by the dominant technologies nor do they suit today's markets. Rigid and mechanical technologies and information systems were hard to separate from rigid and mechanistic organizations. Fluid and flexible technologies and information systems should not be separated from flexible and organic management structures.

This shifts the responsibility of management away from detailed specification of tasks and tight control to leadership based on understanding the capabilities of the enterprise. Values gain special importance as they provide the means of integrating the venture at the lowest cost to the greatest effect. Warren Bennis, former University President, comments:

> ... [traditional] organizations are, by their nature bureaucratic, with a mindset of control, order and prediction. In more stable times, when manpower resources were channelled to make stovepipes or steel these techniques worked well. Now we are moving towards organizations that are more like temporary systems, networks or clusters. The mindset of these organizations will be alignment, creativity and empowerment.

Each of the processes identified by Bennis – alignment, creativity and empowerment – requires a higher level of understanding of the capabilities and competences of the organization than the control and ordering tasks under traditional structures. This is especially true if managers expect to predict with any degree of accuracy the likely results of their actions. The failure to align the capabilities of the organization to the needs of the environment is the best available explanation of the problems of Sony at CBS, Marks and Spencer at Brooks Bros, Imperial Group at Howard Johnson, to name a few.

This failure to align capabilities and needs is equally evident in organic developments. The failure of the EMI body scanner shows how a technological success can turn into a market failure when the capabilities of the firm and the needs of the market are out of sync. EMI had few of the capabilities required to open up the US market for its product or to defend its interests when Jimmy Carter imposed barriers to its development. General Motors' spectacular failures at Hamtramck showed that its old skill at buying its way out of a hole worked well when the solution followed a well worn route. This approach was counterproductive when the need to think was as important as the need to spend. The Mercury Division of Cable and Wireless learned the same lessons in the UK when it tried to win a market share by matching the policies and capabilities of its giant rival British Telecom.

Alignment is not the neat or straightforward process implied by some writers. It involves in-depth understanding of the enterprise and its people, those both inside and outside the organization. It demands a willingness to look beyond the obvious features of the firm's past successes into the real reasons for those successes. Corporations enjoy repeating past successes, even if the world has changed and they turn into modern failures.

The capacity to break the mold and identify new ways forward is closely identified with the notion of continuous discontinuity. Continuity is important but should be a platform for development, not a trap or easy option. The ability to manage discontinuity must be integrated into existing or revised control and operations. This allows the enterprise to focus on the opportunities inherent in change and the value of effective innovation. The ability to manage change and innovation cannot be confined to the product and process aspects of the organization. It must extend into the heartland of the enterprise through its mission, values and culture. Issues like fairness in the workplace, the avoidance of gender or ethnic bias are heartland issues not peripheral topics.

There is some evidence[46] that organizations with a strong gender bias or that fail to create real opportunities for women are more likely to be locked into the old style Taylorite rigidities. Research on women owned or managed businesses suggests that they are more likely to adopt open, integrated and consensus approaches to organization and business development.[47] The gender bias is a major problem for European businesses where women constitute 41 % of the labor pool yet form less than 15 % of the managerial labor pool and only 1 % of main board directors. The business benefits of a stronger female role in decision making positions is clearly articulated by Roger Young, Director General of Britain's Institute of Management. "Female ways of managing – consensus decisions, the ability to handle several projects at a time and strong interpersonal skills – will be even more appropriate in the next millennium." Consensus decision making is especially important in rapidly changing industries where the inability to establish a firm framework for consensus inhibits progress and creativity.

CREATIVE TOLERANCE

Creativity takes many forms in the successful corporation. The most basic is creative tolerance. Established managerial bureaucracies are built around set procedures and ascribed roles. This works well while business conditions are basically stable. Turbulence means that old rules do not work and may be counterproductive. Creative tolerance is needed to endorse a willingness to rethink and reexamine approaches to arrive at the *right* solution rather than the safe solution. Successful reengineering requires this type of creative tolerance. The same tolerance is required to develop the entrepreneurial skills of the managerial workforce. The Economist Intelligence Unit's analysis of *The successful corporation of the year 2000*[48] identified entrepreneurialism as one of the most important attributes of successful senior executives in the run up to the millennium.

The effective management of creativity goes beyond tolerance. It requires a willingness to look beyond the immediate confines when tackling an issue. Hammer's[49] notion of "process orientation" is fundamentally creative. It calls for managers to look at "an entire process" and "cut across organizational boundaries." Hamel adds further dimensions when he advocates looking beyond the organization into the long term, and drawing together the view and visions of colleagues to "stake out the new competitive space."[50] Rosabeth Moss Kanter draws out the need to eliminate the barriers to creativity: "Rarely do bosses in tradition-bound organizations actually have to say 'no' ... to make it clear to people that new ideas are not welcome."[51] The extent of environmental change requires that leaders devise strategies to enhance and draw out the creativity of everyone in the enterprise. It will still be necessary to say no to many proposals. The key management skill lies in saying no in ways that stimulate creativity rather than repress it. International food and drinks companies like PepsiCo rely heavily on sustaining creativity while sustaining a powerful sense of direction and

> *Turbulence means that old rules do not work and may be counterproductive. Creative tolerance is needed to endorse a willingness to rethink and reexamine approaches to arrive at the right solution rather than the safe solution.*

business focus. This partly explains why Roger Enrico, vice chairman of PepsiCo believes he adds most value to the business by concentrating his efforts on developing the next generation of the firm's leaders. He organizes and leads retreats, seminars and working groups so that he can tap into the creative thinking of participants, build a sense of unity and reinforce people's belief that they can make a difference.

The extent of environmental change requires that leaders devise strategies to enhance and draw out the creativity of everyone in the enterprise. It will still be necessary to say no to many proposals. The key to management skill lies in saying no in ways that stimulate creativity rather than repress it.

UNITED WE STAND

Traditional organizations see leadership and empowerment as being in conflict. John Aaker's famous leaked memo at IBM (when he seemed to blame everyone but top management for the firm's problems) symbolizes this view. The proposition that "if people did as I instructed them we'd have no problems" is a classic statement of the command economy. The challenge now is to bring leadership and empowerment together in a new synthesis. The task of the leadership group is to articulate a vision and set of values that reflect the capabilities of the organization, and that, in turn, provide access to competences that generate a competitive advantage and empower their colleagues to deliver the benefits.

This shift is unlikely to emerge in enterprises that sustain the type of fragmented, divided and separated operator and managerial groups which have dominated organizations for most of this century. Current technologies and markets make reintegration practical and desirable. The best production and information systems available today are flexible, interactive and open, enabling operators and managers to intervene directly to improve quality, add value and increase customer benefits. Computer Aided Design and Manufacture can free producers from the machine logic of Fordism by moving away from a preoccupation with the parts to an emphasis on the whole. Mass customization in some form is the likely outcome of these changes.

This is made more likely by the blurring of the lines between products and services. In mature industrial markets the service associated with a product is often more important in sustaining customer satisfaction than its technical features. Finance, warranty, maintenance, availability and product support have long dominated industrial and institutional markets, and now these features are beginning to dominate consumer markets. This reflects, in part, the degree of technological convergence in most markets and highlights the ability of firms to get a competitive edge by development and innovation in service. The synthesis of the physical and service features of the product makes it easier to match the benefits delivered to the needs of the individual – mass customization by another name.

Leadership groups in the service sector have internalized this kind of thinking more easily than those in manufacturing. The nature of their industries forces them to concentrate on intangibles. Jan Carlton of SAS highlights this when he commented that: "the leaders must have a view of the culture required to deliver business results and provide people with an opportunity for meaning in work. You walk the talk and you are credible." This view is gaining acceptance among the more successful leaders in manufacturing. Jack Welch at GE, Percy Barnevik at ABB and others are reexamining their core assumptions to transform their firms.

Deconstructing corporations

In many cases, responding to change means reviewing the nature and structure of corporations. The deconstruction of corporations extends further than breaking them up into smaller units. Dominic Cadbury of Cadbury–Schweppes calls this the creative disintegration of large corporations. Deconstruction means understanding the hidden assumptions and beliefs that bind the large enterprise and using this new understanding to rebuild the organization around smaller, better integrated enterprises. Alan M. Webber argues that "people who manage in the new economy and companies that compete in it, live in the creative tension of creative destruction."[52]

> The renewed emphasis on the values that underpin an enterprise derive from the difficulties of control in the new, more open entrepreneurial environment. This is especially true when the emphasis shifts from management of controllable inputs to less easily controlled processes and outputs.

Breaking up large firms to build more entrepreneurial units creates new opportunities. These units compete successfully against the older, line managed enterprise founded on the division of labor. They gain a competitive edge in two ways. First their unity reflects the unity of the customer needs they meet. Second, they combine flexibility with low costs. They are held together by their value and information systems. The great business leaders of the first and second industrial revolutions, Josiah Wedgwood, Samuel Whitbread, Francis Lowell, Andrew Carnegie, William Lever, Charles Schwab, Pierre du Pont, Werner von Siemens and George Westinghouse were as willing to discuss the values that underpinned their businesses as they were the innovations that drove their firms.

Control

The renewed emphasis on the values that underpin an enterprise derive from the difficulties of control in the new, more open entrepreneurial environment. This is especially true when

53

the emphasis shifts from management of controllable inputs to less easily controlled processes and outputs. Part of the success of Japanese industry lies in their clearer articulation of the core values of the enterprise and their willingness to empower all employees to defend these values. The clearest case of this is the use of the *waigaya* session at Honda. This allows any employee to raise any issue at an open meeting. Critically, it gives employees the chance to question decisions, instructions or procedures which undermine the core value of commitment to quality. Self control, in this form, eliminates the costs and waste associated with external inspection and testing.

The integration of work, expertise (*Fachkompetenz*) and technical competence is a priority in German companies. This is part of an industrial tradition which means that shop floor staff in engineering and production were able to interact with customers, understand their needs and deliver against their specifications. Studies of industrial innovations which compared the approaches of Anglo-US and North European companies found a marked difference in the policies adopted. Anglo-US companies developing new products and services adopted an intensive, separated marketing approach. They preferred to involve customers late in the product development process, preferably when "a finished product was available." Links between suppliers and customers were usually funnelled along a fairly narrow path through sales and purchasing departments.

German firms and other North European companies with shared traditions adopted an extensive, integrated marketing approach. They involved customers at very early stages in the development of new products and services. Idea development, business analysis and early development were often undertaken jointly. Perhaps inevitably, this required the creation of extensive networks of links between people in the supplier and customer firms. Design team talked to design team, production people talked to each other as did engineering, research and development and sales as well as those formally involved in the transaction. The result was that industrial innovation in German companies was less costly as customers shared many of the costs. Failure rates were far lower, partly because problems and likely difficulties were identified early. There was little

Organizations in which there is a high degree of trust are more capable of successfully initiating change and responding to imposed change.

evidence to support the fear among Anglo-US firms, that good ideas would be leaked or stolen. Symbiotic development paid far greater dividends than separated or adversarial development.

The value of these intimate links between customers and suppliers is increasingly recognized. Dell Computers eradicated the middlemen between the producer and the customer to improve quality links (and reduce costs). As the US retail giant Home Depot puts it:

spend whatever time is required with a customer to figure out which product will solve his or her home-repair problem. The company's store personnel are not in a hurry. Their first priority is to make sure that the customer gets the right product, whether its retail price comes to $59 or 59 cents. ... Clerks do not spend time with customers just to be nice. They do so because the company's business strategy is built not just around selling home repair and improvement items but around the customer's needs for information and service.[53]

The same principles of openness and involvement are applied by the growing number of entrepreneurs and chief executives who give their employees a direct line to them to raise problems or concerns. Some even give employees their home telephone number. These actions add a further feature to the value structure of the enterprise – trust. Organizations in which there is a high degree of trust are more capable of successfully initiating change and responding to imposed change.

Trust

The success of trust based organizations contrasts sharply with the problems of corporations in which a blame based culture has evolved. In blame based organizations the priority is to find someone to blame for the problem rather than solving the problem. At its nadir a few years ago, IBM epitomized a blame culture. Top management were too busy blaming others for the problems to take any action. The rest of the managerial labor pool was too busy blaming top management to respond to pressures for change.

Trust based organizations recognized the multidimensional nature of the trust relationship. Trust operates within the enterprise and defines the nature of the relationships between senior, middle and operations management as well as their links with other colleagues in the enterprise. Trust has a public, formal aspect in the mission or value statement of the organization. This has real weight when it is reinforced by the actions and policies adopted in the organization, since it is easier to build trust on the basis of shared experiences and values. In Germany, for example, the shared educational experiences of technicians and engineers who have attended *Fachhachschulen* (technical universities) or other universities added to the unified system of qualifications supports trust building.

Shifting and shaping an organization's value system requires a variety of actions. The hardest is probably the attempt to understand the current values and beliefs. These provide both the starting point for change and the platform on which to build values and beliefs that meet the needs of the different stakeholders in the firm. An effective value statement is more than an elegant piece of prose. It has to go to the heart of the beliefs and assumptions of the people who are expected to deliver these values. The value control and reward systems of the enterprise reinforce each other. A public statement of values which emphasizes quality and customer care has little meaning if control systems emphasize cost savings, or reward systems give other issues prominence. Trust takes a long time to create but can be lost very quickly.

Values cannot be imposed in the way that dress codes, reward systems and other features of business life can be imposed. As Jan Carlton of SAS said: you have to walk the talk. The strongest and most easily sustained values emerge from a real dialog between all stakeholders in the venture about its purpose, operations and outputs. The single most important act of the leader is to empower these stakeholders to have a real say and influence on the purpose, operations and output of the organization.

Trust based relationships extend beyond the enterprise to its suppliers and customers. The approach adopted by Home Depot works because customers trust the firm to give them the best, not the most expensive solution. In Britain, Marks and Spencer established a trust based relationship with its customers by pioneering "no quibble" product refunds. These external programmes of trust building cannot be separated from internal policies. Alienated and hostile employees will not implement successful external efforts to build trust with customers. It is hard to get employees to treat customers well if they themselves are treated badly. The converse of this, treat your staff well and they treat your external partners well, is formalized by innovative companies like Body Shop, but recurs throughout the business environment in successful organizations.

The ethics, governance and environmental attitudes adopted by the firm underpin the environment of trust created within the enterprise and with its partners. The leadership group's role in building a trust based organization often starts with the adoption of a clear and sustainable ethical code and a responsible attitude to the organization's role in the community and towards the environment. At Perot Systems the value statement demands that "we operate with integrity by treating our customers, people and suppliers in a fair and honest manner – as we want to be treated." The former head of Marks and Spencer, Lord Sieff, believed that "business only contributes fully to a society if it is efficient, profitable and socially responsible." Failures to implement responsible attitudes to environment have negative effects both inside and outside the company. The Exxon Valdez disaster cost Exxon almost $15Bn, with clean up costs and fines a minority element of that amount. The largest costs were a resulting discount on share values and loss of market share.

Empowerment

Knowledge and acceptance of and commitment to the goals of the enterprise lie at the heart of thinking about empowerment. Managers who seek to empower their employees add new dimensions to their relationships. They move beyond delegation of activity to the allocation of authority. The empowered individual or group can decide on a course of action and, within accepted limits, take that action. The hardest aspect of empowerment for most managers lies in the need to delegate authority while still accepting responsibility.

In some fields of endeavor empowerment has long been the norm. In a football team, the manager or coach can give his or her instructions before the game but once on the field the players are empowered. Performing artists are empowered to interpret the text. The more talented the performer, the more freedom he or she is given by the director. Academics are similarly empowered. Three aspects of work come together to increase the value of empowerment:

> Managers who seek to empower their employees add new dimensions to their relationships. They move beyond delegation of activity to the allocation of authority.

- unforeseen changes can demand an immediate response;
- the individual talent of the worker can have a marked effect on results;
- lack of freedom may inhibit achievement.

CONCLUSION

Effective management structures match the capabilities of the organization to the needs of the environment. These structures are influenced by dominant technologies and market features. The management structures that emerged a century ago reflected the efforts of organizations to control their operations and direct their workforces along well regulated lines. At the start of the century a divide emerged between the more separated and fragmented structures adopted by Anglo-US corporations and the more integrated approaches which characterized German and Japanese firms. There were enterprises in all these societies which departed from the stereotypes outlined above.

The dominant cultural and social values in the society have a profound effect on the way organizations allocate resources and interpret the technological and market pressures. Change, especially in communication and control and information technologies, is forcing firms to reexamine the way they organize their management systems. This reexamination is raising questions about the value of many of the features which have characterized organizations, particularly those in the USA and UK, during this century. Rigid and elaborate hierarchies fitted well with the needs of the dominant production technologies in industrial and consumer goods. These structures encouraged the introduction of large numbers of supervisory and management staff and delivered the high levels of control required by US and UK business.

This organizational model faces major problems today. New technologies are less dependent on hierarchies and seem to work best with natural, organic structures. Close control and supervision does not work well with newly important groups such as the knowledge workers in telecommunications, information and computing. Elsewhere, the best returns grow out of an emphasis on deploying the talent of people rather than exploiting their labor. Creativity, innovation and business development require more cohesive, better integrated and open approaches to workplace organization. This type of management increases in value as enterprises strive for the greater flexibility of entrepreneurial businesses.

◆

Graduate workers are part of a
new environment that requires
new kinds of managers with
different skills and competences.
An important aspect of this
change will be a blurring of the
line between the leader and the
manager.

◆

Chapter 4

◆

TO KNOW
IS TO SUCCEED

The knowledge based industrial revolution, with its emphasis on innovation, quality and service, extends these principles to a widening set of activities. Robert Eccles[54] noted this phenomenon in his examination of successful investment bankers. the greater the freedom to shape their work, the higher their productivity. Shoshana Zuboff found the same in studies of workers in technology based firms.[55] Increasing numbers of firms and industries find that the same focus on change, talent and achievement produces major gains from empowered workers and managers. This confounds the assumption made by Adam Smith in *The Wealth of Nations* and F. W. Taylor in *Scientific Management.* Their belief (that limiting discretion and breaking jobs down to their component parts is the key to operational efficiency) has dominated management thinking for 200 years.

Successful empowerment calls for major changes in the locus of control in organizations and in the role of managers. Decision making moves from the point in the enterprise that gives maximum control – usually the top – to the point of maximum benefit – usually the point of production, distribution or interaction with customers or suppliers. This shift requires a reduction in the degree of specialization and fragmentation. Customers, for example, are unwilling to tolerate actions, responses or decisions that must be referred elsewhere. Effective communication is essential to hold the organization together and sustain a sense of direction and purpose. Complex hierarchies and multiple layers of organizational bureaucracy become redundant.

Successful empowerment calls for major changes in the locus of control in organizations and in the role of managers. Decision making moves from the point in the enterprise that gives maximum control – usually the top – to the point of maximum benefit – usually the point of production, distribution or interaction with customers or suppliers.

FEDERALISM AND SUBSIDIARITY[56]

The dominant evolutionary trend in business for most of the last 200 years was towards centralization and control. Corporations grew larger and control became more centralized. The renewed emphasis on entrepreneurship, leadership and empowerment marks a move away from this position. Some of the most successful organizations are loose coalitions of businesses. Richard Branson of Virgin forged his business along these lines. He says:

> **Our record company ... was run by a fairly entrepreneurially minded person who wanted to expand and grow. But because I believe that "small is beautiful", whenever the company got too big, I'd ask to see the deputy managing director, the deputy sales director, the deputy marketing director and tell them they were the managing director, the sales director, the marketing director of a new company. They were given a stake in the new company so**

that they too could become entrepreneurs. ... The end result was that we had fifty small record companies around the world with no more than sixty people working out of any one building.

This kind of federal structure is increasingly common as ambitious chief executives appreciate the limits to their span of control and look for ways to capitalize on the entrepreneurial talents of their employees. The federal model is capable of extending beyond the identification of specific, distinct operating units, and can operate satisfactorily within functions such as sales, logistics and R&D. It contains within another subtle shift in the management of organizations. This the shift from the autocracy of top management to the principle of subsidiarity.

The idea of subsidiarity is largely borrowed from politics. It means that, in a federal state, authority for actions and decisions resides wherever possible with the local governing authority. Its application to business means that authority rests with those nearest the action whenever possible. At American Airlines it means that the staff at the ticket desk can decide on upgrades, and probably, therefore, that paying passengers get upgraded rather than staff and people in the travel trade. At Marks and Spencer it means that shop staff can decide on replacing goods, similarly at Toyota the workers can stop the production line to solve a problem.

Integration not separation is central to empowerment.

Integration not separation is central to empowerment. Three integrating assumptions are important:

- the empowered staff know and support the aims of the company;
- staff can be trusted to take action where necessary and learn from any mistakes;
- staff have the understanding, competence and desire to tackle problems constructively.

Each of these assumptions about the workforce places a complementary responsibility on management. People can only know and support the goals of the enterprise if efforts are made to communicate and win support for these goals. Trust goes both ways. Empowered workers require as much support when they get things wrong as when they get things right. Education, training and development are necessary to build up the competences of employees.

Quality

The earliest successes of empowerment in manufacturing were linked with efforts to improve quality. Deming and his followers in Japan adopted a fundamentally integrative approach to work and quality improvement. Deming's 14 points focus on "breaking down barriers," "removing barriers" while "instilling pride in workmanship", and "driving out fear." Supervision exists "to help." Firms should "cease [their] dependence on inspection" and shift the emphasis to "education and retraining" as part of a "new philosophy" founded on "constancy of purpose towards improvement of product."

It was, however, the delivery of this approach in the workplace that highlighted the nature and extent of the change. The Massachusetts Institute of Technology[57] study exploring in depth the revolution in car production produced by the Japanese describes the difference in practice.

"The work pace was clearly harder at Takaoko [the Toyota Factory], and yet there was a sense of purposefulness, not simply of workers going through motions with their minds elsewhere under the eye of the foreman. The emphasis at all levels was in "adding value." Notions like "Total Quality", "Zero Defects" etc. cannot be achieved through supervision or inspection. They come from a unified approach to improvement with managers and workers cooperating over the long term. Authority, responsibility and action work in harmony. Without this sense of integration and harmony it is impossible to have a

system in which "each worker along the line can pull a cord just above the work station to stop the line if a problem is found."[58]

Organizational change[59, 60]

Quality programs such as those described above cannot be grafted on to traditional, centralized bureaucratic organizations. Fundamental change is needed if firms are to adapt to their new environment. It is, however, difficult to produce the kind of change needed without a sustained effort to challenge old assumptions while winning the hearts and minds of those most affected by change. As long ago as the 16th century, Machiavelli pointed out the difficulty of introducing change.

There is nothing more difficult to execute, nor more dubious of success, nor more dangerous to administer than to introduce a new order of things; for he who introduces it has all those who profit from the old order as his enemies, and he only has lukewarm allies in all those who might profit from the new. This lukewarmness partly stems from fear of their adversaries who have the law on their side, and partly from the scepticism of men, who do not truly believe in new things unless they have personal experience of them. Therefore it happens that whenever those who are enemies (of change) have the change to attack, they do so enthusiastically, whereas those other defend hesitantly, so that they together with the prince are in danger.[61]

THE LONG MARCH

Machiavelli highlights the central problem of introducing organizational change: not everyone sees the need for change while many feel they will lose out from change. Even when difficulties are public and widely discussed, it is easy for those involved to ignore the messages. An insider at American Express acknowledged after its crisis in the early 1990s that they resisted change because "we let success blind us. We were inflexible. We were arrogant. We were dreaming." An external crisis is often the most powerful stimulus to change. Ed Artzt, the Chief Executive of Procter & Gamble says that following a crisis "we have a much better view of our own mortality, and that is a great reliever of arrogance." Sir Chris Bonnington the Everest explorer compares this problem with the oxygen starvation that affects mountaineers who stay at high altitude too long. Judgement becomes impaired, errors proliferate, danger signs ignored unless climbers come down occasionally to lower, oxygen rich areas.

Change programs often come unstuck because the leadership group is not ready for the "long march" that change involves.

Clear, outward symbols of change can be a more acceptable substitute than a crisis. Many privatized corporations like British Airways and British Telecom owe part of their success to change in their institutional set-up. The success of AT&T and the "baby" Bells since the breakup reflect the formalization of change. In effect the defender of the old rules cannot turn to them for protection because they no longer exist. Continuity and persistence are equally important. Change programs often come unstuck because the leadership group is not ready for the "long march" that change involves. The implications of the long march analogy go beyond determination and persistence, important though both are. The long march is more likely to reach its destination if people agree about the goal and have a good map. The map has greater value when there are guides who can find new routes if obstacles appear. There will always be people who need different forms

The long march is more likely to reach its destination if people agree about the goal and have a good map.

of support at various times and whose needs ought to be incorporated into the plan.

The resistance to change is often passive and is frequently associated with the helplessness people feel when faced with change. Liddell Hart, the British military historian highlighted the dangers of this sentiment when he commented that "helplessness leads to hopelessness and hopelessness invariably leads to failure." Corporations now face an additional challenge – the institutionalization of change. Endemic change in the external environment forces firms to build continuous change into their own operations. Calls to "consolidate" or "stabilize" are siren calls that must be resisted.

Continuous discontinuity

The ability to manage continuous discontinuity is the key to success especially in those industries where knowledge or access to knowledge is the main driver of market and business development. Continuous discontinuity occurs when discontinuity, that is, a significant shift in the external environment which is not a linear development from the past situation, becomes commonplace. The computer industry faced this when machine size became less important than accessibility, when software became more important than hardware, and again when the priority given to the amount of computing power in a single machine became less important than networking. The materials industries have faced similar discontinuities. The massive effort to produce strong but lightweight composite materials was an extrapolation from past priorities.

> *The ability to manage continuous discontinuity is the key to success especially in those industries where knowledge or access to knowledge is the main driver of market and business development.*

It was overtaken by environmental concerns about the problems of disposal and recycling composites. McDonald's has rethought its strategies constantly over the last decade. Convenience packaging became a liability in the face of environmental concerns. The dominance of beef and the growth in factory farming to meet demand was challenged as worries about beef proliferated. The global growth in demand for meat slowed as vegetarianism grew in popularity. Employment policies which focussed on young workers were hit by claims of exploitation. McDonald's continued success reflects its ability to manage these discontinuities.

> *The value of the knowledge edge has sharply increased over the last decade and the range of industries has increased in which the knowledge edge is now crucial.*

Invention and innovation are causes of continuous discontinuity, and both are essential features in any response. Invention and innovation are stimulated by the ability to bisociate, that is, to link two apparently separate phenomena into a new unity. This is especially important when knowledge is the key to growth. The ability to access different areas of knowledge, bring them together and sustain this capacity over time provides an important competitive edge in the new marketplace. The value of the knowledge edge has sharply increased over the last decade and the range of industries has increased in which the knowledge edge is now crucial.

Cues to the best ways to build and exploit this knowledge edge can be found in industries such as the pharmaceutical industry, which consists of large companies that have survived over long periods. This longevity is closely linked with specific competences. Perhaps the most important of these distinct competences is the ability to foster a high level of specialist knowledge within the organization. Firms like Bayer, Glaxo and Sterling have sustained and developed this expertise over long periods. They have, however, prevented that information from becoming embedded in such a way that it fixed the organization permanently in the past, unable to respond to an ever changing competitive environment. This distinct knowledge competence is closely linked with an ability to sustain continuous discontinuity.

New managers[62]

The scale of the transformation is demonstrated by changes in the managerial labor pool. The notion that managers require specialist training is relatively new. Wharton, the first business school in the USA, was created at the end of the 19th century. The first UK business school dates from the 1960s. Elsewhere, most business schools are even later creations. Business school education largely copies the dominant management paradigm of this century – specialization and yet more specialization. General degrees covering the range of business disciplines became little more than envelopes for delivering specialization. This approach fitted well with

H[ierarchical]-model organizations, for the linear programming, cybernetic feedback, statistical analysis and electronic data processing taught in the academic business school proved useful for management in the H-model firm, where a "high degree of formalization, standardization and centralization" reigned, where "good top-down skills, and a capacity to devise good externally imposed evaluation systems"[63] prevailed.

Specialist degrees became even more esoteric. This process reflected two separate but mutually reinforcing factors. The growth of the managerial bureaucracy in large corporations required increasing numbers of specialists. Demand for these specialists expanded as the division of labor became embedded into management thinking. The second factor lies in the nature of the universities that hosted the business schools. They measure excellence generally in terms of research. Specialization is

71

generally the best route to excellence in research in the sciences. In their efforts to ape the achievements of their academic peers, business educators have largely followed the same route, regardless of its logic or relevance.

This partly explains the failure of business education to play any part in the major developments in business thinking over the last 20 years. The quality and manufacturing revolutions, the debate on corporate responsibility, new thinking on markets, innovations in environmental policies, the transformation in logistics, new thinking on excellence largely emerged from practitioners or consultants (who observed practice). Only in the mathematics of finance and capital market theory have business academics been to the fore. These failures were relatively unimportant when increased bureaucratization was the norm. Training bureaucrats is a defensible role. The managers who are needed in the future require a different, more integrative and wide ranging perspective. This derives partly from the leadership, entrepreneurial, developmental and enabling roles of managers. It is also needed in order to respond to the expectations of the modern workforce in the new economy.

Higher education participation rates across the industrial and industrializing world are increasing. The graduate workforce is already the norm in technology based industries, much of the business services sector and is becoming the norm in many other industries. Companies reinforce this trend by involvement in local and national initiatives. Ford, Unipart and others are systematically creating their own internal universities.

Graduate workers are part of a new environment that requires new kinds of managers with different skills and competences. An important aspect of this change will be a blurring of the line between the leader and the manager. Managers need to relearn the leadership skills that determined the success of their predecessors during similar revolutions. It is sometimes argued that entrepreneurship, a key characteristic of the new manager, cannot be taught. It is, however, clearly possible to exclude or discourage entrepreneurship through policies or training. Entrepreneurial skills will be needed in work and during the career breaks that will be the norm for managers in the future.

The same changes in career patterns call for managers who combine their core competences with a portfolio of skills ranging from organizational sensitivity, people development, learning (and relearning) and "whole business thinking." The value of the latter capacity is illustrated by the continuing success of German corporations. The development of managers in Germany followed a different pattern from that in the USA, UK and other business school dominated systems. The main institutional route lies through the technological institutions or *Fachhochschulen*. These emphasized the integration of management and engineering education. This approach has created a managerial labor pool with greater insight into the core capabilities of the enterprise as well as greater skills in integrating the different aspects of the firm's operations. These are the abilities managers will need to manage the paradoxes and dilemmas they face in the new economy.

THE NEW ECONOMICS?[64, 65, 66, 67]

Discussion of new economics or new economies operates on two basic levels. There are those who claim that economic thinking has become a cul-de-sac characterized by increasingly sophisticated attempts to analyze, model or predict economic behavior based on a set of theories that is fundamentally flawed. Nobel Laureate Wassily Leontief comments that: "In no other field of empirical inquiry has so massive and sophisticated a statistical machinery been used with such indifferent results."[68] The public failure of economists to predict or explain the emergence and disappearance of stagflation, the economic downturn of the late 1980s, the Japanese recession, the collapse

and subsequent recovery of Germany following the re-integra-
tion of the East, the difficulties of the Russian economic
recovery and the turmoil of the Exchange Rate Mechanism has
undermined the discipline's credibility.

The anxiety of policy makers in business and the public
sector to understand the changes facing them gets little
response from economics. Even
relatively small, short-term
changes seem beyond the economist's ability to explain or
predict. In economies like the
UK forecasts on the money
supply, public sector borrowing, inflation and growth rates
are no sooner published by
government economists than
they are revised. While classical

> *The Keynesian consensus
> that held true for the 30
> years after the end of
> World War II collapsed
> under a combination of
> economic difficulties and
> intellectual assault.*

economic theory does not lead to a belief in the predictability of
the future, genuine business concerns remain about such questions as the existence of business cycles and why supply and
demand works on some occasions but not on others.

These concerns were seen as relatively unimportant while there
was broad agreement about economic principles and the economic
environment was generally stable. Neither of these situations
holds true any longer. The Keynesian consensus that held true for
the 30 years after the end of World War II collapsed under a combination of economic difficulties and intellectual assault. The
economic difficulties in the West revolved around three issues:

- a sharp reduction in the rates of economic growth enjoyed in
  the richer, more advanced industrial countries, especially in
  Europe and North America;
- an economic slow down associated with increased unemployment and rapid increases in inflation;
- the reduced competitiveness of Western economies against
  those of Japan and other East Asian countries.

The combination of these phenomena challenged many Keynesian and part-Keynesian assumptions about economic behavior.

The intellectual assault on Keynesian orthodoxy is linked most closely with the work of Milton Friedman and the Chicago School of Monetarist Economists. They highlighted the failure of the Keynesian approach to explain how unemployment and inflation could coexist. They went further to reemphasize the impact of the money supply and especially the impact of government borrowing on inflation and economic performance. The challenge to the Keynesian orthodoxy extended to serious questioning of the role of the state. Keynes had given a prominent and largely beneficial role to the state in economic management. The Monetarists and Neo-Austrian School of Economists highlighted the dangers of

The globalization of world markets extends beyond a shift in economic power.

the state interfering in the working of the market mechanism. The rationalist school of economists led by Thomas Sargent[69] took this argument further by questioning the beneficial results of any state intervention: in sum, the rationalists argued that traditional Keynesian and Classical Economics models were no longer valid.[70]

Despite the vigor of their attacks and the strength of their arguments, the critics of the Keynesian consensus have not come up with a generally accepted alternative. Instead the questions asked go more deeply into the fundamentals, and the traditional core assumptions are open to reinterpretation. It is argued, for example, that land, labor and capital as the building blocks of economics are no longer enough: to them we should now add technology.

THE NEW ECONOMIES

Doubts about the core beliefs of economics highlight the profound changes in the world economy. The globalization of world markets extends beyond a shift in economic power. East

Asia will generate faster growth than any other part of the world over the next few decades: between 1992 and 2000, 40 % of all new purchasing power will be created here. The shift in economic power is associated with new thinking about work and the nature of economic relations.[71]

The important new technologies differ from those which characterized traditional business and economic conditions. Typically these operate to gradually enhance the ability of people or firms to perform existing work. Looking at the car industry, most of the enhancements in production technologies between the 1920s and 1980s made it easier, faster or cheaper to perform the form of work defined by Ford and others during the last industrial revolution. The conveyor belts might break down less often, go faster or the materials last longer. One of Henry Ford's workers of 1924 could step onto a production line in Detroit, Longbridge, Turin or Stuttgart during the 1970s and find the product process recognizable and understandable. The advent of robots, the shift to team working and the "Japaniza-tion" of working methods make today's factory and its operations unintelligible to the old Ford worker. The technolo-gies that are emerging are fundamentally "disruptive"[72] of established work practices. A secretary trained to use a manual typewriter could move easily to an electromechanical or elec-tronic typewriter but word processors changed the very nature of the work.[73]

Writers like Fukuyama[74] have shown that the commitment to team work and the emphasis on quality is more than just another technique for improving productivity – they reflect a different work ethos. Globalization means taking on board this different thinking. The global business is culturally heteroge-neous. It is capable of adapting to the different needs of diverse stakeholder groups across the range of its activities. The nature of trading relations is already evolving in response to these influences. Nobel Laureate Arno Penzras of Bell Labs believes that the nature of personal and business relations rests on shared assumptions and common languages. Communication technologies make extended and extensive contact easier than ever before. Penzras believes that "tomorrow's interactions may depend more on shared understanding than on sharing the same office corridor."

New technologies are an integral aspect of the new economies. These technologies affect supply policies, production and logistic systems and markets. There is even evidence from the growth of biotechnology that the physical science base of technology is altering. Technological developments in energy supplies and materials directly affect the resource base of business while innovative banking technologies make access to funds and money transfer systems unrecognizable from those of a decade ago. Robotics are the most obvious change in production technologies but information systems influence every aspect of production in manufacturing systems.

Logistics are the "enabling systems" of management. Their impact is often underplayed but can change the fundamentals of an industry. The clearest case of this was the effect of Ro-Ro shipping on the global car market. For 15 years I have been asking groups of students, managers and business leaders what they considered to be the most important factor in the global success of the Japanese vehicle sector. Answers vary from "built in accessories like radios" to "skilled imitation." It was, however, the introduction of Ro-Ro that was the essential precondition to enable a country to build up a global car market. The costs and risks of traditional sea borne transport made it impossible to open up world markets, which remained landlocked until the floating car park arrived to transform the economics of the international trade in cars. Once markets could be reached other advantages came into play.

In consumer markets the demand for innovation seems insatiable. Smart technologies like self diagnosing elevators, copiers and computers that detect the likelihood of failure before it occurs are already available. These will soon be followed by machines that are able to take remedial action to repair themselves. The range of smart technologies is extending: materials technologies are being created producing garments that adapt to weather conditions and diapers that change color when wet. Car tires are manufactured that notify drivers of problems. These are all part of a widening array of smart product/technologies.

CONCLUSION

The transformation in markets and economies that is taking place shows all the characteristics of a genuine revolution. The pace of change has accelerated and is qualitatively different from the business environment experienced in the recent past. New firms using novel approaches to work are gaining competitive advantage over well established and resourced rivals. Their successes challenge the assumptions which have shaped the decisions and structures of their rivals. These successes are not confined to specific enterprises. The Anglo-US economies which created and articulated the existing economic paradigm are struggling to cope with competition from economies adopting different approaches to work and organization.

Distinguishing features of the two models are the emphasis placed on people, the organization of work, involvement, trust, structure or hierarchy and opportunity. Successful firms and economies are people based with a powerful emphasis on getting the best from the talents and capabilities of all the people in the enterprise. Jack Welch of GE summarized the people centred approach of the new generation of business leaders. "Above all else ... good leaders are open. They go up, down and around the organization to reach people. ... It is all about human beings coming to see and accept things through a constant interactive process aimed at consensus." This contrasts with the efforts to minimize the scope for human error and substitute machines for people in more traditional organizations.

78

There is a growing emphasis on winning the greater involvement of all workers in the business and capitalizing on their ability to add value. Japanese companies are effective at winning the commitment of their workforce to sustained efforts to add value and customer benefit. This contrasts with the type of Fordist emphasis on breaking work down into its component parts and allocating tasks in fragmented and easily repeated ways. Workers were separated both from the skills they invested in their work and the fruit of their efforts. Greater involvement and the transfer of authority to all those involved in the production of a good or service increases job satisfaction while delivering business benefits in quality, reliability, reduced waste and greater customer satisfaction. A focus on customer satisfaction is fundamental as buyers want a total benefit not a compilation of components.

Major changes can lead to the high costs associated with resistance to change and outright opposition. Trust is, perhaps, the best defense against these negative aspects of change. An organization based on trust has greater flexibility and more scope for innovation. Overheads are reduced as the costs of control and supervision are minimized. The gains from trust and partnership extend across the supply, production and buyer network. Partnerships and alliances have grown in importance as organizations recognize the limits to their capabilities in complex, and changing, global markets. Trust is an important factor in the maintenance of these partnerships. Mazda's turnaround in the mid 1970s highlights the gains from an integrated, partnership based approach to business. The company survived because fellow members of the *kereitsu* (trading network) supported the firm. Its banks provided Mazda with the loans and other finance needed to survive the crisis. Suppliers of goods and services scheduled their charges around the firm's ability to pay. Kereitsu members concentrated their purchasing on Mazda products and the purchasing support extended across the local community, from taxi drivers to local government officials. In return for a no layoff pledge to the union, important changes in business practice were introduced. At one point, large numbers of assembly workers were retrained as car salesmen to sell the thousands of stockpiled cars held by the firm and its dealers. The partnership carried on long after the crisis ended. An employee suggestion scheme, for example, gets tens of thousands of contributions annually.

Rigid hierarchies stand in the way of this type of development. They are especially inappropriate in organizations facing change or those in service, skill or knowledge industries. The key to success in these sectors lies in the ability to adapt products, services and ways of working to need rather than structure. A rigid, multitiered hierachy can force communication, development, policy making and implementation along lines that do not meet market needs. Organizations like ABB show that the enterprise can be restructured or layers taken out with resultant sharp reductions in costs and improvements in performance. These improvements depend, in part, on the preconditions, for example the climate of trust. They also rely on the support systems, values and wider philosophy of the organization. A strong ethical stance, fair approaches to disadvantaged groups and respect for the community and the environment is closely linked with positive business development in the new environment.

> *The paradox at the heart of the new industrial revolution is that technological miracles highlight the ability of people to respond.*

The two central lessons of this new technological revolution are emerging.

- Access both to knowledge and to the emerging technologies is essential to the long-term success of ambitious firms and managers.

- It is not enough to be a master of the technological universe. Long-term success lies in integrating that knowledge with understanding about what makes people tick.

Peter Drucker summarizes the essential feature of this process of integration with his comment that "knowledge flows through technology but resides in people.[75] The paradox at the heart of the new industrial revolution is that technological miracles highlight the ability of people to respond.

◆

The clearest lesson of earlier
industrial revolutions is that
success did not go to those
communities and corporations
with the greatest initial
advantages.

◆

Chapter 5

◆

LEARNING THE LESSONS

OTHER DAYS, NEW WAYS

Earlier industrial revolutions offer important lessons for man-agers, organizations and communities determined to prosper during the current revolution. This does not mean that these revolutions have to repeat themselves: the past is for understanding, not living in. The first industrial revolution can be dated to some time during the last quarter of the 18th century and lasted until the first quarter of the 19th century. The first use of the term Industrial Revolution was probably in a series of lectures by Arnold Toynbee in 1880–1. His use of the term coincides roughly with the start of the second industrial revolution which lasted until the early years of the 20th century.

It is impossible to date these revolutions with any precision. Some of the developments that shape and help to define the revolutions occurred long before the period described. The first industrial revolution was a coal, steam, iron, cotton, joint stock company and factory revolution. The first use of coke to smelt iron, however, was at the beginning of the 18th century. James Watt had completed his work on the steam condenser by 1770. Both the joint stock company and the first true factories were created significantly earlier than 1780. It was the speed and number of changes and their widespread dissemination that marked the start of the revolution.

The same pattern occurred late in the last century. The defining developments were those in the oil, chemicals, engineering, electronics and vehicles industries. The diversified multidivisional corporation had emerged as the dominant form of industrial organization. And yet the first "oil boom," took place in the 1860s, while William Perkin had invented the first synthetic dye by 1856. The dynamo, the transformer and the electric motor existed even earlier. Again, it was the increase in range and pace of development that indicated a qualitative change.

Other days, other ways

The clearest lesson of earlier industrial revolutions is that success did not go to those communities and corporations with the greatest initial advantages. At the start of the first industrial revolution, France had probably the finest scientific base in Northern Europe the German states had the best education system and Spain had access to the greatest supplies of natural resources. Despite not having these advantages, it was the UK that emerged as the dominant industrial power. At the end of the last century, the UK seemed to have a massive lead over its industrial rivals. Yet, within 20 years this lead had been whittled away and the USA and Germany had become the most successful economies. A similar pattern seems to be emerging today with North European and USA companies seeing their advantages being whittled away by East Asian rivals. It is, therefore, vital that today's businesses and managers learn the lessons these past failures and successes have to impart.

The first industrial revolution provides clear indications of the determinants of success during industrial revolutions. The most dramatic was a remarkable concentration of entrepreneurial talent.

The first industrial revolution

The first industrial revolution provides clear indications of the determinants of success during industrial revolutions. The most

84

dramatic was a remarkable concentration of entrepreneurial talent. People like Josiah Wedgwood, Richard Arkwright, McGregor Laird, John Brunner and Sarah Clayton built businesses that were to transform their communities. They were skilled at spotting opportunities, getting access to ideas and deploying resources. Many can be classified as craftsmen/entrepreneurs who used true craft skills to build the machines and products that underpinned their businesses. In modern terms they had a practical knowledge of the capabilities of their businesses. They regularly "walked the talk."

The businesses that drove the first industrial revolution were more internationalist than their rivals. It is no coincidence that Nathan Rothschild moved from Frankfurt, Germany to Manchester, England to set up his banking house. He knew that there were opportunities and relatively few barriers for a German Jew to prosper in that dynamic environment. The same internationalism saw the new firms moving quickly to open markets around the world. Industrialization in Northern Europe was shaped largely by Britons who took their crafts and ideas to Belgium, France and Germany in the first half of the 19th century, although they were not the only entrepreneurs to successfully adopt this global approach.

The roots of US industrialization lie in the decision of Francis Lowell and others to spend years in the UK studying the new industries and trying to find ways to transfer these technologies to North America. This was not always easy since the British government took severe action against people it discovered "stealing" techniques or luring craftsmen to leave their employer and move to a company overseas. There is a special irony in the fact that today the USA is the most active defender of intellectual property rights, 200 years after, Benjamin Franklin, a signatory of the Declaration of Independence, had spent much of his time in Europe after the American Revolution trying to smuggle British craftsmen, ideas and technologies out of Britain to the USA.

The second industrial revolution

The success of Franklin's, and other people's efforts at industrial espionage could be seen in the factories that proliferated in New England, down the east coast of the USA and across country towards the West. The capacity existed to exploit the second industrial revolution. The first industrial revolution was built by craftsmen but the second was created by engineers and technicians such as Edison, Westinghouse, Ford and Schwab in the USA and Siemens, Daimler and Duisberg in Germany. Their success was founded on a new understanding of the process of development and manufacture. Edison once said that his greatest invention was not the filament light, or any of the other 1000 patents he held, but the research laboratory. The industrialization of research and development is a key factor in the century of economic success enjoyed by the USA and Germany.

Breakthroughs in manufacture were equally important. As in the first industrial revolution innovation with adaptation and not innovation alone was the key. Ford was expert at taking ideas from elsewhere and exploiting their full potential. Even Aspirin, the cornerstone of Bayer's growth under Duisberg, was originally synthesized by a French chemist. One important breakthrough was the major improvement in the process of production. This appreciation of the value of process and its corollary, control, was characteristic of the success of many of the greatest entrepreneurs of the second industrial revolution. Rockefeller did not build Standard Oil by being the greatest wild cat discoverer of oil. His greatness lay in his understanding of the process of getting the oil to market and the value of the strategic control of markets.

The industrialization of research and development is a key factor in the century of economic success enjoyed by the USA and Germany.

From oil to steel, food processing and railways, entrepreneurs found ways to manage large organizations by seeking out managerial talent, developing its capability and delegating key tasks. Realizing the advantages of scale became the key to success. Alfred Chandler[76] comments:

the major innovations made in the processes of production during the last quarter of the nineteenth century created many new industries and transformed many old industries. These processes differed from older ones in the potential for exploiting the unprecedented cost advantages of the economies of scale and scope.

The ability to develop systems to manage these vast enterprises provided their major competitive advantage.

The transfer of control of General Motors from William C. Durant to Alfred P. Sloan was perhaps the clearest symbol of the transfer of power from the individualistic entrepreneur to the corporation man. Sloan's own description highlights the change.

Mr Durant had been able to operate the company in his own way, as the saying goes, "by the seat of his pants." The new administration was made up of men with very different ideas about business administration. They desired a highly rational and objective mode of operation.

From oil to steel, food processing and railways, entrepreneurs found ways to manage large organizations by seeking out managerial talent, developing its capability and delegating key tasks. Realizing the advantages of scale became the key to success.

The gap was widened by the sharp increase in the educational qualifications of the managerial labor force. At the end of the 19th century in the USA, virtually all managers emerged from the shop floor, were part of the social group or were related to the ownership group. By the 1930s, almost 10 % were graduates and by the start of the 1950s this figure had doubled. In the 1990s, it is estimated that over 70 % of all US managers will be graduates. The increase in educational qualifications in the blue collar workforce failed to keep pace. The lack of shared education and social experience led to increased gaps between managers and workers at a time when increased cohesion was important to business development.

At the start of the century the new business leaders wanted more scientific management and found the ideas of people like F.W. Taylor fitted well with their aspirations. He wanted to gather together "all of the traditional knowledge which in the past has been possessed by the workmen and then classify, tabulate and reduce this knowledge to rules, laws and formulae."[77] These ideas were soon challenged by alternative views of the routes to operational efficiency in large organizations (see Table 5.1). The battle for ideas which is being repeated today could be seen in the first third of this century. New ideas about management, innovation, the search for new markets and the ability to exploit new financial, control and distribution systems characterized the most successful new firms. Organizations that want to adapt to an information and technology rich technology enabling work mode are forced to break down barriers to communication and interaction while devising ways of allowing information to flow on a need to know basis.

LEARNING THE LESSONS

The last 15 years have seen a new turn in the battle for ideas. The explosion of ideas and debate about management can probably be dated to Peters' and Waterman's book, *In Search of Excellence*. They were probably the first writers to herald the changes in the business environment and practice that required new thinking about the best way to manage. Since the publication of their book, the battle for ideas has extended to address

Table 5.1

The New Organizational Ten Point Checklist	
Issue	*Check*
Is information organized hierachically or on a need to know basis?	☐
Is adding value a recognized corporate goal?	☐
Are opportunities created for all members of the organization to contribute to business development?	☐
Does everyone understand the company mission and/or goals?	☐
Are education, training and development opportunities in place for everyone?	☐
Is everyone customer focussed?	☐
Are fairness and trust building policies in place?	☐
Are disciplinary and control systems consistent across the enterprise?	☐
Do managers "walk the talk"?	☐
Do separate eating and social facilities exist?	☐

the routes to competitive advantage, the nature of leadership in people and markets, the role of strategy and the challenge of implementation. Some of these ideas can trace their roots back to earlier thinking. There are identifiable links between the discussion of corporate capabilities and competences and Ricardo's ideas on absolute and comparative advantage which he was spelling out as early as 1817.

The current debates on the route to success pose major dilemmas for managers and businesses. One body of ideas urges firms to concentrate their efforts around the areas of their business in which they are already strong. The notion of "sticking to your knitting" fits well with arguments for concentrating efforts around areas of overall leadership or distinctive capability. There are two levels of risk with this thinking. It can degenerate into truism: we are best at doing the things we are best at. It can also concentrate the efforts of the enterprise too narrowly. This thinking contains the same weakness of the old 80/20 law in marketing. 20 % of our customers will always generate 80 % of our sales. In the same way we will always be able to reduce our core of distinctive capabilities to a smaller number.

Successful companies like Krones, the world leader in bottle labelling, can operate more experimental, search based approaches to business. It built its US business basis out of an opportunistic response to a business lead. Hermann Kronseder, the founder of Krones, describes how

> **an American businessman approached me. Four weeks later I flew to the United States. ... We visited New York, Chicago, Detroit, and eventually Milwaukee. I came to the conclusion that we needed our own subsidiary in the United States. Two days later we founded Krones Inc. in a room at the Knickerbockers Hotel in Milwaukee. Another two days later we had our first order from a Milwaukee brewery.**

Confidence, a determination to succeed and an expansionist approach to business development are integral parts of this philosophy.

Wolfgang Pinegger, CEO of Bruckner, perhaps the most successful producers of biaxial film stretching systems has a confident, all embracing view of global market development. "We know all our customers in the world. ... We have our own offices and some of our best guys spend 80 % of their time travelling. That's how we cover the world." For these companies, concentration on core capabilities and competences is a growth strategy not a defense policy. Heinz Hanskammer of Brita water filters highlights the difference:

> **Leifheit, one of our competitors, has a thousand products, one of which is a water filter. That's no match for us, because we have only water filters. Five years ago, Melita tried to attack us and**

failed. In America, Mr Coffee, the largest producer of coffee makers lost against us.

This alternative notion of focus and the related set of ideas highlight the value of major changes in organization and structure in response to environmental change. Some approaches to reengineering were criticized strongly in *Fortune* for adopting this position. "Reengineering and other management fads that urge dramatic change on all fronts are not only wrong; they are dangerous."[78] The risks of dramatic change include internal disorientation or lack of a sense of direction, a collapse in morale, the exodus of talent and the loss of comparative advantage.

It is estimated that the failure rate of reengineering initiatives is close to 70 %. This reflects, in part, the intense demands that reengineering places on organizations. It also highlights the importance of solid groundwork and preparation for a reengineering initiative. Trust building, open lines of communication and real management involvement in preparing the ground are the essential first steps in an effective reengineering program. Firms that judge reengineering to be a short time fix are probably doomed to failure. White[79] challenges Hammer and Champy's suggestion that organizations equip themselves with a blank sheet of paper and start again:

> *The risks of dramatic change include internal disorientation or lack of a sense of direction, a collapse in morale, the exodus of talent and the loss of comparative advantage.*

There is no blank sheet of paper. Instead, executives find themselves in a wind tunnel with sheaves of paper being propelled towards them. They catch one and rush around proclaiming they know the answers. All they have found is part of the jigsaw.

Continuity and involvement are important but understated aspects of the second implementation phase of reengineering. Consistent, involved leadership is vital. Inconsistency destroys momentum and lack of involvement undermines trust especially if it seems that the only things being reengineered are those aspects of the organization that do not affect the leadership group.

BUILDING THE CAPACITY TO CHANGE

The clearest lesson from the successes of firms like General Electric, Toyota, ABB, Hewlett-Packard, Disney and Glaxo is that the capacity for evolution and change must become one of the core capabilities of the modern enterprise. The most effective corporations of the last 100 years developed the ability to persist by using their managerial bureaucracies to break down issues into their component parts – reductionism. Once reduced, the component parts could be tackled piecemeal by specialist managers. This specialization was a source of stability and resilience. The task now is to transform that capacity to control and hold a position into the capacity to absorb and initiate change creatively. This will involve a move from reductionism to integration. Effective integration means bringing the parts of a problem together into a new unity.

> *The clearest lesson from the successes of firms like General Electric, Toyota, ABB, Hewlett-Packard, Disney and Glaxo is that the capacity for evolution and change must become one of the core capabilities of the modern enterprise.*

Michael Eisner at Disney specializes in the integration of disparate activities into new unified groupings. His first major success was the integration of Disney's hotel, leisure and conference facilities through a strategic alliance with Marriott, a move that transformed the profits of this part of the Disney Corporation. In the successful Captain Eo project which followed, he drew together the distinct talents and strengths of Michael Jackson, Frances Ford Coppola and Disney. The restructuring of the film making side of Disney into Touchstone Pictures and Walt Disney Productions showed the same ability to draw together disparate strands into a new unity. The pace of change increased but the capacity to manage change was established.

The capacity to manage change can evolve into a core competence or competitive advantage when linked to other capabilities. The structure within which these capabilities are located is the architecture of the firm. The architecture is the distinctive set of relationships inside and outside the firm which determines the ways in which the enterprise mobilizes its capabilities and resources while responding to opportunities and threats. The architecture operates on several dimensions:

> *The pace of change increased but the capacity to manage change was established.*

- the physical structure, often shaped by the investments made by the enterprise;
- the esthetics of the enterprise – the values, rules and relationships within the enterprise;
- the environments inside and outside the enterprise;
- the linkages which bind the people, values, structure and environment together (the understated dimension).

It is easier to change the components than the architecture but the architecture provides tangible limits on the way changes in the capabilities affect the effectiveness of the enterprise.

MANAGERIALISM

The success of any organization depends on the fit between the architecture of the firm, the capabilities and competences of its managers and the needs of the market or environment. For most of this century companies with a stable organizational architecture, that emphasized resilience in the face of external shocks, have been the ones with the "best fit." The clearest example of this was the response of the US automobile industry to the first successes of smaller European car manaufacturers in the 1960s. There were some moves to respond but as soon as possible the industry went back to "normal trading conditions." By the mid 1970s large cars with poor reliability and high petrol consumption were once again the norm.

An even greater psychological problem faces those working their way up the corporate hierarchy. They can locate themselves within the established bureaucracy. They know "how far they've come" and "how far they have to go," in career terms. Change the rules and they cannot locate themselves.

Managers in these enterprises are specialists with a heavy sunk investment in the status quo. This investment can take the form of dedicated, specialized education or training which makes career shifts or changes hard to execute. The specialist manager of a large mainframe computer finds it as hard to switch to a networked personal computer environment as the expert on television advertising policies finds it to learn to use the Internet for promotion. An even greater psychological problem faces those working their way up the corporate hierarchy. They can locate themselves within the established bureaucracy. They know "how far they've come" and "how far they have to go," in career terms. Change the rules and they cannot locate themselves.

In external relationships these organizations and their managers strive to manage or control the environment. Turbulence and change create threats which require a reaction. These reactions frequently center on efforts to reject or oppose the change and funnel it into traditional routes or contain its impact. The immediate impact of business on the growing environmental concerns of society showed all these features. The initial reaction of many firms was to present counterargument or ignore concerns. Firms producing CFCs initially rejected the link between the release of CFCs into the atmosphere and ozone depletion. Corporations using nonbiodegradable plastics in packaging played down the recycling and storage costs. Other firms built spurious "green" images into their advertising and promotion. Only gradually, as customer worries grew and became more trenchant and their rivals won more business, did traditional firms start to respond.

NEW MANAGERIALISM

A revolutionary business environment requires that firms build a capacity to change into their organizational architecture and develop managers whose sunk investment encourages them to initiate, adapt and respond to change. Flexibility, decentralization and the move from a command economy to a democratic and federal economy are integral parts of this shift. Richard Branson's Virgin and Robert Haas's Levi Strauss are two companies that take this literally. Virgin's businesses operate from small buildings and converted houses scattered across North London not from a centralized headquarters. Levi Strauss tried to work from a modern tower block but soon moved back into a more human-friendly building.

Rigid, compartmentalized structures are vulnerable to earthquakes. Rigidity and compartmentalization in management thinking are just as vulnerable to the metaphorical earthquake hitting the business world. The new managerialism breaks free from this because it is founded on a strong sense of the whole organization, its needs, the needs of its stakeholders and its relationships with its wider environments. Organizational and situational sensitivity are more important than the ability to defend a position or a specific point of view. Successful managers will be multiskilled boundary managers able to use extensive networks in response to challenges.

Multiskilling is especially important as it breaks down artificial barriers between areas of expertise. Few real world problems mirror the false divisions between specialisms like marketing, finance, production, human resources and logistics. A successful advertising campaign requires finance. Its value is undermined if production schedules fail to respond to new design. The people in the organization need to buy into the message if they are to support the campaign. Products and services must be available when the campaign breaks. The simplest lesson from successful service companies is that if you respect your employees they will in turn respect your customers. If employees are treated badly poor treatment of customers is the inevitable result.

Gatekeepers are part of a multifunctional, multilayered network of links between the organization and its environment.

Boundary managers learn to operate at the boundaries between these and other areas of activity. Successful technological innovations are, for example, closely linked with the existence of technology gatekeepers. This informal role is performed within the organization by people who continually monitor the technical and scientific environment and draw into the enterprise any relevant ideas or technologies. The gatekeeper role is growing in importance and extending to other areas like finance, people and operations. Gatekeepers are part of a multifunctional, multilayered network of links between the organization and its environment.

Networking by managers gains extra value in this context. It provides access to wider portfolios of knowledge and expertise. It is also a platform on which to build partnerships and alliances. The value of a partnership based approach goes far beyond the gains from any specific arrangement or deal. It further integrates the organization internally and externally by creating a growing web of relationships and links. The organizational web shares some characteristics with the spider's web:

- it works best when it is so fine as to be almost invisible;
- it can be easily repaired if breaks occur;
- the links are as natural and flexible as possible;
- the web is able to grab and hold onto opportunities.

Information technology

The creation of the web based organization turns on the quality and use of computing, information and communications technologies. These give managers access to flows of information which allow them to shape, direct and control the enterprise. They can access the firm's operating systems in ways which enhance their ability to understand, control and direct resources. Modern information technologies differ fundamentally from traditional systems, with, perhaps the most important difference being the scope they provide for integration and easy access. Manual, mechanical and paper based information systems operated within bounds defined by their providers and reflected their assumptions about form and content.

The best current information systems are user specified, and are more accessible because of the relative ease with which material can be formatted and reformatted to meet different needs. The move from centralized processing systems to networks strengthens this facility. It makes it simpler for network members to reorder the material and interact between themselves and other users and providers. Open access and user control are important means to get more value from information technology. In effect the structure is turned on its head with power transferred from the supplier to the consumer.

Managers and management are changing in response to these technologies. It is hard to imagine effective managers in the future who are unable to clearly specify their information needs in ways which exploit the capabilities of the new technologies. The same managers will have a common portfolio of relevant technical skills. They will be as adept at using word processors, spreadsheets, databases, and online information systems as they are at using the tools of their specific speciality. These changes are inseparable from the wider changes in the nature of manage-ment prompted by the new technologies. Shoshana Zuboff[80] points out that information changes the nature of the material the manager uses and, in the same way, management itself.

Information technology introduces an additional dimension of reflexivity; it makes its contribution to the product, but it also reflects back on its activities and on the system of activities to which it is related ... [it] renders events, objects and processes so that they become visible, knowable and shareable in a new way.

Zuboff describes the integrating role of information technology by combining

online transaction systems, information systems and communica-tions systems [to create] a vast information presence that now includes data formerly stored in people's heads, in face to face conversation, in metal file drawers and on widely dispersed pieces of paper.

Relational databases which allow executives to define their own criteria for entry, use and organization are evolving into relational information systems. They combine the capacity to address data sets in different, user-specified ways with the power to integrate operations and allow managers to interact. This in turn creates the ability to adapt and enhance capabilities continuously while breaking down the barriers between people, systems and machines to add value to outputs. The virtual information system, open to all, with its boundaries undefined, and able to constantly improve, is an important aspect of the continually adapting and improving organization. Properly employed, relational databases and database marketing are an effective antidote to "reductional marketing." This occurs when customers are reduced to their parts and classified in arbitrary, spurious and insulting ways. The simplest and often most devastating question to ask of any customer classification is "would it harm us if our customers knew that is how we described them?"

The real meaning of *kaizen*

The ability of Japanese companies to improve the quality and range of their outputs is linked to the notion of *kaizen*. This term describes the search for continuous incremental improvement. It is closely associated with the search for ways to add value to the product or service offered. A distinctive feature of the Japanese approach to both *kaizen* and added value is the recognition that the best route to both ends, lies through the personal involvement of all workers and operatives. The personal dimension is essential because it means that operatives "own" the task and have a self sustaining determination to improvement. Direction and inspection is kept to a minimum, partly because they are largely redundant. Ownership also removes the barriers that are created when the power to correct and improve is taken out of the workers' hands and placed elsewhere.

The human, integrative and developmental aspect of *kaizen* is illustrated by the approach adopted by Herb Keller of Southwest Airlines. He will stay out with a mechanic in a bar until four in the morning to find out what is going wrong and then fix it. He recognizes and values the knowledge of the worker and invests time and effort in drawing out a solution. The approach that respects the personal knowledge and expertise of the individual contrasts sharply with the precepts of scientific management outlined earlier. Corporations that adopt the *kaizen* approach recognize the greater value and contribution of workers who retain the integrity of their expertise. In contrast scientific management can rob workers of their specialist knowledge and potential to add value by taking control "of the traditional knowledge which in the past has been possessed by the workmen and then classify, tabulate and reduce this knowledge to rules, laws and formulae."

Some business leaders suspect that their managers and workers seek easy solutions or answers that minimize the demands on them. Ralph Larsen, the CEO of Johnson & Johnson, contradicts this suspicion. He believes that "managers come up with better solutions and set tougher standards for themselves than I would have imposed." Womack *et al.* point out just some of the gains from this approach at Toyota. "The armies of indirect workers so visible at GM were missing." Space is kept to a minimum "so that face-to-face communication among workers is easier." "Problems are solved in advance." There was "almost no rework." Quality problems were subjected to Toyota's 5 whys, which involves the production workers tracing any fault back to its origins by asking "why" as each layer of the problem is exposed, until the root cause of the difficulty is uncovered and understood.

Stripped of the need to supervise and control supervisors, managers and leaders can undertake more creative and constructive roles.

Stripped of the need to supervise and control, supervisors, managers and leaders can undertake more creative and constructive roles. The greatest challenge is to seek routes to small but certain improvements. Complacency is the greatest short-term problem for the successful company. David Sainsbury of the UK's Sainsbury Group commented in one interview that "the problem with our company is that we're burdened with historical success."[81] This was just months before the group hit major competitive difficulties. In the subsequent year he lost an estimated quarter of his personal wealth of $7Bn as the company's share price dropped. It is hard to disagree with the *Fortune* editorial when it pointed out that success poses almost as many problems as failure.[82]

Creating a vision while pushing the agenda for change and development must be tempered by recognition of past achievements. Boeing CEO Frank Shrontz says: "one of my jobs is to be wildly enthusiastic about the progress we've made and eternally disappointed at the rate we're making it." Andy Grove of Intel is an advocate of competitive paranoia: the sense that rival organizations are catching up, getting level or pulling ahead. "We need a threat, a good target, to get the juices flowing."

Complacency is the greatest short-term problem for the successful company.

It is hard to disagree with the Fortune *editorial when it pointed out that success poses almost as many problems as failure.*[82]

Reengineering

The best reengineering programs link this search for continuous improvement with the capacity to make genuine breakthroughs and an expansion of the competences and capabilities of all members of the organization. Reengineering programs contrast with other approaches to organizational redesign by emphasizing the integration of business operations. These programs start by looking at ways in which the capabilities and competences can be brought into line with the needs of the business environment. There is typically an effort to widen the capabilities of operatives and managers at all levels.

Restructuring and delayering occur naturally as a result of the increased competences of those operating at different levels. There is, for example, less need for traditional first line supervision if the operatives "own their work," seek ways to improve their performance, manage quality and work in self managed teams. The improvements and savings permeate the organization as reengineering programs get under way. A parallel process occurs at senior levels in the enterprise, refocusing the efforts of top management on core stewardship, strategy formulation and implementation while shaping the values and mission of the organization. This reduces the need for corporate bag carriers and related support systems.

Hammer and Champy[83] acknowledge that the central tenets of reengineering can be found in the words "fundamental," "radical," "dramatic" and "process." The first three highlight the link between reengineering and the adaptation of the business to a wholly new business environment. The process perspective emphasizes the need to move away from a fragmented approach which sees operations as a series of separate and discrete transactions. Instead, the emphasis is on the continuity which underpins the developing enterprise.

Some external elements of redesign are inevitable. It is important to move this redesign beyond the superficial, easily accessible features of the business to an appraisal and redesign of core processes. Core process redesign sets out with the specific aim of assessing the core activities of the enterprise and adapting them to current conditions without putting the core strengths of the venture at risk. The remit for redesign can be as broad at the entire enterprise or as narrow as one specific activity within it. Allan Sheppard took Grand Metropolitan Group through a major redesign of its core processes. He moved the group from being a highly centralized, medium sized hotel group with its major businesses in the UK to a global, decentralized, diversified food and drinks enterprise.

Redesign inevitably involves some risks but as Jean-Luc Lagardere of France's Lagardere Groupe commented: "I have never looked for an excuse. When you take risks, you don't blame others when there is a problem." Successfully reengineered companies take difficult decisions about the areas in which they will operate and

A serious assessment of the firm's activities and true strengths frequently leads to a commitment to a degree of outsourcing.

those they will avoid. The latter are often the hardest to take but they bring the greatest short to medium-term gains. A serious assessment of the firm's activities and true strengths frequently leads to a commitment to a degree of outsourcing. In his analysis of the new ecology of competition James Moore drew out the gains:

Everything from designing cars to building factories will get cheaper as auto companies quit making their own parts and rely more on independent suppliers. [Successful producers agree that they're] willing to cede control to suppliers. They know more about their business than we do.[84]

Markets and competition

Fundamental redesign may be an inevitable result of the firm's adjustment to new market conditions. John Kay[85] sees the match between the capabilities of the organization and the marketing challenges it faces as the most important issue in understanding corporate success and failure. Adapting to these changes is made harder by major changes in markets and marketing processes. Some observers have suggested that these changes are so significant that we are seeing either the end of marketing or an alteration of its nature and rules.

These changes range from the increasing sophistication and volatility of customer groups to the greater ability of firms to adapt products and services to their buyer needs. The skill with which customers have learned to discriminate between suppliers has led to a restatement of the old adage – no one ever went broke underestimating the intelligence of the American (British etc) housewife – to – no one ever went broke underestimating the intelligence of those who underestimate the intelligence of the American (British etc) housewife. Persistent high new product failure rates and evidence on the reasons for failure supports that restatement. New product failure rates are around 90 % while those which fail most often are products and services which are worse than existing or rival products at higher prices. These also comprise the largest number of introductions.

CONCLUSION

The bureaucratization of marketing is closely linked with the growing disillusion with the results of marketing. Entrepreneurs like Richard Branson, Anita Roddick, Bill Gates and Akio Morito have criticized both the superficiality and incrementalism which pervade much marketing, and its failure to respect the customer. British Airways and other carriers ignored the lessons of radical offerings like those provided by Laker and People's Express. They concentrated their resources on driving them from the market, and returning to "normality." Virgin and South Western have built their own successes on adapting their operations to the consumer needs exposed by Laker and People's Express.

The failure of the giant soap and cosmetics corporations to respond to the environmental worries expressed by consumer groups left a gap in the market which Body Shop was able to fill. The established firms with

The established firms with their vast marketing departments either missed or chose to ignore a major shift in consumer demand. It is the suspicion that they tried to ignore the movement in demand that poses the greatest questions about the underlying assumptions behind bureaucratic marketing.

their vast marketing departments either missed or chose to ignore a major shift in consumer demand. It is the suspicion that they tried to ignore the movement in demand that poses the greatest questions about the underlying assumptions behind bureaucratic marketing. The failure of the US car industry to learn from the early success of the VW Beetle and its tardy response to Japanese successes raises questions about the value of their marketing investment. In contrast to GM, Ford and Chrysler, Japanese automobile producers spend relatively little on formal, institutionalized marketing. They invest instead in product trials or encouraging their engineers to understand or identify with potential users.

> *The central challenge facing managers and organizations in the current revolution is to integrate their core capabilities with an internal effort to add value to the goods and services offered to the market.*

The highly successful Home Depot retail group in the US places a major premium on this identification with the customer. They require that "every customer has to be treated like your father, your sister, or your brother." Stew Leonard's grocery store company puts the same message in a different way in his company motto:

Rule 1:   The customer is always right.
Rule 2:   If the customer is ever wrong, read rule 1.

The central challenge facing managers and organizations in the current revolution is to integrate their core capabilities with an internal effort to add value to the goods and services offered to the market. In this environment, a company's ability to learn how to adapt and meet customer needs may be its only source of sustainable advantage.

These new strategies work because they break down the barriers between organizations and customers, clients or users.

They become integrated into the enterprise in a real and substantial way. In industrial markets, integrated marketing plays an increasingly important part in breaking down the barriers between buyers and suppliers.

In some forms, the notion of the web based organization might be used to add a new twist to old style separated management.

> **In the high-value enterprise ... office space, factories and warehouses can be rented, standard equipment can be leased; standard components can be bought wholesale from cheap producers; secretaries, routine data processors can be hired temporarily. ... Such arrangements are often more efficient than directly controlling employees.**

This cuts the enterprise off from the capacity of people to contribute and add value to the enterprise. The optimum form of web based organization allows information, insight and value to flow to the center and other parts of the web. Breaks in the web can be easily repaired with a minimum impact on the rest of the enterprise. Like a spider's web, a web based enterprise has astonishing strength and resilience and is a thing of beauty; unlike a spider's web, the web based organization is not a trap for its customers but the basis of a strong and binding relationship.

Part II

◆

ENTERING THE PARADOX

> ◆
>
> **The number and importance of paradoxes increase during revolutionary change as the old beliefs and assumptions struggle to compete with a new environment.**
>
> ◆

◆

The most difficult business
decisions regularly center on the
management of paradox.

◆

ENTERING THE
PARADOX

Charles Handy recounts a tale about change that illustrates not only the fear of change but also contains the type of paradox that recurs in any analysis of revolutionary change. He tells how a meeting of the Synod of the Church of England was addressed by a member, unhappy at a proposal, who asked, "why in this matter, as in so much else in our great country, why cannot the status quo be the way forward?" The hope that the status quo can be the way forward is shared by many, especially those with an interest in the current situation. The paradox is that circumstances today simply do not allow us to hold onto the current position in the hope that it can be the way forward.

The classic definition of a paradox is the coexistence of two seemingly contradictory notions. History abounds in paradoxes. The signatories of the American Declaration of Independence preached the rights of man yet many owned slaves. In the years before World War I, the German Kaiser was a great admirer of all things British. His favorite item of clothing was the dress uniform of an admiral of the Royal Navy and yet he led his country into war against the United Kingdom.

> *The paradox is that circumstances today simply do not allow us to hold onto the current position in the hope that it can be the way forward.*

In most walks of life the existence of paradox is primarily a cause of curiosity or amusement. In business it is not that simple: a paradox that is neither understood nor managed causes confusion and can lead to mixed signals and cues. Many paradoxes are caused by the hangover of one set of assumptions or beliefs into a new age or environment and proliferate when change is dramatic or rapid. Paradoxes emerge when beliefs or assumptions fail to keep up with external changes.

Paradox is common in economics and during economic change. Assumptions often do not fit reality. Nobel Laureate Wassily Leonteff is identified with Leonteff's Paradox, which describes the way predictions about the pattern of international trade do not fit the facts. The Theory of Comparative Advantage underpins most economic analysis of international trade. It argues that it is always in the interest of countries to specialize in the production of those goods in which they have a comparative advantage. In practice, this might mean that a rich country with a strong manufacturing base will specialize on producing capital intensive manufactured goods and concentrate its imports on labor intensive, agricultural produce. When Leonteff studied the patterns of US trade he found that the vast majority of US imports was capital intensive, manufactured goods and not, as predicted, the raw materials and labor intensive goods.

The number and importance of paradoxes increase during revolutionary change as old beliefs and assumptions struggle to compete with a new environment. Fukuyama's analysis of the economic development of Chinese business[1] highlights a paradox that has undermined China's ability to respond to economic change for centuries. This paradox lies in the inability to create mechanisms by which the sense of family and the tradition of dividing inherited wealth between surviving family members can coexist with the need for intergenerational stability. This stability is needed for organizations to evolve and grow over generations. He describes how "the combination of intense familialism, equal male inheritance, lack of a mechanism for adopting outsiders, and distrust of nonkin led to ... no large estates but microscopic land ownings that tended to shrink with each generation."

The same problems exist in Chinese businesses. Entrepreneurs build them and presumably they want them to survive in the way that Japanese, European and US corporations grow and develop long after the founder retires or dies. Yet, paradoxically they remained locked into a system of family based inheritance that works against survival. The decline of the Wang Corporation from being the leaders of the word processing and IT industry to a firm struggling for survival is linked with the apparent determination of the founder, An Wang, to pass control to his son Fred. Japanese, European and North American corporations, however, are also not immune from this problem.

The collapse of the Vanderbilt fortune dates from William Vanderbilt's decision to ignore his father's advice (keep the fortune intact and in the hands of the most skilled son). He divided control of their corporate interests and wealth among his own sons. This led directly to a lack of leadership and the inability to mobilize sufficient resources to manage change. The decline of the Littlewoods retail empire in Great Britain shows the same features. The children and grandchildren of the founder, Sir John Moores, struggle to cope with an inheritance that is declining in value as family interests and business interests blur. The paradox lies in the clash between the motives of the founders, who built businesses for their families or posterity and actions taken that erode the value of the inheritance and reduce their survival rates. Family businesses can survive and prosper but they seldom sustain the growth rates established by their founders. Long-term growth seems to need a separation of the family interest from the business interest.

> *Family businesses can survive and prosper but they seldom sustain the growth rates established by their founders.*
> *Long-term growth seems to need a separation of the family interest from the business interest.*

The most difficult business decisions regularly center on the management of paradox. Those decisions that deal with issues that are congruent or in harmony may be difficult but the way to resolve them can be identified. A firm may wish to enter a market but lacks the resources. Subsequent decisions or actions center on generating sufficient resources for the firm or the market. A company may wish to recruit more women but lacks childcare facilities. Decisions or actions will concentrate on providing inhouse childcare facilities or devising some form of external contracting arrangement. The way forward may be difficult but it can usually be identified. When faced with a paradox this is much harder.

Fred Friendly uses the kind of dilemma managers face in dealing with environmental and fairness problems in his management debates. He poses a problem faced by a US corporation that has a corporate commitment to equal opportunity: all jobs are open to women. It has, however, been warned that one of its manufacturing process means working with materials and in an environment where there is a potential threat to an unborn child, especially in the early days of a pregnancy. Does the corporation sustain its equal opportunity policy and allow women to choose whether or not to work in this area, or does it sustain its health and safety policy and ban women from this part of its operations? The faster the rate of change and the more fundamental and complex the dilemmas, the more important it is for managers to understand and manage paradox.

Chapter 6

◆

THE NATURE OF PARADOX

Most managers are aware of the paradoxes that affect their daily working lives. The most common today is probably the paradox of expectations: the more you achieve, the more you are expected to achieve. This in turn leads to the hope that past success creates some form of buffer against future problems. Salespeople who see growth in sales falter maintain that they were so successful last year, the market must be saturated. They get little sympathy from senior managers who have invested in new plant to cope with rising demand. Tom Peters takes this issue further when he points out that "satisfaction" is no longer enough. You might have once provided a product or service that satisfied customers but now they want to be *delighted*. Their expectations and interpretation of satisfaction and delight change. This places continuing pressure on firms to improve performance and add further value for customers.

Change throws up a host of new paradoxes. Many of these revolve around change itself and the ability of individuals, corporations and communities to adjust to different conditions. The strongest arguments in favor of change often lie in assertions that if you do not change you will lose your job, market or business base. Changes are then introduced involving new working practices, new market opportunities, even shifts in the business base. When new working practices are introduced there is an inevitable challenge to those undertaking the work or to the skills they have developed to undertake this work. Workers face the recurrent paradox that they are at risk if they resist change because the organization becomes uncompetitive, but they are at risk if they accept change because their skills become redundant. This paradox highlights the importance on lifelong learning and continuous personal and professional development.

My work in textiles and the newspaper industries produces many illustrations of these problems. Highly skilled "cutters,"responsible for cutting material in order to get as much usable price as possible from a specified length inevitably feel threatened by computer controlled cutting equipment. They can resist its introduction (possibly undermining the competitiveness of the company) or they can accept the new technology. In the first case, their jobs are at risk as the firm's competitiveness declines; in the second their jobs are threatened by the new technology itself. Typesetters face the same difficulty in the newspaper industry with the advent of computer based full page layout. Gary Hamel describes this as the ultimate paradox: if you don't change you'll lose your job, and if you do change you'll lose your job.[2]

> *The ultimate paradox: if you don't change you'll lose your job, and if you do change you'll lose your job.*[2]

RIDING THE TIGER

Charles Handy widens the analysis of Hamel's ultimate paradox by relating it to broader issues of technological change. He points out that the more we increase our technological capacity and ability to innovate and solve market problems, the more powerless we become[3] in the face of technology, change and rising market expectations. The successful adoption or introduction of a new technology typically highlights the need for additional new technologies and further change. It is a cycle of innovation that is driven by the push of technological change and the pull of market demand. Management's task is learning to ride the tiger.

The underlying principles showing firms and managers how to ride this tiger have emerged over the last few years. The most important principle is the traditional craft discipline of learning to "go with the grain." My father was a cooper who taught me at an early age that it was almost impossible to shape wood by working against or across the grain. Technological change creates the same conditions. It is possible to struggle against change and its implications but better results will be gained more easily if managers work with the grain of change.

A relaxed kind of drive

The work of a good craftsman is like the "relaxed kind of drive" that Charles Wang of Computer Associates claims we need to prosper today. A relaxed drive has two dimensions. The first describes the confident, relaxed approach to work which is a characteristic of craftspeople who understand their work, are confident of their abilities and who gain satisfaction from work well done. The drive comes from the craftsperson's respect for his or her own work and determination to achieve constantly higher standards of quality and functionality. Once this central proposition is accepted people and organizations respond remarkably well. It is, however, a message that needs constant repetition and reinforcement within the institution. The difficulties firms and managers face adapting to change often revolve around their attempts to fit the new conditions into their old ways of thinking and working. Part of the distinctive anthropology of our time is the coincidence of a knowledge revolution with a learning revolution. Educators, trainers and developers have found that people learn in many different ways and the environments in which they can learn are very diverse. Adapting the method of learning or the environment to the needs of the individual can break down many of the barriers to learning.

One feature of this learning revolution is the transfer of responsibility and control from the institution to the individual. Open, flexible, interactive, action, distance and other forms of learning create opportunities for people to learn when they want, how they want and in the form they want. A central plank in the individual's plan for survival,

A central plank in the individual's plan for survival, adaptation and prosperity is a personal development plan. The creation of a learning culture is central to the survival plan of organizations but people have a private responsibility to take this culture beyond the company into the rest of their life.

adaptation and prosperity is a personal development plan. The creation of a learning culture is central to the survival plan of organizations but people have a private responsibility to take this culture beyond the company into the rest of their life. Learning and development may not resolve the immediate difficulty identified by Hamel's ultimate paradox: it may not save a particular *form* of employment, but it will mean the individual remains employ*able*. The information and knowledge hungry manager will be the *employable manager*.

THE HUNGRY MANAGER

Managers who seek knowledge and understanding already find it easier to adapt to change. This ability to adjust extends beyond areas such as new technology. The Economist Intelligence Unit report on *The successful corporation of the year 2000* comments that "the Japanese may have imposed so much turbulence on US and European businesses in the 1980s in part because they have generally excelled at informal learning." This informal learning is a major feature of their ability to manage continuous improvement.

Managing the new hungry managers and workers will not be any easier – indeed, it could be harder – but the returns for success are immense. These people will be putting their millions of brain cells at the disposal of the enterprise. Charles Handy points out that creating the intelligent or learning manager can produce another paradox: the paradox of intelligence. This is that the security of the enterprise lies in the knowledge and brainpower of its people, but this security is fundamentally insecure as the knowledge and brain power are impossible to control using the traditional control systems of the typical enterprise. Knowledge workers, for example, own the means of production in their talent and expertise. They are highly mobile and free from the physical restrictions of the corporate person. They invest in their own capacity and do not depend on the corporation's investments.

The essence of this paradox of intelligence lies in the attempt to impose old style "scientific management" thinking, with its effort to separate employees from their expertise, onto today's business environment. Change the assumptions and the solutions to the paradox emerge:

- stop trying to separate employees from their knowledge;
- turn the integration of the individual and his or her expertise to the advantage of the enterprise by "whole enterprise" thinking;
- link the values, goals and policies of the venture to the values and policies of the individual through sharing, communication and feedback.

This view of the knowledge and learning workplace is relevant to most aspects of the business and fits with Henry Mintzberg's ideas on the craft of planning.[4] He argues that planning in most successful organizations is not the highly formal, structured approach described in textbooks. Strategic planning like the work of a craftsperson requires a full understanding of the materials being used. This understanding is in turn linked to a knowledge of the likely use of the item. The craftsperson's job is to produce a distinctive product from this knowledge.

Managers are craftsmen and strategy is their clay. Like the potter, they sit between the past of corporate capabilities and a future of market opportunities. And if they are truly craftsmen, they bring to their work an equally intimate knowledge of the materials at hand. That is the essence of crafting strategy.

Implicit in this model is the notion of the integration of skills, knowledge and understanding. Great craftmanship is incompatible with either the division of labor or the separation of workers from their skills. This approach adds the ability to respond and adapt that are so often missing from formalized planning. The craftsperson has a "feel" for the nature of the material and this intuition provides opportunities to adapt and respond to conditions.

Honda's early success in the US motorcycle market was founded on just such a capacity. Their initial plan was to concentrate sales efforts around Honda's larger machines, yet the first 50cc Supercubs were important to Honda's employees who wanted mobility cheaply. Even when these smaller bikes provoked interest among potential customers the opportunity was played down. It was only when technical problems emerged with the larger models that Honda followed up this interest, moving quickly so that within

Great craftmanship is incompatible with either the division of labor or the separation of workers from their skills.

The craftsperson has a "feel" for the nature of the material and this intuition provides opportunities to adapt and respond to conditions.

5 years the company held almost one half the US motorcycle market.

Integration is equally relevant in operational areas. Toyota workers concentrate their efforts on the integrative notion of adding value rather than on the separative notion of performing a specified task. This integration is perhaps more important in the service sector. The nature of the offering and the relationship with customers places further emphasis on the integrated skills of managers and workers. Sam Walton at Wal-Mart epitomized this determination to break down the barriers between tasks and roles through his travels around the country and willingness to explore the detailed operations of the stores group.

"IF WORK WAS SO GREAT, THE RICH WOULD HAVE HOGGED IT"

This quotation from Mark Twain finds an application in business thinking. Hunger and greed come together in Charles Handy's wide ranging analysis of paradox in the modern economy. He identifies paradoxes that highlight sharp divides in the ways different groups are adjusting to the changes created by the new industrial revolution. He argues that there is a paradox inherent in the distribution of work and leisure. Paid employment is becoming more concentrated with the successful "hogging it" but the numbers of unemployed and the work available to the poor is shrinking. This means that those in work have less *time* to enjoy their leisure while those not working have fewer *resources* to enjoy it.

This is producing sharp divides in consumer markets. Some companies are exploiting the desire of the rich to spend lavishly in a variety of activities ranging from intense leisure pursuits to the conspicuous consumption of "quality of life" goods from cars to domestic appliances. In contrast, those with less money are focussing their purchases increasingly on products and services that are more durable in terms of both time and money. Cable and satellite television fit neatly into this category. They can consume large amounts of time at a relatively low cost per hour. The task facing companies is how to channel their efforts when faced with this kind of social restructuring.

Similar issues face firms adjusting to other internal and external changes in economies, markets and organizations. Many of these revolve around the dramatic increases in productivity on the land, in factories and in offices. All lead to sharp reductions in prices but the benefits of these price cuts are unevenly spread while the costs are concentrated among those with the fewest resources. The "green" revolution in agriculture pushed up yields and drove down prices. The primary beneficiaries were large agribusinesses and richer consumers in the developed world. Small independent farmers cannot compete. They are driven off the land to swell the populations of displaced people in cities. The same pattern occurs in industry. Increased productivity lowers prices and reduces the demand for labor. The price of labor that can be displaced drops, forcing people out of work.

This vicious circle can only be stopped by increasing the value added through labor and hence its price. The primary route to increasing the value added by labor is greater empowerment,

> The task for corporations is to shift their attention from building production capacity to building people capacity.

and greater knowledge or expertise. More empowered labor changes the nature of the input–output process. Workers and managers can make a difference by adding value. The greater their competence, knowledge, understanding and commitment, the more value they can add to the product, service or process. The task for corporations is to shift their attention from building production capacity to building people capacity.

British Airways illustrate the extent to which this can be shaped and the competitiveness of an organization increased.

They have invested heavily in education and training over the last decade. Ford and Unipart in the UK have extended this investment in people by creating their own "universities" covering the more traditional technical and vocational subjects. They are now expanding their curriculum to wider, more interest driven fields of study. Ford and Unipart are, in effect, letting their employees lead them to areas where knowledge is needed and allowing them to seek it out.

This type of initiative is breaking down the barriers between the worlds of work and learning. Sir Douglas Hague, former advisor to Prime Minister Thatcher, believes that some corporations will become "universities of industry," offering educational and research opportunities on a par with the established universities.

In the 1990s and 2000s, people outside the universities will increasingly be working in similar ways and with similar talents to those within; and they will often do so more innovatively and with greater vigour, because they will come to what they do untrammelled by academic traditions, preconceptions and institutions. The pioneers of the knowledge society will be able to compete with the universities and, increasingly, will do so.[5]

The collegiality option

The management paradigm for these new universities of industry is likely to draw some features from the collegiate approach that has served universities for a thousand years. Parallels with the first and second industrial revolutions can be identified. The first industrial revolution adopted its core management structures from the largest existing institutions for mobilizing "mass labor". These were the armies of the North European states.

With this model, the management paradigm was inevitably a mixture of rigid hierarchies and arbitrary decision making. A mixture of social network and family group determined the membership of the managerial group. The second industrial revolution called for the mobilization of "mass administration." Business leaders looked to the civil service for their models. This retained the emphasis on hierarchy but added a preoccupation with technical and professional qualifications and the bureaucratization of management. The importance of learning and knowledge to organizations seeking to succeed in this economic revolution suggests that the model for tomorrow's business will be the university.

This will not be the simple extrapolation of the collegial model to other enterprises any more than the military or the civil service model was adopted unchanged. Key components of the collegiate model can already be seen in successful enterprises. The erosion of hierarchy is especially important. Collegiate structures assume that leaders are "first among equals" in a structure in which all members of the enterprise share roles and responsibilities. The values

> *The importance of learning and knowledge to organizations seeking to succeed in this economic revolution suggests that the model for tomorrow's business will be the university.*

of a collegiate enterprise provide a bedrock on which a great deal of individual freedom is permitted. In effect, the college assumes that its members internalize its goals and, in return, get considerable freedom. There are many dysfunctional features of the collegiate model which "smart" organizations avoid, including the lack of purpose and the preoccupation with petty politics.

Collegial organizations rely heavily on trust in the other members of the organization and a strong sense of ownership of the organization's role and task. Many of the more intense debates in collegially based organizations center on attempts to define or refine this role. At its best this debate sets standards of sustainable excellence that are unrivalled in other walks of life. At its worst it is corrupt and inward looking. This places considerable demands on those in leadership positions to draw out the strong points and to direct debates about purpose and function along constructive avenues.

Many of the most successful firms in the information and communications industries show features of the collegiate model. Microsoft is perhaps the best known example of a giant corporation deliberately adopting a collegiate approach. Apple, especially during the Steven Jobs era, showed some of the same features. Andrew Grove at Intel has managed to wed the openness and creativity associated with the better universities with a tight management structure. The ability to balance these two apparently contradictory notions might explain why his motto is "Only the paranoid survive." Steven Spielberg, David Geffen and Jeffrey Katzenberg came together to form Dreamworks, an enterprise that initially looked like an especially high powered university development team. The information and communication industries are to the fore in addressing the issues that the rest of business will face in the longer term.

> *The information and communication industries are to the fore in addressing the issues that the rest of business will face in the longer term.*

One of the most important and potentially revolutionary aspects of this change centers on the roles of e-mail, Intranet and the Internet. They create the opportunity for individuals within organizations to redefine, reorganize or simply visualize the organization from their own perspective. John Gage, the chief scientist at Sun Microsystems describes how he uses his Java e-mail list to redefine the Sun organizational structure in his terms. "It lists the people I believe are the real players in Java, my personal view on the power structure." He recounts how this produces wider ramifications. CEO of Sun, Scott McNealy, is on Gage's Java list and notices that a certain Mike Clary is on this and other people's lists. He wants to know:

"Who's Mike Clary ... Mike Clary has been recognized by his peers as an important person."

The existing knowledge industries (universities, communications firms and so on) have survived because they manage to balance the needs of the individual with the needs of the group. Knowledge might be developed through the group but it is held by the individual. Even where teams or partners make breakthroughs it is the way in which they complement one another, not the way in which they replicate one other, that determines progress. Global perspectives, acceptance of diversity and leadership based on achievement not position are other features of the collegiate model that are gaining wider relevance. The diversity of institutional model in universities illustrates the way in which the form of organizational arrangement will become even more diverse in the new environment.

This partly reflects the alternative approach to accountability that universities represent. Most are, in some form, democratically accountable. This model fits well with the stakeholder approach to corporate accountability but less easily with the shareholder or proprietor model of accountability. A synthesis of these models is emerging which weds the short-term efficiencies generated by the market or shareholder approach to accountability of the longer-term, value creation approach of stakeholder or collegiate models. Charles Handy advocates a form of partnership structure. This may resolve some of the internal dilemmas but seems unable to tackle the problem of proprietor or ownership rights without some elaborate system of shareholder representation.

MANAGED OUTCOMES

Some evidence exists that there is a shift in expectations about the relationship between investment and return, at least in those countries influenced by European and North American thinking. Yet widespread anger at excess wage deals for corporate "fat cats" is not confined to any one country or stage in a political debate. Disapproval centers more on the role of the person than on the amounts of money. Risk takers like Bill Gates or Richard Branson are largely immune from criticism on account of their vast wealth in part because they are seen to have taken risks to justify this wealth. Others like Steven Ross at Warner Communications or F. Ross Johnson at RJR Nabisco and Cedric Brown at British Gas do not (at least in the public's eyes) take the risks so they do not merit the rewards.

This shift in expectations is not confined to wages. It affects the working of markets. Conventional economic thinking about markets assumes that people are selfish, profit maximizers. They enter every transaction whether as buyers or sellers, with the clear goal to get as much as possible, for as little as possible. The free market works because, over time, it produces the best allocations and most efficient production of goods, services and money. Inefficient suppliers are driven out of business and inefficient buyers learn from their mistakes.

There are several apparent weaknesses in this model of the market. The most fundamental lies in variations in the difficulty of entering and leaving some markets because of a barrier to entry and exit. A small number of producers dominate most major markets. It is in their interest to replace free markets with managed markets. Buyers face the same problem. It is not in their interest to continually search for and experiment with new suppliers. Cash savings can easily be wiped out by the costs of search or the impact of a mistake.

This approach to managed markets has shaped thinking about industrial economics since Chamberlin[6] and Robinson[7] wrote about imperfect markets in the 1940s. It is the implicit assumption of all those who write about corporations "concentrating on their core capabilities and competences". These organizations are not slaves to the invisible hand of the market. Rather, they make choices and concentrate their efforts where they believe they can gain the maximum competitive advantage from their "monopoly" power. The emerging new economy addresses the other half of the equation – buying.

The selfish buyer is becoming better informed and more willing to take concerted action to achieve goals and adopt a longer time horizon. US petrol buyers boycotted Exxon after the Exxon Valdez oil spill at a cost to Exxon of an estimated $1.7Bn. Wine drinkers across the world stopped buying French wines after the French nuclear tests. The cost to date is $250M. The selfishness of market behavior is being challenged by the selflessness of social behavior in the northern economies. This conflict is less clear in Asian and African economies where maintaining social bonds has equal value with satisfying selfish needs through the market mechanism.

THE NEW DIVORCE COURTS

John O'Neil's book *The paradox of success* takes as its subtitle "When winning at work means losing at life." His implication is that corporate man or woman sacrifices so much to achieve business or financial success they become isolated from their families, their communities and eventually even from themselves. Isolation from families is the best documented aspect of the price paid by the corporate person for success. Loyalty to the organization presupposes disloyalty to the family. This is particularly pernicious as commitment to the company is undertaken as a means of delivering benefits to the family through a better standard of living.

The price paid can, however, undermine the bargain. The executive spends time away from home, is unavailable for key family events and so the sense of betrayal grows. This is a fair description, as the substitution of one loyalty for another is the classic form of betrayal. In the 19th century family breakup was a price workers often paid in their search for employment in the new factories and industries. The journals of migrant workers are full of their sorrow at loss of family. The 20th century saw the same price being paid by managers and the middle class. Nowadays the nuclear family has begun to be sentimentalized in much the same way that workers in the 19th century sentimentalized the extended family.

Separation from families stands alongside isolation from communities as the price paid by managers for success. The relatively low status of managers partly explains the scale of criticism about executive remuneration. But it goes deeper: threats to the environment, urban decay, job losses, indeed almost any sign of diminished competitiveness are placed firmly at the door of management. The contrasting responses to job losses among managers and workers reflects this lack of involvement. Managers losing their jobs are seen as "the biters bit," but when workers lose theirs it is unalloyed tragedy.

The isolation of managers from their communities partly results from the efforts of managers to insulate themselves from their communities. An early form of this was the suburbanization of managers. They moved away from their workplaces, gradually eradicating links as offices became separated from production areas and headquarters units became separated from other parts of the enterprise. Descriptions of the life and workstyles of business leaders like F. Ross Johnson, John Aakers, Asil Nadir, Ralph Halpern and others are reminiscent of the story of a member of Britain's Imperial General Staff who visited the battlefields of France for the first time in 1919, a year after the Armistice, and exclaimed "Did we really send men out to fight in that?"

The popularity of determinist economic or business thinking is another form of isolation or separation for managers. They cannot be held accountable for problems, decline or failure because these are created by forces over which they have no control. Competitive pressures force them to take risks with the environment or their community. Their freedom to act is limited by historically determined "core capabilities" which push them down ever narrower channels. The erosion of the line distinguishing the manager and the bureaucrat is inevitable when managers give up their discretion to act, shape and implement policies.

The blurring of this line produces the third act of separation or isolation. This is the separation of managers from their distinct knowledge, competence and role. The bureaucrats and the managers are separated by the latters' willingness to take responsibility for the results of their actions. Managers who look for others to blame are separating themselves from their distinctive role and becoming bureaucrats. The existence of a blame culture is one of the clearest "lead indicators" of organizational decline. Some time before the problems of IBM became part of the public consciousness I encountered the blame culture raging in that company when leading a development workshop. I struggled to persuade managers that if they were not part of the solution they must be part of the problem – they preferred instead to find scapegoats inside and outside the company.

> *Managers who look for others to blame are separating themselves from their distinctive role and becoming bureaucrats.*

> *The inability to deploy resources is an insufficient defense against change when old ideas and approaches face new conditions and needs.*

Consolidation through growth

Andy Grove, CEO of Intel, summed up the problem facing IBM and other struggling giants when he pointed out that "there's no competitor around who can do as much damage to us as we can do to ourselves." The inability to deploy resources is an insufficient defense against change when old ideas and approaches face new conditions and needs. Gary Hamel describes the problem and gives some indication of the way forward:

Once the diversified corporation could simply point its business units at particular end product markets and admonish them to become world leaders. But with market boundaries changing ever more quickly, targets are elusive and capture is at best temporary. A few companies have proved themselves adept at inventing new markets, quickly entering new markets and dramatically shifting patterns of choice in established markets.

The ability to invest large sums in a solution is most effective when the way forward is known. The USA won the race to put a man on the moon because the means was known; the only question was "Do we have the resources to deliver?" Once President Kennedy had committed those resources the conclusion was never in doubt. And yet President Nixon's attempt to do the same with the search for a cure for cancer failed. The resources were available but right way forward remained elusive.

Organizations face the same problems today and must manage their different portfolios and capabilities accordingly. The concentration of resources on existing core capabilities will generate the best short- to medium-term results. The enterprise that knows how these capabilities work inside the organization and in the wider environment should also understand the extent to which it gains a disproportionate return from this capability. Those leading the enterprise know the features of this capability that make it distinctive from those of its rivals. They will have some understanding of the extent to which these capabilities can or cannot be extended.

The combination of these different pieces of knowledge defines the strategic space within which these core capabilities can be used. Marks and Spencer in the UK have learned how far their core capability to provide high quality value for money goods to a specific set of markets can extend. The firm has a massive competitive advantage in the UK clothing market among those customers who are willing and able to spend a small amount more for a significant improvement in quality and style. At the same time, it has little advantage in selling to those for whom price or high fashion are the primary determinants of purchase. The same capabilities similary convey little advantage in nonanglophile markets. Any attempt by the firm to move into these markets requires the creation of a new set of capabilities and the effective integration of these capabilities into the overall, competitive competence of the enterprise.

Few capabilities convey permanent competitive advantages. Football pools companies in the UK enjoyed a long period of competitive advantage over other forms of gambling derived from their distinctive mix of easy access, large prizes, high profile and low costs. The introduction of the National Lottery led to each of these advantages being lost and as a direct consequence every pools company has lost market share. The decline of ITT coincides with shifts in the competitive environment which

> *Change demands the ability to move beyond current and well understood capabilities to new capabilities.*

made its ability to squeeze cash from underutilized assets less important than the ability to make diverse businesses grow.

Change demands the ability to move beyond current and well understood capabilities to new capabilities. This process does not fit easily into economists' models of factor endowments as the source of mutually advantageous trade. The main endowments in Riccardo's model are fundamentally static. The country, community or enterprise works with a given set of endowments. Organizational development starts from a different assumption – endowments can be employed to build up different capabilities and competences.

The primary task is to adapt endowments, that is the existing resources and capabilities of the enterprise, to meet the needs of new conditions. The problem with adjustment is that it is faced with two unknowns: the future, and the extent to which current capabilities will suit new needs. Successful organizations will need to adjust their cultures in three ways:

- they must move from a "closed" system to an open system view of their operations
- they must invest in capability and competence development;
- they must become integrated, entrepreneurial concerns able to take risks and to learn.

BUILDING THE DODO

A common criticism of management theory is that it has the habit of moving from one all encompassing route to success to another usually contradictory approach. Simplistic interpretations of the focus on core capabilities saw enterprises reduced to a small nucleus of activities. In theory, concentrating their efforts on their areas of greatest competitive advantage provided opportunities for cost reductions and profit increases. In practice, it is not that simple to take out capacity. Some enterprises rely for their competitive edge on seemingly redundant capacity elsewhere. Once a business starts shrinking it is hard for it to stop – when a company leaves the market because it lacks competitive edge, the way is left free for rivals to build up their strength. The 80/20 fallacy, that 80% of my returns come from 20% of my activity, leads eventually to *reductio ad absurdum*. The fewer points of contact the firm has with its wider environment, the less scope it has to learn from new experiences and to create new synergies.

The focus on core capabilities approach has greatest value in stable market conditions. It can produce good profits and a powerful market position. Its greatest weaknesses lie in the deconstruction of the enterprise that is an integral feature of the approach and its difficulty of adapting to change. The deconstructivist approach, breaking an enterprise down into its constituent parts, would be easier to sustain if more were known about the ways in which organizations operate.

It is easy to assume that the core capability underpinning Sony's business success was an ability to convert new technology into user friendly, accessible consumer products. The *Walkman* and a host of other products appear to support this proposition. There is however, a succession of failures that just as readily fit this model; failures ranging from video recorders to computer games. Glaxo's core capability seems to lie in its ability to convert R&D expenditure into successful drugs. *Zantac's* popularity and profitablity seems to attest to the competitive advantage gained but the problems encountered in trying to discover a followup drug raise questions. There are relatively few cases of firms that embark on the road to increased performance through concentration restoring growth. The US airline industry was among the first to adopt this approach, through firms like TWA and PanAm. They eliminated peripheral activities, then fringe routes and, eventually, their own independence.

Experiences and approaches that are suitable for stable market conditions are seldom the best ways to manage change. Concentration on established core capabilities can undermine competitiveness as these capabilities become less relevant to changing conditions. The greater the change, the less useful these capabilities become. The enterprise has the survival power of the Dodo.

Histories of the Dodo tend to concentrate on its road to extinction. They seldom point out how well suited it was to pre-colonial Mauritius, being one of the dominant species on that island, living in vast flocks. It was perfectly adapted to its environment – until the environment changed and it found it had no defenses against the men who hunted it or against the rats, dogs, cats and other creatures man introduced. Gary Hamel argues that some form of internal "biological diversity" is an essential feature of the survivability of businesses.

This internal diversity is founded on deep rooted survival strategies or deliberate attempts to construct and understand future scenarios. Capabilities can be developed which match the needs of these emerging scenarios. Survivalism is not well understood in most companies. In my meetings with business leaders, I often ask them to identify the survival strategies of the firm, those strategies that enable the firm to survive crisis. When these emerge they seldom match any stated core capability. The ability of Chrysler, to survive the series of crises that threatened its existence in the 1970s and 1980s was not the public capability to engineer and design distinctive cars or trucks. The British retailer ASDA survived similar threats to its existence but not because of its distinctive product mix. Chrysler survied because its leadership group framed a survival plan which wedded established strengths to market needs while transforming the organization's culture. ASDA achieved the same internal revolution while focusing on welding the enterprise together within a survival plan.

Envisioning

Survival is seldom enough on its own to justify the role of the leaders or managers of an enterprise. Their primary task is to move beyond survival to prosperity and success. This calls for an ability to envisage the future, shape policies to gain competitive advantage and build the capabilities to deliver these strategies.

Approaches to scenario building exist across the spectrum from logical to illogical extensions of current conditions. The logical extension is extrapolated from the present and asserts that current trends will continue. The

> *Survival is seldom enough on its own to justify the role of the leaders or managers of an enterprise.*

illogical extension assumes that current trends have reached their conclusion, therefore some form of shift is inevitable. IBM

133

successfully adopted the policy of logical extension from the 1950s to the 1980s by realizing that computers were getting larger and faster and assuming that they would continue to do so.

Logical extension can degenerate into tunnel vision. IBM dismissed DEC's success with the Vax because it existed outside its line of vision, and IBM had built up its organizational capabilities and structures to cope with the logical extension of its current marketplace. The illogical development, small, personal or mini-computers, threw it into turmoil, since it lacked the culture, capabilities and structures to adapt quickly to the new environment. In an environment characterized by change, organizations need the ability to envisage the illogical development. They also require the willingness to test their culture, capabilities and structures against the needs of this new environment.

Doing things right and doing the right things

The managerial bureaucracies of large organizations find it hard to shift from their preoccupation with logical extensions of their current situation. They share the fixation of all bureaucrats with the present and current ways of working. They forget the distinction that exists between doing things right and doing the right things. The British chemicals giant ICI showed all these features during the 1970s and early 1980s. Its managers operated along well worn paths to improve efficiency but failed to make serious headway against its European rivals. In the middle of the 1980s a major program of change was initiated by Maurice Hodgson, continued by John Harvey-Jones and completed by Denys Henderson. It took a wholesale restructuring of the firm and its division into two separate firms, Zeneca and ICI, to transform the corporate culture. Bob Haslam, one of the key players in the ICI revolution took these ideas into British Steel and British Coal and led a transformation of both firms that eventually produced two of the most competitive global players in their sectors.

Corporate reengineering is an invaluable tool in this shift in emphasis and attention forcing managers to appreciate the difference between the right things and things right by reexamining the fit between the purpose(s) of the business and its day to day priorities. Almost inevitably reporting systems which loom large in the priorities of managerial bureaucrats are questioned while response systems are reviewed. Reporting systems and processes are important but they are no substitute for an ability to meet customer needs successfully.

I recently worked with a large, diversified consumer goods company, worried about the low rates of success for the new product development program. They described in detail a complex system of targets and performance indicators that centered on an annual launch schedule. Different divisions had "slots" in the schedule that were determined by corporate, marketing planning coordinators. Each division had a specified number of opportunities to launch new brands that fitted into the corporation's sales promotion, merchandising, distribution and advertising schedules. Inevitably a culture existed in which no brand or product development manager wanted to miss the allocated slot even if demand was weak or nonexistent. The result was waste and inefficiency.

Reengineering is designed to prioritize the core purposes of the enterprise in ways that give the best returns to shareholders while ensuring that all assets are employed as effectively as possible. It is an integrated process of improvement that matches radical changes in the external environment with the capacity to undertake radical change in the internal operations of the enterprise. The speed of external change and the extent to which the operational process can be transformed create opportunities for dramatic improvements. These are vividly illustrated by George Stalk's work[8] on time based competition. Firms like Federal Express, Domino's Pizza, Wal-Mart and Matsushita achieved dramatic reductions in the time market, the time it took to replenish stock and the speed with which customer needs were met. In Europe, the Italian motorcycle firm Aprillia reduced product development times by between 50 and 70 %. Each reduction cut costs, improved the firm's ability to enhance quality and features while responding to customer needs. In effect, the business was transformed.

Persistence

These dramatic improvements are not the result of some quick and easy fix. Major changes need major reappraisals of operations and dedication to change. Ray Croc of McDonald's was fond of highlighting the value of persistence in achieving real success and major developments. His famous statement on the topic is worth quoting in full.

> **Nothing in the world can take the place of persistence. Talent will not; nothing is more common than unsuccessful men with talent. Genius will not; unrewarded genius is almost a proverb. Education will not; the world is full of unrewarded derelicts. Persistence and determination alone are paramount.**

The importance of persistence probably explains why stamina is such an important characteristic of those business leaders who have managed to see their enterprise through major change. John Harvey-Jones, former CEO of ICI, claims "the prime characteristic that I have detected in top leaders is mental and physical toughness."

CONCLUSION

Persistence and stamina are aspects of the new mindset that is needed to tackle the eight major paradoxes that managers must face in order to prosper in the new economy. Each paradox contains within it a challenge to the capabilities of managers and their organizations and the key to long-term success. The 8 key paradoxes take several forms but each contains two seemingly contradictory issues that after deeper analysis must come together.

The eight key paradoxes

- Act now for the long term
- Growth through consolidation.
- Building individualistic teams.
- Getting more for less.
- Thinking local, acting global.
- Simultaneous growth of economic regionalism and economic nationalism.
- Winning through action oriented reflection.
- Consolidating internal capabilities while reengineering.

Long-term success depends on the ability of both manager and firm to turn each paradox into a new unity. Out of these new unities emerge a set of approaches to long-term success that fit the needs of the new business environment. Their resolution requires a new form of management thinking based on integration and whole environment thinking.

The virtuous circle is driven by success. The trick is to frame long-term strategies that can be owned by all those involved in implementation.

Chapter 7

◆

REWARDS AND STANDARDS

Three issues recurred throughout the research, development and collaboration with firms that went into the creation of this book. First, business leaders and managers repeatedly commented on the contradictions that occur in their work. The most common is that between the recurrent threats to their business base as new ideas, products, services and rivals appear in the market, while the environment is rich with opportunities as customers seek innovative ideas, are willing to experiment with new suppliers and these new markets emerge. Another contradiction is that there is an ever widening range of skills and knowledge on offer from current and prospective employees, but at the same time equally large gaps and omissions exist. Opportunities for creativity abound side by side with deep rooted conservatism.

Handling these contradictions is made harder by the second issue – the increased expectations of customers and employees. A large scale investigation of industrial and retail buyers was conducted in parallel with this work. It found that an overwhelming majority of buyers required suppliers to be more innovative, expected more innovation of themselves, wanted higher delivery and quality standards, were working to more exacting delivery standards and wanted lower prices. Buyers' expectations are increasing – shorter order lead times, more features and better design but they expect to pay less while imposing more taxing conditions on suppliers (see Table 7.1).

Table 7.1

Changing Expectations of Goods and Services (industrial buyers in Europe)			
Expectation	Yes %	No %	Don't know %
Shorter delivery lead times	95	5	–
More design	75	25	–
More features	75	25	–
More innovation from suppliers	87	13	–
More innovation from self	85	10	5
Shorter order lead times	80	15	5
More concern about price	85	10	5
Tighter delivery specifications	80	15	5

Similar higher standards were expected by key employees, who wanted more support, higher wages, greater freedom and increased opportunities.

Underpinning both the contradictions and the expectations is the third issue – the changes in the rules and assumptions governing business behavior. Well established beliefs and assumptions no longer hold good and ways of conducting business and the business environment itself are transformed. The challenge to rules and assumptions exists at the macroeconomy or industry level and at the microcompany or business unit level. It is no longer acceptable to say "You get what you pay for." People expect to get more than they pay for. At a business level the old assumptions can be fatal. For many years, IBM relished the statement "No one ever got sacked for buying IBM." It came back to haunt them when waves of technical criticism prompted some business leaders to question just why they were buying IBM. They wanted to know whether their equipment was bought because it was the best for the company or the safest for the buyer.

Successfully managing these and the many other challenges facing organizations in the future calls for new ways of thinking. These new ideas and approaches involve both incremental change and logic leaps to create a new form of management and a new generation of managers.

ACT NOW FOR THE LONGER TERM

Thinking about the future in new ways is made harder by the planning paradox facing firms and managers. Two quotations symbolize this paradox. The first was made by the chief executive of a large and successful UK manufacturer interviewed as part of the UK's Institute of Management's *Management development to the millennium* study. He argued that

These new ideas and approaches involve both incremental change and logic leaps to create a new form of management and a new generation of managers.

looking to the millennium is too short sighted when talking about issues of development and organisational structure. It takes at least two years to get any value out of good management development and then its effect can still be developed over a ten year period.

Another senior manager commented that "we have the groundwork in place and some of the superstructure but we are still not getting the best from it. It will take at least ten years before we get the best from it."

Microwave magic

Business leaders in North America and Europe are impressed by the ability of East Asian firms to plan for the long and very long term. The success of Samsung in the microwave oven market illustrates the way long-term strategic planning is used to gain competitive advantage. In the early 1970s Samsung committed itself to winning global leadership in the microwave market. At the time the firm had few of the resources and little of the expertise to be able to achieve this goal. Lee Byung Chull, Samsung's chairman, was determined to build up a powerful position and was willing to invest for the long term in research and development, engineering and quality staff as well as technology transfer deals with foreign companies like General Electric.

By the end of the 1970s, Samsung's production was still tiny especially in the face of a world market of over 5 million units a year. By then, they were producing their own models and were beginning to benefit from their investment in R&D. The first international sales breakthrough came at the start of the 1980s when J.C.Penny, the US retail group, approached Samsung to produce a retailer brand for their stores nationwide. In the first year Samsung produced almost 100,000 units. A year later this had doubled, and by the late 1980s, major US producers like General Electric were looking to Samsung for collaborative ventures. Total output broke through the one million unit mark at the end of the 1980s. Fifteen years of patient development had produced the desired outcome.

The devil is in the detail

This approach was replicated by Japanese, Korean and other East Asian producers as they grew to dominate markets as diverse as zippers, golf clubs, whisky, video recorders and a host of other products. Gradually, North American and European corporations started to learn the lessons and struggled to stretch their time horizons, just when the rules seemed to change. Mitsubishi are one of many Japanese companies achieving breakthroughs in the time taken to develop new products from original conception to market introduction. On a typical product range, Mitsubishi has moved from a 3 to 4 year new product development cycle to a 1 year development cycle or even shorter.

These breakthroughs in cycle times reflect a shift in the pace of operations and work. Now, when I talk to managers, they often react by saying "Five, ten, twenty year time horizons: if I could plan for five, ten, twenty days, I would feel that I was ahead of the game". Managers face the paradox that they must manage for the moment while adopting a long-term vision. It is the ability to mix incrementalism and vision that marks the effective leader.

Incrementalism is founded on the kind of attention to detail which is summarized by Sir Richard Greenbury of Marks and Spencer when he commented that "The devil is in the detail." Detailed work was once viewed as painstaking and slow but urgency is the key feature of contemporary leadership. The ability to set a pattern of short-term wins which become a platform for further progress is a key characteristic of success-ful enterprises. The success of

> Managers face the paradox that they must manage for the moment while adopting a long-term vision. It is the ability to mix incrementalism and vision that marks the effective leader.

Stew Leonard's Dairy in the USA is characterized by the mixture of urgent attention to detail. There is a famous story about Stew which shows the effectiveness of this approach. Leonard regularly sits in on customer focus groups. On one occasion a woman commented that she did not buy fish at Stew Leonard's because it was always shrink wrapped and displayed in a plastic container. Within days the fish were displayed unwrapped lying on a bed of ice. Sales soon doubled.

Attention to this kind of detail and a fast response are not merely features of successful retailers. 3M have built much of their success on this kind of attention to detail and a refusal to prevaricate about introducing improvements. Akio Morito built the same determination to improve constantly and incremen-tally into the Sony philosophy. BMW in Europe share this approach to improvement and have little patience with attempts to equivocate in the face of opportunities for improvements in products, processes and relationships.

The features of painstaking urgency are easy to describe but involve deep rooted changes in an organization's thinking. A preoccupation with problem solving is integral. The challenge is to get the line flowing, tackle the reasons for customer dissatisfaction and then allocate responsibility for getting at the causes. If Richard Branson arrives at the airport and finds long queues and angry passengers, he helps out by distributing tickets and clearing those queues. Once the customer care problem is solved, he works to identify the cause of the problem and ensure it does not happen again. This type of hands-on management confounds traditional, hierarchical approaches to management. Branson pays less attention to issues like "undermining the authority of line managers" than to "getting the job done."

Glass boxes

Hands-on managers are willing to break the rules of the bureaucracy to meet customer needs. Sam Walton's constant travels around the USA to visit his stores to test their service and quality was matched by Marcus Sieff's stated commitment to buying everything he could from his own stores. Leaders who do not share the experiences of their customers soon lose touch with their needs. Nothing shows how far some companies have drifted from the roots than the "customer awareness" presentations advertising agencies provide for major clients. These video, tape, slide and talk events take place in the company headquarters or agency. They purport to show top managers how their customers live, buy and use their products. Of course they get it in a nicely sanitized and comfortable presentation.

> *Hands on managers are willing to break the rules of the bureaucracy to meet customer needs.*

This type of presentation operates like a glass box. Business leaders think they are seeing the real world of their business when in fact they are getting a purified version of it. It takes time to fit store visits, talks to customers and buying and using products into a busy schedule. Demands on time are heavy enough with budget meetings, strategy committees, board meetings, discussions with investors, public ceremonies and other duties. These are active demands on the managers' time that contrast strongly to the passive demands made on their time by customers and operations. One of top management's biggest challenges is to smash the glass boxes that their staff build around them. They have to ensure that they have a real feel for the guts of the business and its markets not the version dreamed up by someone else.

Attention to detail is not enough by itself. A long-term vision is essential especially if incrementalism is to become a route to change and not a barrier. Hammer and Champy argue that all too often "incrementalism is the path of least resistance for most organizations. It is also the surest way to fail at re-engineering." The solution is to link incrementalism to a long-term vision, a strategy to deliver that vision and a program of planning for and creating short-term wins.

Peters and Waterman summarized important features of the relationship between long-term visions and short-term action in the notion of the tight–loose approach to policy, which in short implied that top management was responsible for defining a clear and tightly fixed sense of direction on the enterprise. They identified its destination. Operations management and people were responsible for implementation and chose the means or route to take. This approach has much to commend it but it is gradually being overtaken by events, technologies and shifts in individual competences.

THE SHINE ON THE PENTIUM

The successes of firms like Cummins Engines in the USA, ABB and Glaxo in Europe and NEC in Japan show that this type of rigid demarcation between strategy and implementation is no longer sustainable. Strategy and implementation are parts of the same process. Undertaken properly they interact and adapt to one other. The least valuable strategies are those that are not or cannot be implemented. Intel has been especially successful in milking the best returns from a strategy through effective implementation. John Crawford, who was in charge of the team developing the Pentium chip, describes the importance of keeping the research team focussed on implementing the policy in hand.

> **We had launched another team in Oregon to build a more advance microprocessor, and they were coming up with ideas of what they could do with their transistor budget. They were making good progress towards another leap in functionality and performance from that other product, and a lot of the new research was already bearing fruit for the next generation. The shine on the Pentium processor was beginning to pale in comparison to the gleam in the engineers' eyes for the generations to come. So I helped to keep our team focussed in getting the Pentium product to the market.**

Richard Branson of Virgin is a firm supporter of rooting policy deeply with implementation. He looks for deeper involvement and says that "I have not depended upon others to do surveys, or a lot of market research, or to develop grand strategies. I have taken the view that the risk to the company is best reduced by my involvement in the nitty gritty of the business."

New technologies, particularly, information and communication technologies, have eliminated many of the barriers between those involved in framing and implementing strategy. Physically remote senior managers can get feedback on actions and responses as quickly as those much closer to the point of implementation. The "reach" of top management has increased dramatically as fast, user friendly management information systems become more widely available.

The double helix

The same technologies provide increasing scope for inter-activity. This creates opportunities for those with a primary responsibility for implementation to play a full part in policy formation. The unified enter-prise is driven by leaders and managers who frame policies that capitalize on all the assets of the firm and by operational staff who own the policies and

> A strategy that cannot be communicated cannot be owned.

are determined to play their full part in their implementation and development. A virtuous circle is created between policy and implementation. The corporate double helix uses an under-standing of the genetic code of the enterprise to shape the policies that direct its work and ensure the effective implemen-tation of policy.

The virtuous circle is driven by success. The trick is to frame long-term strategies that can be owned by all those involved in implementation. Some basic principles can be applied to this type of long-term strategy. The immediate task is to ask whether the strategy can be communicated. A strategy that cannot be communicated cannot be owned. The second require-ment is to ensure that members of the enterprise understand and accept the part they can play in implementation. This means articulating long-term strategies in ways that identify the roles of particular groups and individuals: opportunities must be provided for all people in the enterprise to spell out their vision and their understanding. The implementation process is driven by people who have the confidence to believe that they can make a difference. This means framing programs that allow members of the firms to undertake tasks that provide opportunities for small wins and real successes.

This means not limiting people's visions. We are looking for ways to transform the organization from a 19th or 20th century enterprise to a late 20th or early 21st century business. This requires a radical shift in the kind of operations and management, and needs people who are confident of their ability to make a difference. Bill Marriott Jr. of Marriott Hotels is one of many business leaders who argues that "people who think they can make a difference make a difference."

The paradox of thinking long and acting short is solved by integrating a long-term view of where the enterprise is going with wide ranging freedom for people in the enterprise to take action. The vision and the values come together in the minds of people who know how to act and have the self confidence to act. They appreciate their role in delivering the big picture. James Barksdale of Federal Express spoke at a seminar in which the difference between the mindset of new integrated enterprises and that of old separated enterprises came to the fore. He was talking about the speed with which Federal Express reacted to an incident in which a woman had become trapped underground and her rescuers urgently needed special equipment airfreighted to Texas. "But how did they get permission from head office to ship the goods overnight with no certainty of payment?" was the question. Barksdale replied "There wasn't any management authority needed. The operator who answered the call in our regional center, just said yes

> *Vision, integration, confidence and trust are the watchwords of the new management paradigm which resolves the paradox of long-term vision and short-term action.*

and started the ball rolling ... if that person calls me at home in the middle of the night to okay something that important I've failed as a manager."

Vision, integration, confidence and trust are the watchwords of the new management paradigm which resolves the paradox of long-term vision and short-term action. Building, expressing and forming the vision are an ongoing task for all members of the organization. Articulating the vision and finding ways to integrate everyone into the task of specifying the future is essential to its implementation. Short-term wins give everyone ownership of a winning streak. This builds confidence across the enterprise. Confidence is part of trust and together they empower people to take action. Mao Tse Tung once said "The longest march starts with the first step." This is the vision which resolves the first paradox of the new revolution.

Scenarios

The struggles to survive, prosper and dominate the future are built on an understanding of the present and the possibilities of the future facing the firm. They provide a notion of the ultimate destination, a sense of alternative directions and indications of the equipment needed to achieve the "desired" destination. Organizations take different approaches to constructing scenarios. In the UK, Shell is well known for looking into their possible futures and constructing scenarios based on linear developments from known, current conditions. The trident model constructs a future that takes the present as a fork in the road with three alternative ways forward. One is created from the most favorable current conditions; the second is constructed from an especially negative combination of events; the third tries to construct a balanced picture.

The challenge to management is to test current endowments, capabilities and competences against these conditions. Endowments are made up from the historic mix of products, technologies and resources. These can be tested against three simple questions applied to each scenario:

- Can we survive?
- Can we prosper?
- Can we dominate?

Survival is typically the most fundamental question and faces the closest examination under the most threatening scenario. The decline of Wang Laboratories illustrates the danger

149

of not testing endowments and capabilities against a negative combination of events. They failed to test themselves against market conditions in which personal computer manufacturers and software firms produced cheap, highly portable and effective word processing software. The company did not construct a realistic scenario in which successive problems would blight the firm's ability to move forward. There is little evidence that they added to the scenario they had created the capital shortages which were initially serious but which worsened as rivals overtook Wang's early lead and the succession crisis loomed.

This type of scenario building is important if existing capability and investment in capacity building is to keep the firm ahead of its rivals. At General Electric Jack Welch uses 5 key questions to assess the corporation's ability to prosper. These are:

- What are the global market dynamics today, and what are they going to be over the next 3 to 6 years?
- What actions have competitors taken to exploit or upset these market dynamics?
- What have we done to exploit or upset these market dynamics?
- What are the most dangerous things our rivals could do in the next 3 years to exploit, upset or harm our position in these market dynamics?
- What are the most effective things we could do over the next 3 years to exploit, upset or dominate our rivals' position in these market dynamics?

Prosperity is seldom sufficient in today's marketplace. Dominance is required to generate the returns and scope for long-term investment especially in manufacturing. This explains why companies like Sharp, Toshiba, Sony, Daimler, Aerospatiale, Boeing and General Electric link long-term investments based on scenario building on short-term competence building.

These companies realize that entry costs in new technologies and new markets are lowest at the early stages in the development of an opportunity. Sharp's and Toshiba's investment in flat screen technology was relatively small in the early years but they were also the largest investors, so the relative scale of their investment won a large share of the best expertise and built a competitive lead. They reinforced their position by intensive protection through patents, licenses and contracting. As the scale of the opportunity emerged, new entrants were forced to invest far more heavily to catch up. The entry costs of late entrants were pushed up by the need to follow routes not protected by Sharp or Toshiba. Eventually the US government was forced to intervene with a massive support program to establish a US capacity to produce flat screens.

The logic map (see Figure 7.1) provides a valuable perspective on scenario building at times of rapid change. The easiest route to follow in constructing a scenario is to concentrate on logical continuities.

Figure 7.1

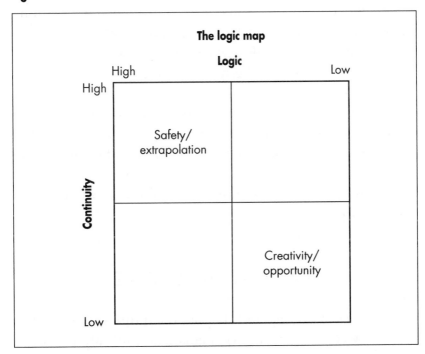

This future assumes a logical and consistent flow from current conditions. Under normal circumstances this is the most likely outcome in the short term. Logical inconsistencies can be constructed logically from current conditions but involve significant inconsistencies in trends. It is, for example, logical to assume that the telecommunications market will continue to expand. The consistent line of development calls for continuing dominance by large utilities offering "dumb" services to a mass market not interested in novel technology. It is plausible to construct a scenario based on the current logic which does not involve the continuous development of "dumb" services by large utilities. The Internet, for example, offers both a technological alternative and more variety in suppliers. A telecommunications future built around networks of smaller enterprises offering smart services to an ever more demanding and technological aware customer group is a further possible scenario.

The third alternative is a consistent development from existing assumptions: large utilities and "dumb" products still exist but change is driven by some illogical likelihood in the future environment. This could be the technological possibility of sending telephone signals down electrical wires. The electrical utilities could become the major players. Another illogical development might be a switch from intermediary or system control of telecommunications industries to producer or user control. The extreme outcome is an illogical discontinuity. The most immediate example of this is the power of the producers of software for personal computers whose influence in the contemporary IT industry confounds the logic of most of the last half century.

FINDING THE FUTURE

Approaches to finding and shaping the future vary considerably between organizations, managers and entrepreneurs.

Approaches exist as five dominant types: explorers, trappers, pioneers, builders and migrants. These categories have many similarities to the groups that opened up and developed new regions and unexplored tracts of territory on the earth. Understanding their characteristics is important not only in tackling the first paradox (acting now for the longer term) but for dealing with the second (growing through consolidation).

Explorers

These are the individuals and firms that open up and map new opportunities and markets. They are often known for their willingness to enter unknown territory and for the strength of their personalities. William C. Durant explored the possibilities offered by the early automobile industry. He showed that it was possible to establish ranges and knew the value of branding but he also mapped the territory that managers from Alfred P. Sloan to Lee Iaccoca subsequently developed. Erik Rotheim was one of the first people to develop a practical aerosol. He showed that it could be used for products as varied as paints, insecticides and cosmetics. Unfortunately he was never able to exploit his development and like many explorers died young and relatively unknown.

All industries need explorers who are willing to embark on new ventures in new environments. The first personal computer was developed by Ed Roberts whose Altair computer influenced the thinking and development of companies such as the Apple Corporation and Microsoft. Roberts had spotted the potential but did not manage to turn it into a major corporation unlike Clarence Birdseye who realized the potential of frozen food while working in Labrador, Canada. He used a technique developed elsewhere to set up his company "General Seafoods Corp." which he eventually sold for $22M in 1929.

Trappers

In some ways Clarence Birdseye was more trapper than explorer. He spotted an idea that was already in use and exploited it commercially. He described his experience while working on a US government survey of fish and wildlife. "That first winter I saw natives catching fish in fifty below zero weather, which froze stiff as soon as they were taken out of the water. Months later, when they were thawed out, some of these fish were still alive." Trappers are skilled at spotting opportunities and exploiting them and often may do little to actually build up capacity or develop the idea.

Smart companies learn how to use the trapper to identify technologies and ideas that can be turned to their own advantage. 3M showed the value of this approach while illustrating the value of an integrated approach to people with their Post-It Notes. The adhesive for these notes was originally developed by Spencer Silver in 1970 as an offshoot of his search for a powerful super glue. The main features of this adhesive were that it could be reused and left no residue. It was not until the 1980s that a colleague, Arthur Fry, found a use for the glue on Post-It Notes. He sang in a church choir and found paper with drops of this new adhesive on it were invaluable for marking his place. His private pursuit turned into a major profit earner for 3M.

Pioneers

New markets, like new territories, need pioneers. These are people or businesses that will take the risks associated with establishing themselves in new environments or markets. Pilkington Group in the UK were pioneers of the float glass method of glass production. This was a radical innovation in an industry in which Pilkington was not yet a major producer and the development costs were massive for a firm of its size. Waste product alone cost the firm $3.6M while other R&D costs were more than 20 times that amount. This was at a time when the Pilkington Group made net profits of less than $5M per year. It took 3 years of intense development to produce a marketable product but eventually royalty sales alone would net Pilkington $250M.

Pioneers often face severe difficulties as the costs of development threaten the viability of the enterprise. This can happen at any stage. John Moores, the founder of Littlewoods Pools in the UK, found out early. After spending almost $1000 in their efforts to get the business off the ground, his early partners wanted to pull out. Moores bought them out for $600. He ended up as Britain's richest businessman with a personal fortune of over $3Bn. Tom Watson Jr. of IBM faced the same problem in the 1960s. He wanted to upgrade the entire line of IBM machines through a revolutionary new line of computers – the System 360. The costs and risks were immense: the development costs of the range alone eventually exceeded IBM's total assets of $5Bn, but the success of the range ensured IBM's domination of the computer market from 1964 to 1990.

Builders

The most successful pioneers become builders. This is a process that can take place within firms as well as in markets. Alfred P. Sloan was a builder who created the success of General Motors out of the disparate collection of businesses assembled by William Crapo. Builders typically establish systems that sustain the development of the enterprise over long periods and in different conditions. Ryder Trucks in the USA achieved market leadership in the truck rental industry by simple but practical steps in industry building. The two most important elements were the creation of business systems which enabled them to sustain a much newer fleet than their rivals and a determined effort to give customers an easier to use and more reliable service. These two elements recur throughout the history of business building.

Migrants

Once a market or business is established it attracts migrants. These are new entrants who penetrate the market usually by introducing lower prices or niche trading. They are strongest where the costs of entry are lowest. They push prices down and break up the monopolies that can emerge when the builders use their power, knowledge and scale to dominate an environment.

Some companies have become adept at migration into new opportunity areas or out of those in which opportunities have declined. Virgin is a good example of the business migrant. Each of its areas of strength – entertainment, retailing, air transport and financial services – was dominated by large and stable corporations before Virgin entered the market. The company's mixture of low costs and high enterprise has won it important segments of the market. Japanese corporations are not only adept at entering markets, they are equally adept in market exiting. Matsushita Electrical has expanded its operations rapidly over the last 20 years. It is, however, quick to pull out of markets where its ability to combine technical proficiency, time based competition and intensive marketing yields diminishing returns.

Rot and decay

Hamel and Prahalad point out that "competing for the future requires not only a redefinition of strategy, but a redefinition of top management's role in creating strategy."[9] The challenge of competing for the future while competing for the present goes further. It demands an approach to business development that sees growth in terms of a series of platforms for further development. Progress on to the next platform can only be made if the first platform is secure.

Securing the first platform relies on several core disciples. The first is avoiding rot, or any other process which weakens the platform or its foundations. Corporate rot is caused by the erosion of the core strengths. Erosion in a business is like all erosion, occurring when parts cease to fit together and start to rub. The signs are there to see if anyone cares to look: groups in the firm stop communicating; empire building becomes more important than business building; form is more important than content; core capabilities are neither understood nor maintained. All this leads to organizational decay.

The most common form of decay in an enterprise occurs when the edifice and image remain rosy but since tests of capabilities are rare. Leaders of the enterprise begin to believe their own propaganda. Each of these features was seen in IBM before its crisis. The corporation had lost the ability to initiate or deliver major integrated technological projects such as the 360 range, concentrating instead on trivial product adjustments. The PC launch appeared to break the mold but was a minimalist development based on "catch up" not "get ahead" technology. Its success exploited old achievements instead of creating capacity for new achievements. Belief in its own propaganda could be seen in the firm's approach to marketing.

IBM was a sales driven business. Its massive salesforce had perfected a number of the techniques that characterize dominant manufacturers, especially the ability to swamp customers and rivals. IBM convinced itself that this large salesforce indicated an understanding of marketing which was an image confirmed in many popular textbooks. Closer examination suggested that the level of real marketing insight was far more superficial. The approach to branding the personal computer market vividly illustrated the weakness of IBM's marketing. The firm's early success showed that customers were seeking brand reassurance in a technologically diverse and complex market. IBM pioneered the term PC for personal computers but did nothing to protect "PC" as a brand name. The same failure occurred after the launch of the advanced technology (AT) range. When IBM did start to invest in brand name protection it was to protect the name PS/2. By that time the firm was in the unusual position of seeing clones selling for a premium on the originals.

The control of rot calls for a willingness to turn the corporate spotlight on weaknesses and to remove any obstacles in the way of the clear out that must follow. Jack Welch's approach at

General Electrical links illumination of problems with the confidence to tackle them.

We took out management layers. Layers hide weaknesses. Layers mask mediocrity. I firmly believe that an overburdened, over-stretched executive is the best executive because he or she doesn't have the time to meddle, to deal in trivia, to bother people.

MANAGING THE PRESENT TO SHAPE THE FUTURE

Growth through consolidation means managing present internal capabilities to ensure that competitive competences are created which shape the firm's future. The choices are surprisingly simple when there is a clear determination to make choices. All too often managers and leaders fight shy of making choices, perhaps hoping that something will turn up to make the choice unnecessary. Yet the evidence reveals that if nothing does turn up the later choices are usually harder. Equally often, the choices are not made for fear of the internal reaction to choices that mean abandoning a colleague's pet project or favorite scheme. The bulk of available evidence on organizational success indicates that clear decisions made early minimize losses, maximize gains and sustain organizational commitment.

Growth through consolidation means managing present internal capabilities to ensure that competitive competences are created which shape the firm's future.

Managing the present to shape the future requires an understanding of likely scenarios backed by determined efforts to invest to ensure that the enterprise is ready to capitalize on its opportunities. Sustained capital investment works best when it is concentrated on those core capabilities that maximize competitive advantage. Tight cost control is not an optional extra in these conditions, rather it is the measure of responsible investment. Intense supervision of people and other resources is compatible with the freedom of people to maximize their contribution when it is seen as adding the weight of support to their endeavors.

Simplification and integration are becoming the mantras of effective managers. They work equally well with inputs as with outputs. Products that are designed for ease of manufacture usually end up cheaper to produce, are more robust and provide better value for customers. The same commitment to simplification produces gains in logistics, operations and support services. Tight, disciplined internal structures create the capacity to adapt and respond to new and changing conditions. Complexity is especially harmful for internal networks and close coordination both internally and externally.

German and Japanese producers have gained an outstanding reputation for effective networking during the research, development and innovation processes. Product or service development interactions can be mapped along the two axes of intensity and proximity (see Figure 7.2).

Early, intense involvement is a characteristic of those German innovators that involve likely users early in the development process. They extend that involvement beyond the sales and purchasing function to include engineering, design, marketing in an intense network of collaborators. Other companies involve a less intensive group, mainly sales and purchasing, but again involvement is from early in the product development process. Some organizations have intense collaboration but late in the development process. The lowest success rates seem to characterize those firms that involve buyers both late and across a narrow range of partners.

Figure 7.2

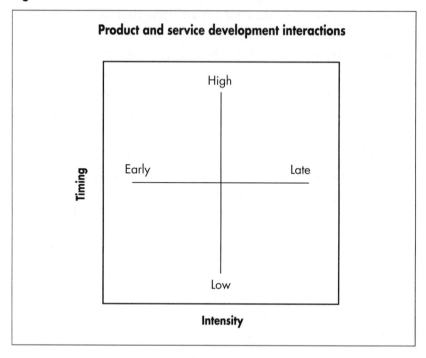

ARTICULATION

Growth through consolidation blends networks and relationships as much as it does competences and operations. Articulation, that is the process of building seamless links between discrete processes, provides the means to bridge the two activities. The task of management is to use consolidation to assess the future relevance of existing capabilities and competences. These must be measured against their value in securing current competitive advantages and their potential contribution in ensuring future advantage. Close analysis of current and potential rivals is integral. Their capabilities and competences can be tested against those which are important to the manager's firm. Investment in detailed competitive analysis pays major dividends if it provides an understanding of the capabilities that determine competitive success.

An appreciation of the ways in which existing capabilities articulate with desired or needed capabilities provides guidance on change strategies (see Figure 7.3). Ideally the shift is a seamless process in which the firm adopts the S shaped curve approach to organizational change. The S shaped or sigmoid curve describes the elements involved in building capabilities and the ways in which their contribution alters. The first stage is early learning: the company starts to build its capabilities and learns how to use them effectively. This early learning stage varies considerably in length of time, has different building blocks and is usually important because it is in this stage the company must win ownership of the capability, embed the capability in the firm and test the means by which competitive advantage is won.

Figure 7.3

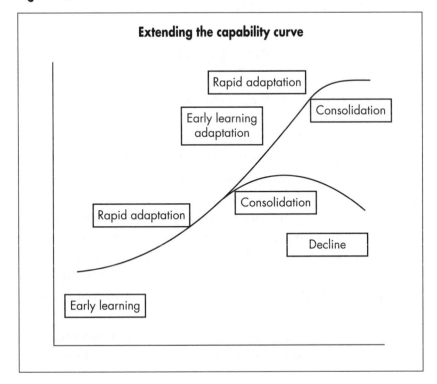

Once capabilities are embedded they can be rapidly adapted to different opportunities and used to create organizational competences. This is the time when the greatest competitive advantage and operational efficiences are won. It is the testing time for capabilities as the advantages deriving from them are made apparent.

Those capabilities that provide a real advantage are eventually absorbed into the central architecture of the organization. This is the period of consolidation when capabilities are transformed into the corporate endowment. Competitive pressures will eventually undermine the true competitive advantage from a capability. Organizations that fail to renew their capabilities will struggle to survive. Successful firms develop strategies to renew their existing capabilities and to build new ones. This recreates the cycle of learning, adaptation and consolidation but from a higher platform. It also provides an inner dynamic as managers realize that their advantages have finite lives and must be renewed or replaced constantly.

CONCLUSION

Robert Woodruff, former chief executive of Coca-Cola, summarized the competitive edge provided by discontent and impatience with the status quo with his comment that "The world belongs to the discontented." Sustaining a constructive sense of discontent or its corollary, the ambition to do better, is an important skill for business leaders who want to resolve the paradoxes of acting now for the long term and growth through consolidation. Effectively managed, discontent produces the mixture of impatience and determination that pushes a company forward. Ambition provokes people to push themselves to their limits. Both characteristics are integrative and creative; both are essential attributes for the 21st century.

Discontent has its negative features which can be minimized or avoided if leaders are sensitive and provide constructive outlets for them. Sympathy and projection are valuable tools in converting discontent to a positive. Sympathy is based on a knowledge of the concerns that create the discontent and a willingness to trust people sufficiently to legitimize these concerns. There is a tendency among leadership groups to exclude the worries and reservations of others.

The leadership uses a variety of ways to dismiss or reject these worries. Sometimes it is believed that those with worries do not understand the big picture or that they merely want to protect their own interests. These sentiments can easily degenerate into the kind of "group think" that rejects all dissenting views. It is more productive to start from the twin assumptions of trust and respect. This starting point requires that leaders accept the need to win the argument not the power play. Winning the argument eventually means that the leadership gains the trust and respect of all the people in the firm. This in turn becomes the platform which allows the first paradoxes to be resolved.

◆

The recognition that team work is
increasingly important to success.

◆

Chapter 8

♦

THE ENTREPRENEURIAL PRICE

THE ZIGZAG MANAGER

The eminent sociologist C. Wright Mills once wrote about the emergence of a new kind of business leader, whom he called the zigzag manager because he built his business by zigging and zagging between the areas of business ignored or under-developed by traditional corporations. When the giant soap companies pruned brands like Pepsodent from their ranges, zigzag managers bought them up and exploited the residual demand for these products. The major US and UK car companies decided in the 1970s to apply the 80/20 rule to their dealer networks. They withdrew their backing hoping these "less successful" dealers would quietly disappear. Instead, Japanese car firms zigged and zagged between these dealers, signed up the best and solved what had been the biggest barrier to their entry into the US and UK markets – lack of dealer support.

Illustrations abound of entrepreneurs performing their classic economic role as "gap fillers," "boundary managers" and "risk takers." They fill the gaps in markets left by large firms, which is what, initially, Anita Roddick's Body Shop did, filling the gap left by the giants Lever Bros, Procter & Gamble and Colgate. The "boundary manager" role is harder to define. Virgin Atlantic and

South Western Airlines zigzag along the price and service boundaries of the airline industry. They succeed because they voluntarily push the boundaries further than their larger rivals are prepared to. Risk taking involves the ability to zigzag between the opportunities and threats that exist in new developments. Ted Turner survived because he was skilled at zigzagging between the opportunities created by 24 hour television and the risks of a totally new approach to TV news broadcasting.

Sharp increases in entrepreneurial activity coincide with economic turbulence and revolutionary changes in markets. The list of entrepreneurs who emerged in Britain in the first half of the 19th century seems endless. These were people who overcame religious, national, ethnic, political and social barriers to transform the UK, and eventually, the world economy. From across Europe entrepreneurs like Nathan Rothschild, Ludwig

> *Risk taking involves the ability to zigzag between the opportunities and threats that exist in new developments.*

Mond and Hans Renold were attracted to cities like Manchester and Liverpool because they recognized the turbulence and opportunities created by entrepreneurs like them.

ENTREPRENEURIAL SHIFT

The spark of this enterprise did not die with the end of the first industrial revolution; it simply spluttered and flared less often. The flame was transferred to North America and Germany, both nations enjoying a surge in entrepreneurial activity at the end of the last century that matched and sometimes exceeded the earlier explosion of talent. Vanderbilt, Rockefeller, Ford, Edison, Carnegie, Westinghouse, Schwab, Morgan, Siemens and Krupp are but several on another long list of entrepreneurs who created and transformed industries and markets. The surge in entrepreneurial activity over the last few years shows many similarities and some important differences to earlier revolutions.

Two of the differences have special relevance to this analysis. The first is the geographical dispersion of entrepreneurial activity. There is relatively little migration of entrepreneurial talent to the most entrepreneurial or opportunity rich locations. This might show that it is harder for migrants to establish themselves in the most dynamic economic locations. Japan and Korea, for example, are far less welcoming to migrants than was 19th century Great Britain, USA or Germany. The greater mobility of the means of production, capital and technology, might mean that there is less need to physically move the opportunity center. There is some evidence that successful large enterprises are learning to respond to the challenge of enterprise.

The second difference is that internal corporate entrepreneurs play an increasingly important role in the achievements of larger firms. The story of Thomas West, one such entrepreneur, was described in *The Soul of the New Machine*. West mixed a willingness to take risks, follow unconventional routes and make creative leaps with the ability to mobilize resources, develop people and manage a complex administration. At 3M there exists a company culture that enables, encourages and endorses the work of internal entrepreneurs who seek out new business opportunities and turn them into successful businesses. Robert Devereaux, head of Virgin Communications, has the freedom to develop the business as an internal entrepreneur. John Neill at Unipart and Percy Barwise at ABB are corporate entrepreneurs who encourage the entrepreneurial spirit across the enterprise.

Many of the most significant entrepreneurs emerge from outgroups. During the first and second industrial revolutions religious, ethnic and migrant groups played a disproportionate role in entrepreneurial activity. The Rothschilds were Jewish migrants in the main economic centers where they established their banks. Surprisingly large numbers of US and UK entrepreneurs were members of minority religious groups. There are some indications that similar processes are at work today. Women owned businesses are making up a large proportion of the successful new starts across the world. Some data suggest that women owned businesses survive longer, employ more people and are more economically stable than male owned ones. This may reflect the skill at integrating diversity and building consensus based enterprises shown by women entrepreneurs. One of the earliest signs of corporate decay is the failure to spot cloning and reluctance to acknowledge the value of outgroups. Clone driven corporations reflect the weaknesses of top management and soon become sterile and decay. In biological systems health is closely linked with the ability to absorb diversity.

Teams

These entrepreneurs are aware that enterprise is not enough. The parallel strand in business development is recognition that team work is increasingly important to success. The team rather than the unit or group within a hierarchy lies at the center of Japanese and many other East Asian success stories. The picture that emerges from the successes of firms like Toyota, NEC and Hitachi is of enterprises that involve teams in activities that range from strategic decision making to optimizing operations. Winning consensus from the team is the first step in any development even in giant corporations with powerful leaders like Matsushita.

Gaining this support and involvement is not easy. Time and effort is spent building the sense of team by breaking down institutional barriers between people. The lack of barriers is used to draw people into the decision making, use their knowledge and expertise to minimize risk and maximize gains, and ensure their support for policies. The prevailing view is that time spent in winning predecision support is more than compensated for by time saved in post decision implementation. The pattern is repeated elsewhere in Asia. Jim Rohwer of First Boston in Hong Kong describes how the intensive networks that characterized Korean and Chinese society are replicated in the group behavior in the firms that emerge in these societies. The ability to mobilize the talents and endeavors of the group provides these firms with significant advantages over their more individualist and less cohesive rivals.

The gains include access to a wider set of experiences, insights from team members with special knowledge and less resistance to change. The team becomes both the proving ground for ideas, and the means of delivering added value and innovation. Teams can be created on the vertical, the horizontal and on a mixed plane. They can be relatively permanent or short lived. *Vertical teams* bring together managers from every level of the organization enabling the mobilization of strategic, distributive, communications and operational insights that reside at different points in the hierarchy to tackle a task or challenge. This form of vertical team is especially effective at undermining and even changing the hierarchy by drawing out the distinct competences of managers.

> *Mixed teams are increasingly popular with enterprises that aim to get the right people to work together in the right way to produce the right results.*

Horizontal teams pull in people who have the same type of seniority, drawn in from different functions and having various types of expertise. They can tackle specific tasks while reinforcing bonds between functions. Effective horizontal teams shift the enterprise philosophy from an assembly of different (sometimes competing) groups to a multifunctioning and multiskilled unity.

Mixed teams are increasingly popular with enterprises that aim to get the right people to work together in the right way to produce the right results. The potential to contribute is more important than status or claimed expertise.

The paradox facing managers and organizations lies in wedding the twin themes of entrepreneurship and teams in modern business. The vast bulk of evidence on entrepreneurial aspirations and behavior emphasizes the entrepreneurs' desire for independence. The earliest entrepreneurial success stories show how important it was for individuals like Josiah Wedgwood, Conrad Vanderbilt, Werner Von Siemens to strike out on their own and prove their independence. The same desire persisted in Carnegie, Lever, Beecham, Morito, Dassault and endures today with Branson, Roddick and Gates.

The struggle for independence is more important as a motivator for entrepreneurial activity. This does not sit easily with the notion of team playing or building entrepreneurs. The same problem exists when the team players act entrepreneurially. Available evidence on the most effective or successful team players shows that they seek satisfaction in forms which contrast sharply with the aspirations of entrepreneurs. They prefer structure, relationships, peer recognition and comfort to independence, power, creativity and risk.

Individualistic teams

Despite the paradox implicit in the notion of the entrepreneurial or individualistic team, there is burgeoning evidence that such a thing can be created and once created can provide a powerful spur to business development. The success of 3M symbolizes the benefits that can derive when individualism and team work combine. 3M has created a culture in which individual enterprise is married to a cohesive organizational structure in which team working provides an edge over isolated enterprise. Nestlé has invested heavily in creating a culture in which the enterprise of all its managers is wedded to team goals. Reto Domeniconi of Nestlé describes both the scale of the task and the nature of the opportunity.

To get excellence the greatest source of untapped resources is from middle management down. But people play old games; knowledge is power and initiatives get blocked.

There is no fundamental reason why enterprise, individualism and entrepreneurship cannot be wedded to team goals or why teams cannot show enterprise. The histories of sport, the arts and business are full of examples of the success that can be won when this paradox is resolved. The greatest US football teams, from the Green Bay Packers in the 1960s to the San Francisco 49ers and the Dallas Cowboys in the 1980s and 1990s, linked and integrated stars whose enterprise created a platform for greatness that made a difference to teamwork. Joe Montana of the San Francisco 49ers was the playmaker but he was protected and converted by others. In soccer, Hungary in the 1950s, Brazil in the 1960s, Holland in the 1970s, Germany in the 1980s combined players like Puskas, Pelé, Cruyff who could redefine their own role in the game with others like Mattias who created the opportunity. Cricket, baseball, basketball, hockey and other team sports illustrate the capacity to link entrepreneurship with team work.

It is easy to argue that this link is an integral feature of the sport itself. At Dallas, Troy Aikman simply could not perform without the offensive line to protect him, or without Emmett Smith to convert his efforts. The same might not be true for an entrepreneurial firm like Virgin. Does Richard Branson need Robert Devereaux or Will Whithorn? Are they interchangeable with other managerial bureaucrats? Eric Cantona's enterprise and talent transformed two "win nothing teams," Leeds United and Manchester United, into champions. So was it the team or the individual that made the difference? In team sports an individual like Dennis Lillie, the Australian cricketer, can be a talisman who has an effect far beyond his individual contribution. Individuals within enterprises can seldom produce the same immediate effect especially when moving from one to another. Even Kodak's $3Bn man, Christopher J. Steffen, did not last long enough for a proper assessment of his potential.

A flock of eagles

Individualist or entrepreneurial teams combine the strengths of enterprise with those of teamwork. The problem they pose was well summarized by Ross Perot who complained about General Motors. He felt GM stifled enterprise, summarizing his view with a philosophy that "eagles don't flock." There is a school of thought that believes entrepreneurial eagles can flock in firms combining the right leadership with supportive systems and the right atmosphere. Leading entrepreneurial teams has been described as "learning to herd cats." This means finding the right inducements to maneuver them on routes they feel they do not necessarily want to follow.

Leader/managers have many of the classic characteristics of other types of leader but they have learned to display and use them in different ways. Vision is important to get other entrepreneurs to buy into a way forward. Alex Ferguson at Manchester United and Jimmy Johnson at the Dallas Cowboys

> *Leading entrepreneurial teams has been described as "learning to herd cats."*

communicated a simple vision: the return of their teams' former greatness. In business it is hard to convey the vision in such simple terms. It is also difficult to provide the immediate feedback and reinforcement that sport provides. The leader/manager of the entrepreneurial team must provide a simple but clear vision. He must combine an ability to articulate this vision with a willingness to accept challenge and provide continuous support or reinforcement.

Talent and entrepreneurship go hand in hand yet surprisingly little attention is given to the management of talent in business with the possible exceptions of the finance sector and research laboratories. Clear and strong incentives provided through the leadership group matter a lot. Talent often shows little respect for the powers of office. What is more important is the ability to perform.

It is hard for some leaders to cope, familiar as they are with using the powers of office to reinforce their position. They are able to get their way, in part, because they can hire, promote and reward, but punish and demote. Their powers are employed to reinforce certain types of behavior and to deter other types. Subordinates respond because their freedom to react or withdraw is limited. The eagles in our team have fewer inhibitions. They are confident of their talent and enterprise. This confidence inevitably reassures them that they can withdraw or leave if their abilities and contributions are not recognized. Loyalties center on their fellow team members or on their talent itself. Relatively little is given to the specific firm. In the words of a New York investment banker: "If you want loyalty, get a dog."

Leaders of these entrepreneurial teams tap their talent by supplying a vision and nurturing the support of the team and its talent. Sometimes the vision is hard to sustain once the first goal is achieved. Bill Kenwright, the theater impresario, tells the story of his production of *Piaf*. For weeks before the part of Piaf herself was cast, Elaine Page frequently approached him. She was so anxious to get the role that she promised total dedication. She was cast and her interpretation of the role on the first night was a great success. The following day Elaine telephoned Bill to say that she was not willing to perform matinées: she was changing the rules.

> In the words of a New York investment banker: "If you want loyalty, get a dog."

The ability to change the rules to the organization's advantage is one of the great strengths of entrepreneurial teams, but direction and control are required if the firm is to reap real benefits. Rule changing places a premium on the ability of the leadership to articulate the vision in ways that compel the support of team members. A compelling vision must:

- win team members' support;
- energize the members;
- give them the confidence that they can deliver.

Leadership involvement at this stages adds extra value as it endorses the shift in behavior. Effective behavior change is reinforced when examples and models are set and achievements are recognized and celebrated.

THE END OF THE ANONYMOUS MANAGER

Management support for the entrepreneurial team gains greatest value when it is clear and public. Anonymity has emerged over the last half century as a cloak behind which managers hide, enabling them to avoid responsibility. The worst feature of IBM at the end of the Aaker era was the proliferation of anonymous managers who were fond of the phrase "Managers are only human," a phrase that was used to minimize their own responsibility to address the challenges facing the company.

The rise of the anonymous manager is a feature of organizations in trouble. There is the famous cartoon of a manager behind his giant desk . His comment to an aggrieved customer is "I don't know how you managed it, madame, but you have got through to someone in authority." It is a sentiment that is familiar to many of those inside organizations. The leaders and managers are just as anonymous to their colleagues as they are to their customers. They have become bureaucrats not managers.

Close analysis of some of the most successful firms indicates that most have leaders and managers who are confident enough to communicate their views. They identify themselves with their vision and can break out of the strait jacket of anonymity, Sam Walton at Wal-Mart, Michael Eisner at Disney, Gerry Robinson at Granada and Jack Welch at General Electric are cases in point. It is harder to achieve in older established firms than in new ventures. Managers from chief executive down are tempted to "let the figures do the talking" or a similar line. This leaves their colleagues unclear about their vision, and, more dangerously, leads them to think: if the leaders will not stand up for their policies why should I?

FOOLS' GOLD

Anonymity provides managers with the appearance of security. If they don't know me, how can they blame me? But this is the fools' gold of management. Anonymity emasculates managers and turns them into bureaucrats since the primary difference between the two is the accountability of managers. It is intriguing to read letters from lawyers, some of whom take this move away from accountability even further by signing their letters in the name of the firm and not the person. Accountability has its positives and negatives. There is a temptation to minimize personal involvement and hide behind process, procedure and time. Effective managers learn to take responsibility for rewards and reward systems. Ed Crutchfield, CEO of First Union Corporation, argues that

recognition and reward has to be done on a very short interval basis ... given immediately after the service was rendered. [It's] not something that you get in your pension 35 years from now, but it's something you can buy bread with on Monday.

Immediate rewards add three important dimensions to the entrepreneurial team:

- senior managers get involved;
- there is immediate feedback;
- team members bond together because response is due to endeavor and achievement not position.

Rosabeth Moss Kanter describes the changes that occur in the team. Social psychologists have shown that the maintenance of an authority relationship depends on a degree of inequality. If the distance between the boss and the subordinate, whether it be social, economic or other, declines, so does automatic deference and respect. This is further aided by the existence of objective measures of contribution. Once a high level of performance is established, the subordinate no longer needs the goodwill of his or her boss quite so much. One more source of dependency is reduced, and power becomes more equalized. Proven achievement reflected in higher earnings produces security. Security produces risk taking. Risk taking produces speaking up and pushing back. In short, if you want colleagues who are deferential and averse to risk maintain large, position based reward differences. However, if you want entrepreneurs who will work in teams, take risks and push the company forward, get involved, reward achievement publicly and quickly. You have to walk the talk and show you mean it.

High performance entrepreneurial teams break down other barriers. They can, for example, resolve the "act short term, think long term" paradox. They have the confidence and resolve to act immediately to tackle issues, and the breadth of knowledge to take an expansive, long-term view of the environment. Their development requires a shift in managerial attitudes. Coaching and mentoring of the kind more closely associated with team sports is more important than controlling and directing. Peer group pressure has the same effect in entrepreneurial teams as in sports teams, in that it puts the onus on the individuals to develop and manage themselves. Self development, training and the search for new ideas are part of the ethos which the entrepreneurial team creates.

NAPOLEON'S KNAPSACK

Feedback from within and without the team guides the team as a whole and each individual team member. One of the less publicized features of successful Japanese firms is the role of group feedback in stimulating improvements, sustaining quality and pressing for added value. At Canon the task was defined in relatively simple terms, initially "Beat Leica," it later became "Beat Kodak." Behind this simple proposition were teams that shared a determination to deliver that message, teams that supported, cajoled and challenged one other until they won. Similar approaches were adopted by Toyota, Komatsu, NEC and other Japanese firms. They learned that it was possible to square the circle of bringing people together if you had them working in teams as well as working as individuals.

It is not a uniquely Japanese approach. 3M prides itself that it is a company made up of 90,000 entrepreneurs working in teams. The teams at 3M can be stable over time but new teams can also be constructed to handle specific tasks. The company works hard to keep its main operating units small, division managers are expected to know their staffers by name and when a unit becomes too large to meet this test, it is broken up. Managers get to know their colleagues and support them through both success and failure.

Risk taking is encouraged and resulting failures tolerated as long as the lessons are learned. At 3M, Napoleon's old maxim, that every soldier has in his knapsack a marshal's baton, is taken literally. People who come up with an idea that the firm wants to use are given the freedom to recruit their own team, shape a work plan and implement the program. Even when an idea lacks official support people can spend part of their working time trying to prove its value. There is even a venture capitalist side to 3M's operations: each year Genesis grants of up to $50,000 are available to support people's ideas.

Michael Milken adopted a similar philosophy during his glory days at Drexel Burnham Lambert. He claimed:

There is no second in command. You could say that on some days there's one hundred seventy people that are second in command, and other days, you know, there's ten. It depends on what's happening, what the situation is. People have responsibilities, rather than a formal organizational chart.

Milken overreached himself and went beyond the bounds of the acceptable, but not before he had created a powerful, achievement oriented team of entrepreneurs.

In Germany some of the most successful firms confound their image by building their success on flexibility, enterprise and personal freedom. Hoechst, Bayer and BASF dominate their markets in Europe and elsewhere because they build on the culture of quality training and personal competence to allow entrepreneurial freedom. The German national training system has created perhaps the most skilled workforce in the world, with management training integrated into engineering education to create effective polymaths. The best German firms provide the freedom for these trained people to deploy their skills to the full.

It is easier to sustain this kind of culture than to create it. General Motors are battling to regain their leadership in the world automotive industry by shifting their culture. They want to move from an adversarial, fragmented and controlled culture to a cohesive and integrated but entrepreneurial culture. The work on the Saturn Plant symbolizes GM shift from the technosolution to the businosolution. Their technosolutions concentrated on investing in technology to beat the opposition. This is fine when technology is the problem and you know what technology to develop. It does not work when technology is not the solution or you do not know what technology is right.

Businosolutions take a whole business approach to problems. The Saturn Plant links technological capacity with people's capabilities. It draws on the knowledge, insights and involvement of workers to design and create an open and integrated working environment. This process has led Skip LeFauve Head of Operations to comment: "Managers don't wear suits, this breaks down the barriers between bosses and workers." This is a far cry from the formalism and separatism that characterized so many US and UK companies until recently. When I got my first job in management there were 11 different restaurants, one to cater for each tier of management. Now all employees at Saturn are involved in solving problems and creating added value, they are expected to work together until the right solution is produced. This has improved every aspect of production from the use of components to the process of manufacture. According to Skip "[this] is revolutionizing the assembly process ... it is a ten cent solution to a million dollar problem."

CONCLUSION

Perhaps the one universal feature of successful business development is the central role played by entrepreneurs. Rothschild's Bank, Unilever, Ford, General Electric, Siemens, Bayer, Sony, Toyota and Microsoft are inextricably linked with the ability of specific individuals to envisage the kind of enterprises that would succeed at a particular moment. In some cases their visions created businesses that survived far longer than the individual. Their enterprise allied with the distinctive opportunity of spotting the gap filling role of the new or small firm shapes the economic outcomes of the technological and market revolutions.

This entrepreneurial spirit is in turn reshaped by economic circumstance. New types of enterprise are more likely to benefit from team based entrepreneurial development than are traditional firms. This is especially important in learning organizations which strive to take on the potential of the knowledge based industrial revolution. Peter Senge sees learning organizations as based on "systems thinking [that] leads to experiencing more and more of the interconnectivity of life and to seeing wholes rather than parts." This integrated and unifying approach is well illustrated by the team based approaches adopted by more public entrepreneurs such as Anita Roddick, Richard Branson and Bill Gates, and is sometimes expressed in institutional approaches to reward. At EDS, for example, according to Mort Meyerson: "more than 60 per cent of the company is owned by people who run the company. So if we go public someday, we'll still make a lot of our people very rich." An approach such as this creates the kind of shared vision and unity of purpose that makes individualistic or entrepreneurial teams work, confounding Ross Perot's assertion that eagles do not flock. They will flock if the conditions are right, if there is no threat from the other eagles and the rewards are sufficient.

◆

Companies that perform well
refuse to take the path of
least resistance.

◆

Chapter 9

◆

GOODBYE TO ALL THIS

The shift in behavior and attitudes in new generation companies heralds a deeper change in the relationship between leaders, entrepreneurs and managers. The business literature of the last two centuries is full of attempts to define these groups and to draw lines between them. Leaders were often thought of in terms of the famous military or political leaders of history. Parallels are drawn with people like Churchill, Napoleon or Lenin who led nations or armies to great triumphs and disasters. People who inspired others to follow them when all seemed lost, people whose followers achieved the seemingly impossible, people who even, when in the minority, can still win through. This heroic view contrasts sharply with the more mundane view of leadership adopted by some equally successful leaders. Prime Minister Asquith struck a chord with many when he said "I am their leader, therefore I must follow them."

HEROES

In many business circles there is a stated or latent wish that heroic leaders will emerge and transform the business. These heroes will face up to crises in the manner of Churchill, be as decisive as Patton, have the credibility of Eisenhower, show the strength of personality of Kennedy, be as brave as Gandhi and be as visionary as Martin Luther King. The fact that close scrutiny of all these lives shows that all had their weaknesses does not dim the ardor of those wanting heroic leaders. The contribution of these leaders is often contrasted with the limited, operational work of management. It is, however, obvious that the dividing line has never been as clear as some imply, and is nowadays blurring even more as managers face the challenge of creating visions their colleagues can buy into. Pressure, challenge and change call for managers who can communicate, mobilize their colleagues, supply focus, tackle crises and get more out of their colleagues than they believed they could achieve. The old line is becoming redundant. The best managers are leaders.

A similar divide is often drawn between entrepreneurship and management. "Entrepreneurs are born not made" is a common refrain, so can anyone be a manager? There is something special about Lever, Ford, Lilley, Gates and Roddick that sets them aside from the mass of managers. The features are well rehearsed:

- They seek independence.
- They are risk takers.
- They view opportunities in different ways.
- They show resilience in the face of adversity.
- They are builders.
- They are leaders.

These same features are increasingly part of the set of assumptions made about good managers. They must cope with independent decision making in the increasingly fragmented decision units that make up contemporary businesses. They are expected to take risks, and to learn as much from their failures as from their successes. The new industrial revolution is an opportunity rich environment. Those managers who spot and exploit opportunities build their business; those who do not, can destroy their business. The line between the entrepreneur and the manager is disappearing even more quickly than the line between the manager and the leader. This has profound implications beyond the day to day work of managers and their companies. It affects the training and development of managers and the cultures in which they operate. The paradox of the entrepreneurial team becomes less the more the manager and the entrepreneur come together.

THE FULL PRICE

Entrepreneurial teams play a part in tackling the most pervasive of modern paradoxes: the pressure and desire for more for less. This shows very clearly a major study of industrial buyer behavior in Europe undertaken as part of the preparation for this book which found that buyers expected more innovation, more features and more design but at lower prices, with shorter lead times and tighter delivery specifications. A parallel investigation of retail buyers found broadly similar requirements.

The same phenomenon is found inside organizations. Resources are being tightened but targets increased. The "lean, mean" organization is expected to operate with fewer layers of support systems and fewer backups but simultaneously must move down new avenues, be more entrepreneurial and innovate. The old notion that widening the range and scale of activities means more resources is disappearing under resource constraints and new assumptions.

This paradox of more for less was, perhaps, the first of the great paradoxes to be widely recognized and this recognition grew from two sets of problems that beset companies in the late 1970s and early 1980s. First, the search for growth pushed firms into diversification programs that led firms overseas, into new activities and into new ways of working. Most failed to recognize the risks they faced by trying to buck Ansoff's strategy matrix, which indicated that the greatest costs and difficulties

185

face those firms moving into new markets, with new products. Second, some companies compounded their problems by introducing new ways of working into their attempts to move into new markets with new products. Costs rocketed and returns were small.

At the same time, researchers became aware of the financial and commercial gains from an alternative approach: concentrating resources on markets the firm knew, with products it knew. The Boston Consulting Group and others highlighted the gains from applying a learning curve to economies of scale. Those firms that knew the most about a market had the best chance to dominate that market. Market dominance was associated with economies of scale in production and barriers to entry. The higher the barriers to entry the easier it was to win good margins. The notion of "sticking to your last" became one of the great managerial truths of the 1980s.

THE SEEDS OF DESTRUCTION

Like virtually all social truths, sticking to your last contains elements both of wider realities and the seeds of its own destruction. The wider truth in this case was that the role of organizational capabilities and competences is more important and more complex than hitherto assumed. Companies cannot move from one business to another merely because of an act of will or a clear business opportunity. Their freedom of maneuver is constrained at least in the medium term by a mixture of their historic endowments, their capabilities and competencies and the architecture of the firm.

All firms have endowments, that is the assets that the company has accumulated over time. These assets provide a foundation for all future developments, and have the great advantage that their costs are typically sunk, that is they were paid for in the past. Current costs are primarily those of maintenance and protection.

Intel's endowments include the intellectual property rights sustained through patent legislation across the developed world. Glaxo has a similar endowment with the protection afforded to Zantac. Marks and Spencer has an important endowment in its retail outlets and strong supplier base. Many automobile firms have an important endowment in the differential trade in relationship with past customers. Banks in the UK have an important endowment in the limits put on companies applying for retail banking licenses. A strong balance sheet, good R&D, patents, licenses and brands are all part of a company's endowment. Endowments can ironically become liabilities: Littlewoods Stores in the UK are heavily endowed with large stores in declining city centres.

The ways firms use these endowments are largely a function of their capabilities. These capabilities define the ability of firms to use their endowments. The extent to which this use is unique or specific to the organization converts a capability into a distinctive capability. Intel, as mentioned earlier, is endowed with many valuable patents, but its distinctive capability is its ability to build a commitment to successful innovation on this endowment. A competitive advantage is created if it is better than its rivals at using this innovativeness commercially. It is as easy to fritter away an endowment by failing to wed it to the enterprise's capabilities as it is by failing to build on it.

The problems of diversification, especially if companies try to move beyond their capabilities, prompt many to renew their focus on their distinctive or core capabilities. When asked which activities put their endowments to the best use many companies replied the activities that created those endowments in the first place.

Michael Porter was to the fore in advising companies to look at relationships with their markets. Close examination of the links in the chain of relationship highlights aspects in which the firm has distinct or differential advantages when it comes to creating customer value. Concentrate resources here and results will improve. This type of reductionist approach works well when market conditions are generally stable or contracting, although any edge or leadership position as Peter Drucker points out "is likely to be short lived."

Close examination of the links in the chain of relationship highlights aspects in which the firm has distinct or differential advantages when it comes to creating customer value.

Capability building for the for future and future competitive advantage is as important as capability maintenance for the present.

Figure 9.1

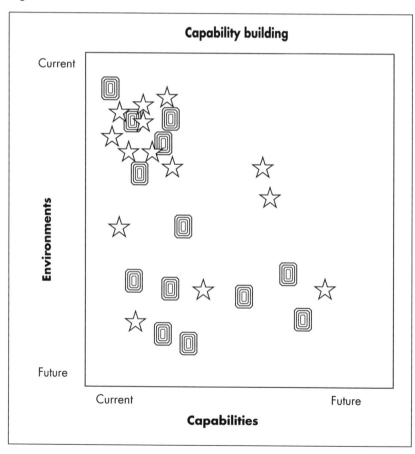

Building capability for the future while sustaining present capabilities within existing or fewer resources poses problems for managers that compare with those of providing better products and services at lower prices and requires a novel approach to focus which builds on two related strands of development. The first is the effective audit of the organization's capabilities; the second is the creation of scenarios that describe possible futures. Current capabilities are mapped against future scenarios and gaps in capabilities or the need to adapt capabilities are identified and ways to overcome these weaknesses explored.

> *Capability building for the for future and future competitive advantage is as important as capability maintenance for the present.*

SHORT-TERM, LONG TERMISM

This process imposes major demands on firms as they juggle current capabilities and possible future capabilities against future scenarios. The answer lies in challenging assumptions about the way capabilities are used and leveraged. Short-term, long termism provides people with the power to act now while continuing to look for ways to adapt current capabilities to new needs while simultaneously building the capabilities that are needed for the future. Numbers can be a great help in both refining existing capabilities and building new capabilities to fit new conditions.

Federal Express has built much of its reputation on the quality of its service. This is only one of its current core capabilities and president, James Barksdale, constantly seeks higher standards.

If we have 98 per cent overnight delivery of eight hundred thousand packages and letters, then sixteen thousand – 2 per cent – of our customers did not receive their packages absolutely, positively

overnight. I'm not inclined to brag too loudly about sixteen thousand packages gone astray.

The problems are worse for frequent users. Assuming that the 2% failure rate is distributed evenly across all users, it will not be long before every frequent user is affected. It is a theme that the head of Britain's post office endorses: John Roberts points out that a 2% failure rate is the equivalent of 2 jumbo jets crashing every day at Heathrow.

Building capabilities for the long term means trying to understand the long term and taking early action to adapt to it. Derek Wanless, Chief Executive of NatWest Bank, talks about how short lead times really are in most markets.

If, for example, Britain decided not to participate in the single European currency, we would need to start repositioning ourselves now. This is needed so that we have the capabilities required to succeed in an environment in which London's role as an international banking centre would be affected profoundly.

This form of capability building requires a greater emphasis on local leadership and the ownership of competences. Both are easier to create in a high trust environment. Motorola gives much of the credit for its transformation over the last few years to the high trust environment created by CEO Bob Galvin, a situation summed up in the following story. One of Motorola's senior managers was working to complete a major job when he was asked by a subordinate if he could leave early as one of his sons had been involved in an accident. The manager said it would be difficult in the circumstances but that he'd check with Bob Galvin. Galvin's immediate reply was "Is it Tom or Ralph who was injured?"

High trust, high involvement environments are high performance environments, part of which involve the creation of local leadership strategies. This process transfers leadership roles to those responsible for operations especially those involving customer support. At Motorola (Europe) the program to make local leadership a key capability was the cutting edge of a wider program of development design to get more for less. It was especially important to symbolize the new approach in the related development initiative. Motorola (Europe) contrasts its approach to traditional capability development programs (see Table 9.1).

Table 9.1

Traditional vs Motorola – Two Capability Development Programs	
Traditional	**Motorola**
Expert led	Self led
Technical jargon based	Own language based
Takes 3–6 months	Takes 1–5 weeks
Significant external costs	Nil external cost
Roll out needs selling	Organization owns it
Based on push from centre	Based on pull from operations

Some firms have changed their language to effect this type of change in ownership and control. Rover Group, the UK based subsidiary of BMW, calls all its people "associates". At Quad/Graphics in Milwaukee all 3500 employees are called partners. At Disney the term used for all those working at the theme parks is "the cast".

Employee involvement and leadership allied to involvement, the desire to maximize their contribution and focus are the three factors that produce more for less. Ron Zemke in *The Service Edge*[10] tells the story of an H.B. Fuller employee who symbolized all three of these features.

A secretary at H.B. Fuller (Louisville, Kentucky) took a 'phone call. from Macon, Georgia, where a valued customer was running out of the glue required for a specialized manufacturing operation. This particular glue wasn't one of the products it bought from H.B Fuller, but since it wasn't working properly anyway, the customer

figured maybe someone in Louisville could help. Without immediate help his whole production line would stop.

The prospects were bleaker than they knew. This particular morning the secretary's boss was out of the country, and the local salesman was on vacation. Time to take a message, right? Instead, the secretary took the initiative. After calling the regional technical centre she found that only suitable stock was in Louisville. She then took her own car, collected the product and drove it to the airport, where there was good news – there was a flight to Macon in 30 minutes – and bad news: her employer did not have an account with this airline. Although the bill was over $300, she paid it herself rather than let the customer down. By early afternoon the product was with the customer and his line was running, uninterrupted, better than ever.

The cash cost of this level of service is virtually nil to the employer who creates as customer oriented, leadership capability. This contrasts with my experience of a certain English soccer club, that several years ago built a new set of ticket offices and installed new ticketing equipment. Any beneficial effect was lost when the ticketing staff put up a large notice behind their desk which read: "What is it about NO that you don't understand."

Too little too late

Firms that attempt to tackle the "more for less" paradox are prone to underestimate the initial effort required to change thinking and may therefore move too late to address the issues. In part this reflects the strange love/hate relationship that managers have with crisis and difficulty. A crisis causes stress and can be extremely harmful. But it does concentrate the minds of all those involved. Those managers who successfully manage a crisis often get more credit than those who tried to avoid the crisis in the first place. Bob Eaton at Chrysler is probably the least well known of the recent CEOs of Chrysler. In part this reflects his deliberate efforts to avoid the crises that marked the careers of his predecessors, even though he also knows that their subsequent recovery won them their place in the business Hall of Fame. Shortly after Eaton took over at Chrysler he assembled all his senior managers together to communicate this message: "Let's stop getting sick. ... My personal ambition is to be the first Chrysler chairman never to lead a Chrysler comeback."

He started by trawling the company for best internal practice. This was compared with best practice elsewhere. The practices that matched or exceeded best practice in other companies became the building blocks for future development in Chrysler. Eventually much of the work at Chrysler became the standard against which manufacturers across the world measured themselves. However, crises can became addictive because managers who solve them become heroes. They may find they want to repeat the experience in the knowledge that if no crisis occurs it is fairly easy to create one.

The link between performance enhancement programs and evolving outside conditions is an important feature of the work of Paul Strebel at IMD, Lausanne. He points out that the strength of the pressure for change and the scale of resistance determine the type of change strategy that is most effective (see Figure 9.2).

The coincidence of powerful external pressures for change with little internal resistance makes rapid adaptation relatively easy but also makes it hard for changes to stick. In contrast, the willingness to change when external pressures are weak provides the opportunity to initiate bottom up experiments in change that once established can survive because of local ownership. High levels of resistance to change when pressures for change are weak call for radical leadership of the kind shown by Paul Allaire at Xerox who decided to transform the Xerox culture after a decade of comfortable decline. Mediocre performance but little external threat created a situation in which Xerox needed to change but felt no sense of immediacy. The

Figure 9.2

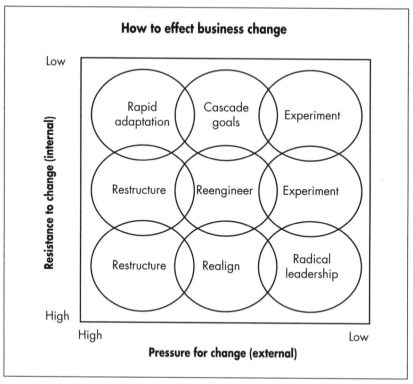

How to effect business change

Source: Strebel, P. (1992) *Breakpoints: how managers exploit radical business change.* Boston, Mass.: Harvard Business School Press.

company still dominated the large photocopier market but had seen markets as diverse as small copiers and graphical user interfaces (GUIs) snatched from them.

Top down experimentation works best when there is little external pressure for change aligned with medium internal resistance. Akio Morito at Sony and Colin Marshall at British Airways are among the business leaders who have become effective at initiating top down experimentation. The combination of medium strength resistance to change and moderate external change creates the best conditions for process reengineering. Strong resistance to change while external pressures are considerable can only be overcome by the kind of downsiz-

194

ing and restructuring that Jan Timmer introduced at Philips. The group's financial crisis forced Timmer to confront his management team with a "change or else" restructuring which took out swathes of the bureaucracy that had prevented the firm exploiting its technological potential.

CHALLENGING PRICE/PERFORMANCE ASSUMPTIONS

Organizational change is an integral feature of the effort to challenge assumptions about how markets operate. Behind these challenges is often a powerful sense of mission and determination to ensure that the organization serves the purpose of the business rather than the other way round. Many enterprises implicitly assume that the market exists to meet their needs. Products or services are produced, policies are adopted or initiatives developed because they meet the organization's goals or are simply "the way we've always done it." Available evidence suggests that firms often introduce new products simply to attempt to match some innovation by a rival. "Me-too" brands, products and services dominate the launch programs of many firms; they also dominate the lists of failures and poor performers consuming resources that could be better employed elsewhere. Marketing programs are not the only aspect of corporate activity where "easy to do, have little value" initiatives dominate. Analysis of the recent initiatives of 20 major corporations found that the vast majority fell into this quadrant of the activity map (see Figure 9.3).

CONCLUSION

Companies that perform well refuse to take the path of least resistance. They realize that it may cost as much to do a poor or inadequate job as a good job. Matsushita refused to compromise

Figure 9.3

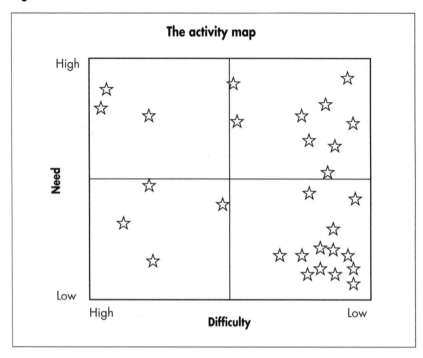

in their efforts to perfect the videotape machine. They ignored the compromise adopted by RCA of building machines that could not record, and moved beyond the short duration tape to the 3 and 4 hour machine. The determination to "get it right" gave them a technological lead which they used together with licensing and pricing policies to build up market dominance.

In 1979 Canon adopted the same approach when it set itself the task of producing a copier for $1000 or less.[11] The clarity of the goal and the refusal to compromise led to a series of innovations in design ranging from the "desktop" styling to the cartridge based toner system. It also meant that Canon still had the option of pricing their products against Xerox and other office copier producers. This might produce larger short-term profits but at the price of minimizing their market power; they rejected that option.

Hamel and Prahalad recommend a "naive" approach to some aspects of price and product development. "Be as little children" is their advice in testing the boundaries of acceptability and moving beyond the conventional. It is, however, clear that the firms that get the most value from this "naïveté" have a deep understanding of their environment, focus their efforts along paths that fit their capabilities and take an integrated, whole person approach to their people. This means that by resolving the paradox of entrepreneurial teams they create organizations capable of producing more for less.

◆

The pattern of international trading
relationships is no longer defined
by the boundaries of the nation
state or the enterprise.

◆

Chapter 10

◆

GLOBAL ACTION

Among the main characteristics of earlier industrial revolutions was a major shift in the nature of international trade. Those countries and companies that spotted and adapted to this shift were the most successful; those that failed to adapt struggled in the new environment. The first industrial revolution was an export revolution. Companies in the UK prospered because they recognized the opportunities that existed to move goods "ex port" from one country to another. British broadcloth was shipped from the UK to North America, across the Empire and to Europe; almost everywhere where demand was sufficient to justify trade. The same pattern was followed in goods as diverse as iron and steam engines. In return, raw materials and commodities were exported from countries abroad to Britain. The scale, reach and continuity of this trade differentiated it from anything that had gone before. This first "global" economy was fatally undermined by the great recession of trade in the 1870s and by the time economies had recovered a new industrial revolution was under way.

The second industrial revolution produced two major shifts in the pattern of international trade. First, the emphasis on exports declined. The most successful companies had set up overseas assembly and even manufacturing operations, and the most powerful corporations were those that had broken free from the confines of individual nation states. In 1885 Standard Oil battled for control over the Russian oil fields with the Nobel family interests. A few years later Standard was involved in merger discussions with Shell. Ford established its first over-seas manufacturing operations in Manchester, England before the outbreak of World War I. General Motors followed shortly after the end of World War I. This was not a one way process. Lever Brothers of Great Britain and Bayer of Germany had already set up manufacturing and distribution operations in North America in the first quarter of this century.

Second, once established these operations were often given considerable freedom and autonomy. Alfred P. Sloan describes the reasoning behind their development in Germany while he was Chief Executive of General Motors at the start of the century.

I viewed the case there something like this. If the idea was to make a very small car, much smaller than the Chevrolet, assuming that was an economic thing to do, then we might be better off dealing directly with Opel. I felt that we would get off to a better start that way than we would by trying to compete on our own in a country with which we were largely unfamiliar.

These overseas operations grew in importance but they remained largely offshoots of the parent business., since most were largely ethnocentric. The home market could easily be identified, most of the top corporate managers came from the home market and its values permeated its operations. A recent study of corporate, charitable giving shows how strong this home market focus remains. Major corporations like Exxon, Coke, Eli Lilley, for example, can be shown to gain higher prof-its and to have a larger turnover outside the USA although the vast bulk of charitable donations is firmly based in the USA.

The scale of international activity grew and the pattern shifted from the narrow focus of the first industrial revolution to a much broader one. This was the era of the international firm or the national company operating in some or many other markets. Some commentators have argued that the global economy of the second industrial revolution reached its peak before the great slump of the 1930s. The post war international business order has never matched that era for such freed movement of trade and low barriers to market entry.

The latest industrial revolution is seeing comparable changes. Growth in the scale and scope of operations is only part of the picture. Perhaps the most important change has been that the ethnocentricity that used to be so prevalent has been shattered by the success of firms with diverse backgrounds. The language used by Robert Cawthorne, the Chief Executive of France's successful Rhone-Poulenc Rorer pharmaceutical corporation, about his attitude to change could be used as easily in North America as in Asia. Cawthorne says "I love change. I hate status quo. It is very hard to win in a status quo environment. In a time of change, you get winners and losers – so at least you have a chance to win." Bill Gates of Microsoft talks constantly of "the power of change to create change" and how these changes "create opportunities." Similar themes are adopted by Sir Denys Henderson of ICI, Lee Byung Chul of Samsung and Ratan Tata of India's Tata Group.

WHO IS US?

Of equal importance is that the values, cultures and operations of some of the most successful organizations challenge traditional approaches. The dominant business paradigm is no longer homogeneous but heterogeneous. The pattern of international trading relationships is no longer defined by the boundaries of the nation state or the enterprise. Kenichi Ohmae argues that the changes go to the root of what makes up an organization and its markets:

In a borderless world, however, it is increasingly difficult to manage functional activities across so wide a spectrum of operating environments from a single central point. Moreover, advances in digital networks and information technology allow these activities to be disaggregated on a global basis and outsourced, creating, in effect,

a virtual functional network spanning the globe. Seen in this light, companies are no longer stand alone institutions but, rather oddly and often asymmetrically, parts of transnational webs of functional activity. And in a world defined by such webs, traditional notions of centralized control rapidly lose their meaning.[12]

Robert Reich took this theme further in two articles in the *Harvard Business Review* in which he challenged traditional assumptions about the nature and form of international competition by asking "Who is us?"[13] And "Who is them?"[14] He concluded that the logic of the national interest and the logic of the national business interest had diverged in recent years. Companies were adopting a new global logic to advance their commercial interests and it was a logic that did not necessarily fit with any local logic.

Think local, act global

This approach can be summarized in the paradox that underlies the popular comment "think local, act global" and its corollary "think global, act local." Central to the notion of thinking local and acting global is the paradox that awareness and interest in diversity provide the dynamic for much global business development. Successful global businesses like Unilever, General Foods, Procter & Gamble, Honda, BASF and News Corporation International build their global business up from their knowledge of local markets. They have detailed local market knowledge but incorporate this into a worldwide pattern of development. Most are able to go beyond the confines of the nation state. News Corporation's success with the *Sun* newspaper in the Irish Republic is driven by the skill with which they distinguish it from the British version of the *Sun*.

Procter & Gamble has learned to distinguish between hard and soft water areas within countries when framing its distribution policies. Their global success is driven by their ability to "think local" and to use this local attention to detail as a driver of their global strategies. Those firms that try to "buck the market" and ignore this heterogeneity soon hit problems. The public face of this "think local and act global" principle lies in the marketing and product development policies adopted by firms, similarly the most public failures and errors from ignoring this principle lie in marketing. When firms fail to think local they are saying that if the choice is between changing themselves or trying to change the tastes, culture, values or behavior of customers, they prefer to change the latter.

Thinking local extends beyond the marketplace. It calls for a recognition that workplace behavior and cultures vary between operations: just because the same equipment and even procedures are *used*, it does not mean that the same methods and approaches will *work*. Terms and ideas which work in one environment to motivate and control people will not work elsewhere. There is a tendency today to be blinded by our limited understanding of words. US and European companies adopt from Japanese business culture terms like *kaizen* (the search for continuous improvement through adding value), *shibui* (working in tune with nature or natural feelings), *amae* (the concept that underpins the "trust based" relationship) in the belief that they can be usefully extracted from their wider cultural and behavioral context. The danger of simply extracting terms and their approximate meanings was vividly illustrated in the years after World War II when companies in the UK adopted the US business language with few of the underlying processes. It proved in business the truth of Mark Twain's comment that "The British and the Americans are two nations separated forever by a common language."

THE FISH EYED CORPORATION

Sensitivity to local conditions, culture, social conditions and norms, calls for the creation of a new kind of corporate consciousness. This consciousness is open minded and capable of integrating different kinds of thinking into its ways of operating. This awareness operates in many ways and along a number of different levels. There is, for example, a need to extend the peripheral vision of the corporation. Focus remains important but its nature has moved from the narrow, sharp focus of traditional businesses to the kind of focus achieved by the best fish eyed lens on a

> *Sensitivity to local conditions, culture, social conditions and norms, calls for the creation of a new kind of corporate consciousness.*

modern camera. This builds awareness of the differences which surround the activities lying at the centre of our attention. It means, for example, the reward systems that work well in Germany will not be as effective in the Czech Republic.

Francis Fukuyama challenges Western assumptions about the homogeneity of Asian business thought and practice.[15] He points out, for example, how Japan's success at building large corporations contrasts sharply with the much smaller scale of private Chinese corporations. Similarly in Korea and Japan structures that look and sound the same operate differently. Korean *chaebol*, the networks of enterprises that link individual businesses, were deliberately based on the Japanese *zaibatsu* or *keiretsu* (or the later *shogu shosa*). The Chinese characters for *chaebol* and *zaibatsu* are the same, yet their operations are very different. In Korea the *chaebol* account for a much larger share of gross national product while the role of the family is much stronger in the firms that make up the *chaebol* and the associated networks.

Breadth of vision in global markets is not merely about seeing diversity and variation, it is about codifying those variations in ways that make sense to the corporation. Sometimes the outcomes are consistent across markets. Benetton have identified a customer niche which exists in different forms in many countries. This niche admires the mix of total look, color coordination and radicalism that is delivered through a world-wide franchise operation. The franchise approach is especially effective at wedding the think local, act global approach to market development. Benetton, Body Shop and McDonald's use the franchise formula to create opportunities for locals to provide the detailed local view that allows the parent corporation to act global.

The fish eyed lens works best in this global environment if linked with acute sensors at the point of customer or operator contact. The dual focus eye of the vulture provides a useful analogy. The outer lens of the vulture's eye has wide peripheral vision. It avoids the confusion that can result from taking too many images into account by learning to recognize certain signals. In the vulture's case any signals that

> *Inability to learn and accommodate different mindsets is the biggest barrier to success in global markets.*

suggest all is well and healthy in creatures that come into view are ignored. Distress signals produce a different effect. The vulture uses an inner, sharper focus eye to examine the nature of the opportunity created.

Successful global companies operate in the same way. They scan the environment constantly. They have learned to recognize signals that indicate opportunities. They then turn the recognition of an opportunity into action.

Part of their success lies in learning to learn from others. Inability to learn and accommodate different mindsets is the biggest barrier to success in global markets. Ethnocentricity is no longer a sustainable position in global markets. Christopher Bartlett calls the new approach a new mind matrix: "[the ability] to view problems from both global and local perspectives, and that accepts the importance of the flexible approach."

NEW RULES

The think local and act global paradox is tackled by recognizing and adopting a new set of rules of global business practice. The most basic rule is that the global marketplace is your nearest high street. The closer the firm is to understanding the factors that make this a global marketplace the closer it is to understanding its position in other global markets. Managers can ask what imperatives prompted Benetton from Italy, McDonald's from the USA, Hyundai from Korea or Toyota from Japan to adopt their approaches to success in this local environment. In part their successes reflect their commitment to breaking out of the constraints that a specific market or set of business relations impose. Many of these firms were rule breakers before they became rule makers. The challenge is to understand the explicit or implicit rules that inhibit or create opportunities.

The value of the alternative view of the paradox think local and act global, that is think global and act local, lies in confounding ways of thinking that limit organizations to their current environment. These are not constraints that customers are willing to accept any more. Industrial buyers seek the best sources of supply regardless of location. My own work in business education demonstrates that users choose the best provider regardless of location.

The challenge is to understand the explicit or implicit rules that inhibit or create opportunities.

Buyers of senior management training from Coats Vyella, British Aerospace and the UK's National Health Service agree that the opportunity cost of the manager's time far outweighs the cash cost of the program.

The ability to compete in the global marketplace is part of the core capability of those companies seeking long-term success within the new economic paradigm. It is not, however, an ability confined to firms from any specific region of the world. The first rule of the new mindset is an acceptance of the fact that best practice is found where it exists and not where it should exist. The second rule of the new global competitor is that the toughest challenge lies in building a global dimension to all existing capabilities. Those that can add this dimension, transform their local capabilities to a global competitive edge. Benchmarking plays an important part in this. Most benchmarking approaches focus attention on the best local

The struggle to create a world class organization starts with the determined effort to understand international rivals in order to benchmark performance against them.

standard. The struggle to create a world class organization starts with the determined effort to understand international rivals in order to benchmark performance against them.

The third rule in learning to act global is that the biggest barriers exist within the company. It is easy to slip into convenient stereotypes about rivals, build psychological barriers between management and their people or customers and try to adopt a separated approach to globalization. A global company integrates this frame of mind across the activities of the firm, even into those that seem to be domestic or isolated. This integration provides the key to resolving the paradox.

New rivals

New rivals and rivalries push the ability to adopt this perspective further up the corporate agenda. Institutional barriers to market entry were eroded by the progress made at GATT. Equally important, technological, management and financial barriers to entry have declined while the priority given to internationalization has increased. The success of East Asia has highlighted the opportunities which international success offers to other Pacific Rim countries as well as to China and India.

Properly and sympathetically developed Hong Kong will provide China with an invaluable platform for the move of
Chinese products and services into global markets. The rapid
recent growth of the Indian economy has prompted successful
Indian manufacturers like the Tata Group and service companies like the Taj and Oberoi Groups to strengthen their
international position.

The opening up of these markets as well as those in East
Europe has direct parallels with the opening up of markets that
occurred during the first and second industrial revolutions. The
first industrial revolution saw UK, then European companies
establish trading centers on the periphery of new markets
notably in North America and the empires of the European
countries. The second industrial revolution saw the most
"open" of these markets, the USA, Germany and later Japan,
build up their home markets, open up other advanced markets
and develop new markets. The third industrial revolution sees
the new markets building up their home markets while seeking
their place in the global marketplace.

Established companies and economies face the twin threat of
new rivals from new markets and new entrepreneurial rivals
from within their own markets. The new rivals from new markets provide an opportunity as well as a threat: the opportunity
they offer is access to their large and growing domestic market;
the threat is rivalry in home markets. This mixture has
prompted many organizations to find a new solution in redefining the nature of their enterprise. Many are breaking out of the
traditional boundaries of the organization to build strategic
partnerships or alliances wedding their capabilities and reach
to that of their partners.

Blind alleys

Despite the interest in alliances and partnerships, the track
record of partnership based development is mixed. The alliance

between Microsoft and IBM linked Microsoft's software development and marketing capabilities to IBM's institutional strength. Eventually it became a blind alley for IBM which shut more doors than it opened. Some people attribute this to the distinctive approach of Microsoft. Ruthann Quinlan, who was involved in Microsoft's public relations, claimed that "with every negotiation Gates and Microsoft have an 'I win' mentality. I win and you lose is not a platform on which to build sustainable strategic alliances."

Strategic alliances that succeed are partnerships founded on an "I win, you win" approach. The classic case of this occurred in the microprocessor industry in the 1980s. Fierce competition between Intel, National Semiconductor, Motorola, NEC and other microprocessor producers was forcing prices down to the point at which technical and market development was suffering. Faced with a lose–lose scenario, the leading producer and user companies created a series of strategic partnerships such as those between Intel and IBM, and Motorola and Apple. Those firms that created and maintained their alliances prospered while those that failed to create or maintain these partnerships struggled to survive.

In some markets strategic partnership are more the norm than the isolated corporation. Pre war Japanese *zaibatsu* used alliances and networks to paper over gaps in the skill and knowledge base of member companies. Post war Japanese *shogu shosa* show some similarities although there is often a dominant member who controls access to the market. The

> *Strategic alliances that succeed are partnerships founded on an "I win, you win" approach.*

three largest Korean enterprises, Samsung, Hyundai and Lucky-Goldstar, are *chaebol*. These are, typically, networks of autonomous enterprises that are held together by trading, production, logistics and shared ownership. Other successful Asian economies such as Malaya have adopted variations of this model, at least in certain industry sectors.

The creation of strategic alliances or partnerships is sometimes a useful "quick fix" when firms facing complementary problems come together. The Honda–Rover partnership during the late 1980s won Rover access to new technology, superior quality production and new finance. Honda won early access to European markets and novel design thinking. It was a bridge across which both companies could move forward. The collapse of the alliance when Rover was acquired by BMW merely highlighted the progress both firms had made during the partnership.

The next stage in strategic alliance building or partnering lies in the closer integration of operations through integrated process reengineering. This takes the principles of process re-engineering and works it through from one partner to another, thereby creating further opportunities to merge several jobs into one. Marks and Spencer in the UK have built much of their recent business success through alliances with suppliers and logistics companies. The integration of their design, development and information systems is creating new opportunities for improved effectiveness and enhanced customer service. Partnerships create major opportunities to develop business processes around natural orders of behavior or action. Organizational or institutional structures provide more barriers to this type of ordering than internal structures. In the UK, the National Health Service, is allocating resources in partnership with its supplier and user groups along this type of natural process.

Successful partnerships have taken this focus on the "natural order" to concentrate work "where it makes most sense." The European Airbus project showed some of the worst and some

of the best features of strategic partnerships. The political economy of the partnership with its powerful, national interest
inhibited the use of natural ordering and total process engineering. There were, however, some outstanding examples of
completing work "where it makes most sense," particularly in
areas like the design of control systems and aspects of the air-
frame production. The integration of business process
reengineering and strategic alliances will become a crucial
source of competitive advantage over the next decade.

The mosquito

Sometimes it seems that the notion of thinking local and acting
global is relevant only to large firms. It is, perhaps, another feature of the giantism that characterized the last few decades of
the last industrial revolution. Yet the paradox creates special
opportunities for smaller companies whose greater integration
gives them a head start in linking the two concepts. Entrepreneurial concerns that break free of the inhibitions that size
sometimes imposes can think local and act global more easily
than their larger rivals. Anita Roddick uses the analogy of the
mosquito to challenge those who think small firms cannot compete in today's markets. She says: if you think being small
means you cannot get noticed, think about a mosquito in a tent.

Mosquito management uses freedom and flexibility to break
out of the limitations of size. It challenges established expectations to create a new environment. Expectations analysis is
useful in tackling old assumptions, where we test the expectations we believe others have against the expectations they truly
hold. I got my first real taste of the value of expectations analysis when I used it in an undergraduate class. I wanted to test the
expectations of the students taking the class with the expectations of faculty.

Students were asked what they thought was expected of them
and what they expected of faculty. Faculty were asked the same

211

basic questions. There were striking differences between the two sets of answers. Students thought that they were expected to be interested in the subject, creative, participative. Faculty, on the other hand, expected students to be punctual, attentive, disciplined. Use of expectation analysis in public and private enterprises has found the same differences in approach. Those in positions of authority set control expectations while their subordinates believe they should be creative partners in development. Effective management requires an understanding of these different expectations and some attempt to integrate them.

The new pattern of global trade is hard to bound within either the structures of the nation state or those of the private or public organization. The mixture of push from technology and pull from markets is proving fatal to older "bounded" structures. Firms that try to confine themselves to the limits of a specific nation state struggle to compete with those that cross borders to create, develop and build markets. This is not solely the case in sectors like pharmaceuticals that have long needed larger international or global markets to win sufficient returns from their investments in R&D. The same pattern is seen across broad swathes of manufacturing, services and retailing. Some public services are feeling the same pressures. The speed with which newly privatized utilities in the UK have adopted a global perspective suggests that there is pent up demand for this type of structure. Partnerships and alliances are emerging in areas as diverse as health care and fisheries protection.

> *The new pattern of global trade is hard to bound within either the structures of the nation state or those of the private or public organization. The mixture of push from technology and pull from markets is proving fatal to older "bounded" structures.*

WHOSE FISH ARE THEY, ANYWAY?

This shift towards global or international collaboration contains within it another paradox, since the move coincides with increasing economic or local economic nationalism. The paradox of simultaneous demands for economic regionalism and economic nationalism is easy to dismiss as a clash of interests between the demands of "big business" for big markets and isolationists for protection. Across the world, the macroeconomic pressures are prompting the creation of cross border collaboration. The European (Economic) Union (EU) and the North American Free Trade Area (NAFTA) are merely the best publicized of the regional groupings that cover virtually the entire globe.

The macroeconomic arguments are well rehearsed. These regional blocks cut costs by eliminating the waste involved in cross border transactions, different regulations and duplication. At the same time, they create opportunities for greater investment in research and development as investments are pooled and returns earned over a larger market base. In some parts of the world there is a hope that economic integration reduces the risks of conflict between nations. An inherent feature of the EU and some other economic unions is the assumption that "levelling up" will occur. This means that the business, workplace and financial standards of the most advanced nations will be matched by others. Levelling up is part of the implicit contract which underpins the formation of economic unions. The more prosperous countries are, in effect, saying: "We will help you to catch up – if you do not use your membership of the club to compete unfairly."

This implicit contract lies at the root of the tensions which characterize the economic nationalism or localism that has emerged alongside the move towards regional aggregations. Within the more prosperous countries there is the inevitable fear that their part of the contract is easier to enforce with more tangible sanctions than the poorer countries' part. The latter face a similar concern: that progress is not fast enough to satisfy the economic aspirations of their citizens. Beneath both of these spoken concerns are other issues. The heterogeneity of most nation state economies is a constant source of worry.

The richest economies contain sections of the population suffering from serious economic difficulties. This is as true in Germany as in the USA, and the phenomenon makes it harder to accept the diversion of "national" resources to support countries that contain sections that are richer than the poorer part of the home economy. These concerns grow almost in proportion to the success of the "catching up" process. They are sharpened every time a member of the economic group highlights their achievements in, say, inward investment. Similar problems occur because of the uneven distribution of natural resources. The intense debate within Europe on "the UK's oil" has parallels in NAFTA and elsewhere.

The greater the success of the regional grouping, the greater the pressure to expand its coverage and challenge the nation state itself. The demands for wider coverage grow out of the ways economic and business activity permeate other aspects of life. The relationship between, say, education, training and development and economic performance is reasonably well documented. An economic grouping which had wide variation in standards and performance in the former is not likely to produce convergence in the latter. This creates pressures on any regional agency with responsibility for convergence to devise policies which provide some form(s) of transnational framework for education, training and development. The expansion of this remit is as significant a threat to national identity as are moves towards currency convergence.

The internal diversity within nation states creates a parallel set of challenges from economic regionalism. Groups that have subordinated their interests to the national interest have less need to sustain this position within a larger grouping. Those

214

seeking devolution for Scotland, for example, argue that the "subordination" of Edinburgh to London has no validity when London is "subordinated" to Brussels. National interests are not the only groups that challenge this dominance. The existence of trade or economic courts and appeals systems often leads to erosion of the independence of the national legal system as appeals move to higher, nonnational courts in trade disputes, workers' rights, stewardship, contracts and other issues.

WELCOME TO MY WEB

The principle of subsidiarity has evolved to address some of the concerns about the "top down" erosion of national interests by regional interests. Although it goes some way towards resolving the problem, difficulties occur especially in highly centralized nation states such as Great Britain. The logic of subsidiarity might mean national governments conceding some of their authority to local assemblies. Many have shown themselves reluctant to go that far. The principle of subsidiarity, however, provides some cues as the optimal approach for managers and corporations striving to resolve the paradox of the coincidence of economic nationalism and economic regionalism.

Organizational structures are capable of being operationally disaggregated while being held together more strongly by improved planning, information and control systems. A specific activity can be transferred to local control or outsourced with little loss in control or the ability to manage inputs, processes or outputs. This allows the firm to acknowledge the diversity in production, logistic or marketing conditions while sustaining a cohesive business structure. The notion of the web based business is highly relevant to this approach. It changes the notion of the web from something that traps its prey to a network that survives because those at the centre are highly sensitive to actions across the web.

The most important area of corporate sensitivity in resolving the national/regional paradox is cultural sensitivity. Anglo-Saxon approaches to management generally assume both the universality of business techniques and their separateness. The principle of universality gets its greatest endorsement from developments like scientific management, operations research and mass production. The notion of separateness is symbolized by the efforts to separate business and economic life from other aspects of society. The business schools in North America reinforce this attitude by their separation from other aspects of university life, notably engineering. In the UK the process goes further. Serious commentators argue that business and education do not mix and training, for example, has little place in the university. Both these features are in sharp contrast to the traditions of uniqueness and integration that characterize German, Japanese and Korean approaches.

The same issues of universality and separateness provide cues to the ways managers and organizations can tackle the local/regional paradox. The answer lies in finding ways to provide and use greater local autonomy. The acid test of this local autonomy does not lie inside the firm but in the ways it integrates its work with others, notably its business partners. Tom Peters highlights this when he describes the reluctance of firms to share strategic information with partners. He comments on the

propensity of managers to share strategic information with their customers. Almost one-quarter of respondents (23%) say they never share such information. Only one quarter share often (26%) and just 7% always. The remainder report sharing sometimes.[16]

These figures provide an overall view of the ways respondents across the world view their partnerships. The aggregate figures disguise wide variations in behavior between nations and firms. The most successful firms are those that share and integrate most.

216

This confirms research carried out in Europe on the most
successful innovators in industrial markets which examined
the industrial innovations in the

*The most successful firms
are those that share and
integrate most.*

largest European economies (see Figure 10.1). It plotted firms
along the two axes of timing of involvement and intensity of
innovation. Intense innovation was measured in terms of the
number of people and functions involved in customer collaboration. Where the link was confined to sales and purchasing
intensity was low. When the links extended to design, engineering, production, marketing and finance intensity was high.

Successes were concentrated in the early and extensive
quadrant. These results highlight the ways in which barriers
are breaking down between corporations in the new global
environment.

Figure 10.1

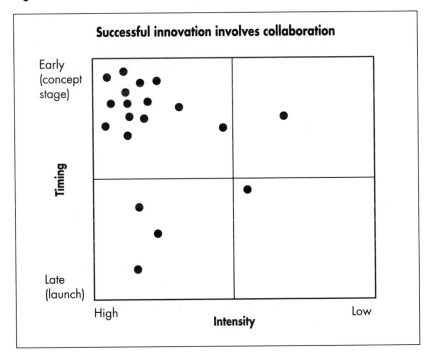

217

The pressure for outsourcing further erodes the lines between organizations, their managers and their partners, since it comes from a mixture of the desire of organizations to concentrate their work on the activities they know and a realization of the scope for minimizing their overheads by pushing activities outside. The sharp contrasts between the scale of US and Japanese firms reinforces the image that the latter obtain much of their flexibility from concentrating their efforts on areas of genuine competitive advantage. In 1995, for example, Mitsubishi overtook General Motors as the largest automobile firm in the world in terms of sales turnover. It achieved this with a labor force of some 65,000 in contrast to General Motors' 650,000 plus. Outsourcing works best when the lines of communication between suppliers and users are short. This suggests that the best outsourcing decisions are made close to the point of production, purchase or use. And yet the dominant trend in outsourcing decision making is from the centre. This in turn produces major diseconomies especially in international trading partnerships where lack of ownership produces lack of involvement and poor or late communication.

Partnerships based on local ownership or subsidiarity are more capable of delivering the hidden benefits of alliances and partnerships identified by writers like Francis Bidault and Thomas Cummings. These benefits can extend the gains beyond the formal "goals" to improved performance across both enterprises. When Bekaert of Belgium and Bridgestone of Japan set up their joint venture the goals were specific: for Bekaert, it meant a local partner to support its entry to the Japanese market, Bridgestone wanted access to technology. The creation of an early and extensive program of collaboration produced a range of unexpected benefits that led to dramatic improvements in productivity. Aprillia, the Italian motorcycle producers and BMW produced the same synergy when they created a strategic partnership in motorcycle frame design and development. One of the best documented examples of early and extensive alliances exceeding expectation occurred with the development of the Renault Espace following the formation of a partnership between Matra Automobile and Renault.

CONCLUSION

The pattern of development that seems to work best highlights the value of adopting an intercompany, reengineering approach which is grounded on local ownership and control. This ensures that joint operations are fully integrated to ensure reengineering around the "natural order" of operations. Barriers between business and activities inhibit the potential gains, and some of the greatest barriers reflect the peripheralization of alliances. Unless, therefore, the best people see that working on alliances matters in their career development, this integration work will remain at the periphery of the business. Effective alliances improve the peripheral vision of the business. Improved peripheral vision together with an emphasis on subsidiarity means that firms can resolve the paradox of local, economic nationalism and regionalism. They can then develop a climate in which a business mindset exists which can think local while acting global.

◆

Companies cannot and probably
should not try to separate
themselves from their past.

◆

Chapter 11

◆

ADVENTURES IN WONDERLAND

The corporate motto of Nike, "There Is No Finish Line," illustrates the challenge facing business as it moves towards the end of this century. Organizations build assets and acquire liabilities but they have to move forward or lose ground as others sustain their advances. Eleanor Roosevelt once said: "The day you cease to contribute is the day you start to die." That is as true for organizations as it is for individuals. When they cease to contribute to meet market needs, to realizing the potential of their people and to giving a return to shareholders and other stakeholders, they start to die. The organizational challenge goes still further as this contribution is being made in a competitive environment in which others are refining and developing their skills, are meeting needs, are realizing potential and are giving a return.

The choice of the way forward is partly a reflection of the capabilities of the enterprise and partly a reflection of the new environment it faces. Companies cannot and probably should not try to separate themselves from their past. The answer the Cheshire Cat gives Alice in her *Adventures in Wonderland* is as common in business as it is useless:

> "Would you tell me, please, which way I ought to walk from here?"
>
> "That depends a good deal on where you want to get to," said the Cat.
>
> "I don't much care where," said Alice.

"Then it doesn't matter which way you walk," said the Cat.

"So long as I get *somewhere*," Alice added as an explanation.

In tackling questions about the choice of direction, organizations depend not only on their sense of direction but on their capability to get to where their strategy takes them. Managers often face the problem identified by the countryman's answer when the visitors asked him the way to their destination. He replied that he "would not have started from here."

Questions of starting and end points grow more complex during times of rapid change. Business history shows the dangers of carrying forward old assumptions into new environments. The fate of the pre-first industrial revolution munitions industry highlights both the risks of and the opportunities for change. The revolutionary wars at the end of the 18th and start of the 19th century had created a massive munitions industry in Europe. The American War of Independence, the French Revolution and the Napoleonic Wars meant that some of the largest private and public organizations of the time were the cannon makers and armourers. These were people with vast amounts of skill. They were well networked with their likely customers especially at the senior levels in the military. Complex sets of relationships, even staff exchanges, produced enterprises that were well integrated with their customer groups. Their importance and scale grew through the colonial wars and up to the American Civil War. After this, within 30 years, the entire industry was overwhelmed by new technologies. No European cannon maker of the 18th century adapted to the new conditions. Those that survived did so as foundries or in other sectors. The technological revolution of rifled guns and artillery passed them by because they failed to successfully address two paradoxes: wedding action with reflection and, concentrating on core capabilities while reengineering.

THE DYNAMIC LAST

The action/reflection paradox poses some of the most complex and practical challenges to managers. Management books from Peters and Waterman's *In Search of Excellence*[17] to Treacy and Wiersema's *The Discipline of Market Leaders*[18] and business leaders as diverse as Murofushi Minoru of Itochu Corporation, Ho Kwon Ping of Singapore Power, John Crawford of Intel and Peter Bonser of BT all highlight the importance of an action orientation. Their motto could be: "Don't think it, do it!" In many organizations this approach pays massive dividends as customer frustrations are relieved, work forces are energized and returns improved. One of the most widely expressed gains from delayering organizations is the reduction in the lead time between request and action. The client does not need to fight through layers of bureaucracy to get a need met. Management priorities do not need to fight their way through bureaucracy to be implemented.

The action orientation focusses attention on the deliverables and outputs of a business rather than on the philosophies and processes of the business, and is, in part, a reaction against the paralysis through analysis that seemed to bedevil many large organizations in the 1970s and early 1980s. There was a great deal of organizational satisfaction from in-depth analysis of financial ratios, performance ratios, regressions and correlations.

> *One of the most widely expressed gains from delayering organizations is the reduction in the lead time between request and action.*

The difficulty arose when trying to translate this work into successful policies. There is the story of a Cambridge mathematician who, when asked why he chose to study mathematics, answered: "because there is safety in numbers." W. Edwards Deming, the quality pioneer who helped transform Japanese industry after World War II, has this to say:

223

Management in America (not all) have moved into what I call retroactive management; focus on the end-product – look at the reports on sales, inventory, quality in and quality out, the annual appraisal of people; start the statistical control of quality and QC-circles for operations, unfortunately, detached from management's responsibility; apply management by the numbers, management by objectives, work standards.

The follies of the systems of management that thrived in the expanding market that followed the War are now all too obvious. They must be blasted out, new construction commenced. Patchwork will not suffice.

Rejection of retroactive management in favor of integration and action is part of the blasting out apparatus. The focus on action sits well with a culture that encourages experimentation and risk. Organizations that build a climate in which managers work out their solutions "on the job" soon become organizations that accept risk and the related successes and failures. This climate offers both satisfaction and, for managers, the chance to satisfy their need for results and feedback. The greater the turbulence in the environment the greater the rewards for those who are first to market or first to respond. Murofushi Minoru of Itochu highlights the challenge and the pace of development. He comments that "[Itochu] constantly strives to achieve more growth by developing new businesses in fields and regions with strong potential. The company is assigning greater priority to investment of management resource in high growth sectors in general and Asia in particular."

The focus on action sits well with a culture that encourages experimentation and risk.

The propensity to act is right for the times, the manager and the company and acquires its greatest value when linked with an understanding of the firm's capability. Actions that are firmly rooted in the organization's capabilities and competitive advantage will produce more consistently positive results than those which are not. John Crawford of Intel comments that that company's constant push to innovate is a result of "a combination of technical curiosity on our part, encouragement by upper management and forces of the marketplace."[19] Each of these capabilities could produce either long, slow and unproductive responses or tangible and beneficial action. Companies like Acer of Taiwan, Daiei of Japan, Ford and Shell, all of which have either achieved growth or succeeded in a turnround, can be seen to have adopted some version of the Shewhart Circle (see Figure 11.1) which consists of four steps:

- Plan.
- Do.
- Check.
- Act.

The process is perhaps more accurately described as a spiral because effective action leads to new plans – further tests or experiments – more checks and further action.

Figure 11.1

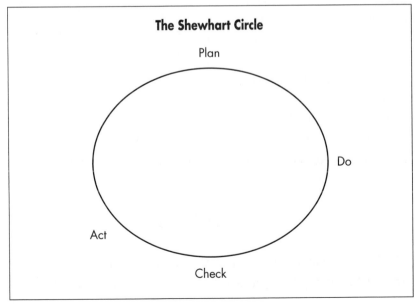

225

Despite the importance of action it is obvious that not all action is useful. Writers like Deming and leaders like Akio Morito are especially critical of the firefighting mentality of Anglo-Saxon business leaders. Firefighting might solve a problem but it does not move the company forward. Even when fires are fought, the emphasis lies in learning from the problem and using the lessons to move the firm forward. Jurgen Schrempp of Daimler-Benz is adopting this approach in his efforts to move the German giant out of its current torpor. He uses simple questions, gaps in awareness, attention to detail and close contacts throughout the company to provoke a transformation in action. Schrempp places special emphasis on getting rid of grand ambitions and turning strategies and policies into terms everyone in the corporation can understand.

It is early days in the Schrempp revolution but in trying to follow the path set by leaders like Jack Welch at General Electric he has adopted Welch's emphasis on the use of the firm's core capabilities to focus attention on the areas that require action. The diversification programs developed by his predecessor were sharply reversed, loss makers like Fokker are being closed and divisions like AEG, DASA and MTU are under close scrutiny.

> *The focus on action and current capabilities has a great deal of appeal to managers who are "up to their neck in crocodiles."*

He has gone as far as Jack Welch in saying that the firm will only stay in markets where it is first or second. The implications of this are clear: activities that fit with Daimler-Benz's core business interest and build on its distinctive capabilities are the priority.

FUTURE FIT

The focus on action and current capabilities has a great deal of appeal to managers who are "up to their neck in crocodiles."

There is, however, growing evidence that the greatest success stories of Asian business emerge more from their sense of vision than their speed of movement. The survey of business leaders that supported the *Management Development to the Millennium* report found that strategic thinking is the priority management skill for the year 2001. The leadership group believed that the ability to rise above the detail was "the extra dimension organisations needed to succeed." Brainpower not manpower provides the competitive edge in a growing number of industries. The kind of brainpower that makes a difference in business has five dominant features:

- an intellectual hardness or the faculty to sustain a position in the face of persistent argument;
- whole system thinking to integrate different facets of an issue into a coherent unity;
- a vision of the future and of the pressures that will create, challenge or undermine that future;
- a sense of exploration to closely identify and examine issues, ideas or trends and to test them out; and
- an ability to interest and involve others in the process.

The paradox lies in the twin demands for managers to be both action oriented and reflective.

The pressure for more reflection is driven by parallel demands on those that encourage a willingness to act. The most immediate pressure lies in the complex nature of the analysis that underpins attempts to understand the capabilities and competences of organizations. Traditional analysis emphasizes the physical and tangible assets of the enterprise – its capital base, plant, equipment or personnel. These assets can be measured and deployed and are, therefore, easier to grasp. When we move beyond the tangible or physical a different level of analysis is required. Prahalad and Hamel's analysis of the core competences of Canon[20] highlight the quality of thought that is needed to understand the nature of these core competences and the way in which they operate to give Canon a competitive edge.

The core competences of Canon are not the tangible items on the balance sheet or their successes in the product fields of photography, copiers or printers. These product successes grow from the core competences Canon have created in precision mechanics, fine optics and microelectronics. These technical competences are deployed separately or together to move into or to create new opportunities. Technical competences are *enabling* competences that provide routes for Canon to move out of their traditional areas of business into new areas. They can then employ their *engaging* competences to open up the market by integrating technologies and simplifying products, and then use their *exploiting* competences to expand the market. Canon is not the only firm that has formally or informally engaged in this type of review of capabilities and identification of the best way to mobilize their core competences to gain a competitive advantage. The same article by Prahalad and Hamel describes how NEC went through a similar process to arrive at its view that it was "a portfolio of competences [not] a portfolio of businesses."

John Kay's analysis of competitive competences[21] reaffirms the importance of moving beyond the obvious to an understanding of the nature of competences and the ways in which they work. He shows how the UK retailer – Marks and Spencer – successfully moved into financial services. Marks and Spencer realized that their core competence did not lie in the ability to retail clothes or in the number of stores they operated nationwide, but in the trust and confidence of their customers: the *exploiting* competence. The *engaging* competence was their ability to bring together a mix of financial offerings that fitted the needs of their customers in ways that were seen as good value. The *enabling* competence was the mix of search, selection and support systems that were developed in clothing, foods and other aspects of their business that were now deployed in financial services.

Success is determined not only by the ability of organizations to manage the current complexities and intangibles. The nature and pattern of change means that the priority for most organizations is to position themselves to prosper in a future environment they will struggle to understand and predict. The fact that the future will be different poses a fundamental challenge to organizations positioning themselves to keep head of their rivals or trying merely to survive, for the rules of engagement will change as surely as the environment.

There is a sense in which the same message is reaching the boardrooms of US and UK corporations. Future competition will call for different skills and competences. These skills cannot be created overnight nor can firms build up the enabling, engaging or exploiting competences quickly or easily. Some of the most successful organizations in Asia, Europe and North America have learned to think and plan years ahead. They do not assume that they will build up an exact picture of the future but the planning process forces them to explore the fit between their current capabilities and those they expect to need in the future. Derek Wanless of NatWest Bank identified the most striking feature of the bank's long-term future as its tendency to overestimate how long it would take for developments to occur.

Lord Laing of United Biscuits highlights the value of long-term thinking when he points out that "it takes about seven years to build a viable business in today's competitive environment." This 7 year time horizon extends even further in both directions if companies include development time and opportunity to earn returns. The typical development time for a new business in a sector like food is between 2 and 4 years which extends Lord Laing's time horizon to 9 years at least. Few businesses pay off their early investment immediately. In foods the pay off period is unlikely to be less than 3 years. A venture that did not survive for that time is probably not worth the initial investment. I have often used these arguments for long-term thinking in workshops and meetings with management groups in the UK and USA. Most react by saying: "If we could think three, five, seven or ten days in advance we'd be content!"

These managers feel overwhelmed by the diversity and turbulence of the environment they face. It seems easier to react than to respond. The difference between the two is that reaction is immediate and physical: the "you kick me, I kick you" phenomenon. Response is just as immediate but involves thought. Reflection is essential if these managers are to understand the causes of the phenomena that affect them. Thinking was not viewed as one of the key management skills of the last industrial revolution. In part this reflected the emphasis on

The link between action and reflection relies on creating an environment in which high performance thinking occurs.

the division of labor but it was, also, a function of the bureaucratization of management. Bureaucrats do not need to think; they merely follow rules. Analysis of all forms of competition, especially the most intense and well documented, war, supports the contention of Basil Liddell-Hart, the military historian, that "intelligence is a further factor of which sufficient account is rarely taken in setting out the balance of strength."

HIGH PERFORMANCE THINKING

The link between action and reflection relies on creating an environment in which high performance thinking occurs. This type of thinking is characterized by the mnemonic OFTEN. The mnemonic highlights the importance of Open (minded) Focused, Task oriented, approaches that Engage people to act Now. Thinking OFTEN means first and foremost having an open mind on the issues and the environment in which the organization is operating. There is the old saying "The human mind is like a parachute; it functions best when it is open." Failure to appreciate the implications of this message is probably the single most important reason for the failures of large and well resourced organizations to identify or respond to change or threat until it is too late. The recent acquisition of Forte Group by Granada in the UK vividly illustrates the danger of a closed approach to business thinking. Forte saw itself and acted as a closed system with little input from outside into its strategic thinking. This made it vulnerable to a predator with a much stronger open system view of its developments.

Some companies confuse openness with lack of focus. The task in business thinking is to link focus with openness. Michael Porter[22] gives a depressing picture of the success rates of those corporations that lack focus in their developments especially in the areas of acquisitions and diversification.

My data paint a sobering picture of the success ratio of these moves. I found that on average corporations divested more than half their acquisitions in new industries and more than 60% of their acquisitions in entirely new fields. Fourteen companies left more than 70% of all the acquisitions they had made in new fields. The track rate in unrelated acquisitions is even worse – the average divestment rate is 74%.

Focussed thinking in business need not be narrow but it must concentrate attention on corporate issues that:

- are within the current or accessible knowledge and experience of those involved;
- provide a platform for further, progressive development;
- create or employ opportunities for sharing identifiable synergies;
- employ existing or accessible skills and competences;
- are solvable.

Focus on issues that lie within this five point plan fits well with the task approach to reflection that is the most important way to resolve the paradox of action oriented reflection. Lean thinking of this kind is analogous to the kind of lean production that eliminates barriers between thought and action, slashing time spent, focussing on outcomes and making goals tangible and measurable. This is best achieved by following the other precept of lean production: engage as many people as possible in the process. Pushing responsibility for ideation and development on to the operator groups closes the loop between reflection and action in a positive and constructive way. It also produces such lateral thinking as in the Southwest Airlines' decision to involve frequent fliers in some of its appointments' boards. The final element is resolving the gap between action and reflection is immediacy.

The jolly giant on the high wire

The problems of diversification and innovation identified by such authors as Porter have made many firms wary of moving outside their areas of core capability and competence. Many corporate leaders have taken to heart Ansoff's famous grid with its associated data on differential failure rates (see Figure 11.2). His work indicated that failure rates increase as firms move away from markets and products they know well. The highest success rates, sometimes as high as 80%, occur when the firm is dealing with products and markets it knows. The lowest success rates occur with new products in new markets.

Richard Branson is clear that "the biggest risk any of us can take is to invest money in a business that we don't know." The message has been taken even further in sectors like

Pushing responsibility for ideation and development on to the operator groups closes the loop between reflection and action in a positive and constructive way.

manufacturing where "dominate or die" has become a principle adopted by senior business leaders and academics alike. The notion has a long history in all forms of competition. Sun Tzu the Chinese general and military thinker commented that "weakness comes from having to prepare against possible

Figure 11.2

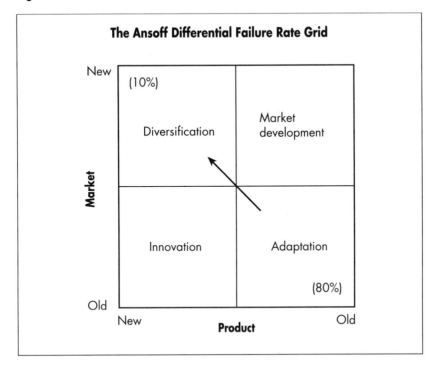

The Ansoff Differential Failure Rate Grid

attacks ... strength, from compelling our adversary to make these preparations against us." The notion of domination, or determining the rules of engagement, is closely linked to the principle of concentrating the organization behind those capabilities or competences that give it a genuine competitive advantage. This will not only give the organization the edge in head to head conflict but will also provide the maximum scope to gain maximum leverage from its assets.

The focus on core capabilities and their continual refinement allows the organization to choose those aspects of development and competition where its competences provide the best use of resources and the greatest opportunity for success. Some universities in the UK have decided that their strengths lie in teaching and research, not in property management, and are transferring control of their student residences to hotel groups or property management companies. Local authorities and hospitals are following the same route, businesses are contracting out services that they have traditionally kept in house. And the same pattern is seen in market or business development: Hanson Group in the UK has restructured its businesses around four tightly defined business units, Philips has cut back on the diversity of areas in which it does business, Continental Bank has retrenched to concentrate on those areas that maximized shareholder value and competitive advantage.

This concentration on the inner workings of the organization and its core strengths creates a paradox when put alongside the pressure on organization to reengineer its operations to meet changing conditions. The central principles of reengineering call upon organizations to be willing to engage in "fundamental," "radical" and "dramatic" reorganization of the business and its "processes." The willingness to rethink and even "break" the rules that have guided the organization is an integral part of the thinking behind reengineering. There is little doubt about the successes that have been achieved through successful reengineering programs. The transformation of Asea Brown Boveri's structures and operations dramatically illustrates how performance and returns can be transformed by a radical rethink of the way the business operates. Aprillia the Italian motorcycle company changed its design and development program after taking a fundamental look at the way this work was undertaken, having a radical rethink and then implementing a new approach. This cut its design cycle by half, increased the scope for innovation and reduced costs.

EMPIRICAL SELF CRITICISM

The difficulty lies in wedding the kind of fundamental rethink associated with reengineering with the concentration on core skills that is so closely associated with success and survival. A key element in the effort to reconcile this paradox is a true understanding of those distinctive capabilities that give the firm a genuine competitive edge. My work with corporations highlights the reluctance of firms to engage in the type of empirical self criticism that is part of the search for an understanding of those core capabilities that provide a competitive edge. Core competences that provide a real competitive edge meet five criteria. They are:

- distinctive;
- sustainable;
- appropriable;
- usable; and
- measurable.

Those competences that are not distinct to the firm, that is are generic to a sector or can be matched elsewhere, cannot provide a competitive advantage. Sustainable competences or capabilities persist, probably through deliberate action. A temporary or accidental competence, perhaps created by an aspect of national government policy, cannot be sustained in isolation, is vulnerable to future uncontrollable changes and is not an integral feature of the organization. Appropriable competences benefit the firm. Usable competences can be affected by the deliberate action of the organization and may be deployed against more than one situation. Measurability allows those leading the enterprise to define the parameters and scale of the competence.

Organizations seldom subject the competences they attribute to themselves to the type of close scrutiny inherent in this type of analysis. Empirical self criticism provides a basis for the firm to identify those capabilities around which the reengineering process is built. The reengineering can then build on the strengths of the organization rather than running the risk of undermining these strengths. The starting point of the reengineering exercise is the plots on the map of the organization that mark its strategic assets.

Organizational profiling is an increasingly important feature of efforts to define the enterprise, its capabilities, competitive advantages and opportunities for development. The most useful profiles build a picture of the architecture of the firm – its borders (the outer skin); the inner structure; lines of communication, authority and action. An effective picture of the organization's architecture describes not only those aspects that create its distinctiveness but the "load bearing" walls, hazards and risks. The externals are important: the inputs, process and output, together with the feedback loops, current and potential partners. The architecture defines the context and capacity of the enterprise. An understanding of this is an essential prerequisite for resolving the paradox of core capabilities and reengineering.

Information and communication technologies are changing the nature of the internal workings of the enterprise. Perhaps the most important shift is the change in the fabric that alters the relationship between the enterprise and its environment.

The new industrial revolution is changing the architectural potential within the business environment. The features of this are especially relevant to handling the paradoxes created within the revolution. Architecture is creating the potential for smart structures that exploit the potential of the knowledge based industrial revolution. Simultaneously, information and communication technologies are changing the nature of the internal workings of the enterprise. Perhaps the most important shift is the change in the fabric that alters the relationship between the enterprise and its environment.

THE GENETIC CODE

The value from the genetic code of organizations is shaped by the new environment. The genetic code of the organization largely prescribes how it responds to conditions and stimuli, and it is deeply embedded in the enterprise and rooted in the culture and values of the organization. The search for an appreciation of this code involves deep and intense scrutiny beyond the normal confines of the executive suite and boardrooms. Jack Welch spent years visiting GE plants, talking to managers, operatives, suppliers and customers to get some sense of the code which determined the way the firm responds. Jurgen Schrempp is engaged in the same type of process at Daimler-Benz. An understanding of the genetic code of their business, through long and detailed involvement in the highways and byways of the

> *The great skill of competitive advantage in the new industrial revolution lies in devising a mix of defense and attack strategies that build on strengths while understanding weaknesses.*

organization, is one of the key advantages that Japanese business leaders have over their Western rivals. This reflects the greater integration of their business lives with the evolution of the organization. The *parachutist* manager who drops in and flies away has little place in the Asian business environment.

CONCLUSION

Involved management own the message of corporate development and sustain their involvement. This provides the long-term perspective that sustains competitive advantage despite environmental turbulence. This approach sees business development and competition as less of a frontal attack and more a war of position where the skill lies in sustaining a competitive advantage for the long term. The flanking attack which seeks the weak points of rivals or finds ways to outflank them minimizes losses while keeping rivals unhinged. The great skill of competitive advantage in the new industrial revolution lies in devising a mix of defense and attack strategies that build on strengths while understanding weaknesses. Attacks can be based on frontal attack, flanking or outflanking, encirclement or guerrilla warfare if the organization understands its capabilities and matches its capabilities against those of its rivals in the struggle to add value and meet customer needs. The same principles hold true for defense: fortresses can be built, mobile defense, preemption, flank position attack, counteroffensive or deterrence can be used to hold on to markets and positions. All require new kinds of managers to deal with new kinds of conditions. This new thinking provides the route to resolving the paradoxes and welcoming the revolution.

Part III

♦

THE MILLENNIUM MANAGER

> ♦
>
> **The kaleidoscope organization contains many distinct parts which come together in ways that maintain the integrity of the whole, in a unique format which retains the separate identity of the parts.**
>
> ♦

◆

Structures

Operations and

Strategies

could almost be the call sign of

those managers who are striving

to build organizations that will

make managing paradox easier.

◆

THE MILLENNIUM
MANAGER

The first and second industrial revolutions were driven by changes in technologies and markets. The use of coal drove steam powered machines made from iron that produced goods in larger quantities at lower prices than ever before. Clothing, food, transport and other markets were transformed. Later, oil drove the new machines. Engineered products replaced the cast products of the former revolution. Markets were created for chemicals, pharmaceuticals and mass consumer goods. These were the more obvious changes of the first and second industrial revolutions. Beyond these, new institutions were created. The factory system, the international trader and the trades unionist were children of the first industrial revolution. They emerged to meet the needs or respond to the demands of the new joint stock companies. The second industrial revolution produced the giant, hierarchical, multidivisional company and managers to run it.

The kind of organizations that prosper are intimately connected with the nature of the economic, technological and social environment in which they operate. The type of machines, the available control systems, the nature of the dominant industries, and the social structure of the day led to the success of the unified, large, single site manufacturing operation that prospered during the 19th century. Textile production is well suited to large aggregations of labor whose main role is "machine minding." Public organizations were small and highly distributed because of the lack of any real economies of aggregation. The industries of the second revolution produced a shift in the optimal organizational form. Large aggregations of labor are needed for car production and they were joined by new specialists in design, research, marketing. The scale and nature of the product makes distributed production profitable. Proximity to markets gives additional advantages. In the public sector and administration similar shifts occurred. The typewriter, adding machine and telephone created genuine economies of scale in aggregating labor. The organization that prospered during this century was shaped by the dominant technologies and market needs. The current changes in these technologies and markets are altering again the forms of organizations that will prosper this time round.

It is not easy to describe in detail the kind of organization that will emerge to dominate a specific economic paradigm. Richard Arkwright built his first factories because he wanted to exploit new technologies and give his business an edge: a grand vision of building a new type of enterprise was probably far from his mind. John D. Rockefeller knew that he wanted to get control of the distribution of oil, and built Standard Oil which maximized his control of a highly distributed company, then devised systems to increase his grip while enhancing quality and controlling costs. Alfred P. Sloan built on these lessons to increase control and quality while decentralizing operations. He needed a managerial labor pool which adopted these measures professionally and consistently to give General Motors an edge. This was an exercise in business management not organizational engineering.

It is, however, possible to identify the key characteristics of the enterprises they created, and how these related to the needs of markets and technologies. Their operating systems and organization were shaped by these pressures. We are now able to identify not only the external pressures but the features which organizations will need to build into their Structures, Operations and Strategies in order to succeed. SOS could almost be the call sign of those managers who are striving to build organizations that will make managing paradox easier.

Chapter 12

◆

THE CHANGING FACE OF ORGANIZATIONS

THE KALEIDOSCOPE ORGANIZATION

A series of recent studies has highlighted the characteristics of organizations that seem to be best suited to the needs of the challenges of the new industrial revolution. There is surprising consistency between the picture emerging from studies as diverse as the Massachusetts Institute of Technology,[1] The Economist Intelligence Unit,[2] The (British) Institute of Management[3] and other work in North America, Europe and Asia. The kaleidoscope organization contains many distinct parts which come together in ways that maintain the integrity of the whole, in a unique format which retains the separate identity of the parts. The parts can come together to create new patterns out of the same pieces in response to new forces. The environments in which they exist act like the mirrors in the kaleidoscope to add new dimensions to the form and its operations. The features that shape the successful enterprise of the future are determined by its Structure, Operations and Strategy.

Structure

Successful businesses are changing their structures to exploit the potential of new technologies to meet new market conditions.

They are breaking the barriers between themselves and their customers by making themselves more responsive, flexible and adaptive.

Flatter structures

Flatter structures are an integral feature of this change, and firms must take out those layers of the bureaucracy that have increased costs and imposed barriers between policy and implementation. The complex and elaborate managerial bureaucracies that emerged over the last century were needed to run the large and complex enterprises that had developed. The electromechanical technologies which dominated information and control systems required large numbers of people to implement them. Computer based information and control systems do not require either the numbers or the tiers. Firms are using the freedoms which new technologies provide to take out layers of management.

Percy Barwise, Chief Executive of Asea Brown Boverie (ABB) is totally dedicated to the twin principles which underpin the efforts to build flatter organizations. He claims that "we have not reached the limits of our ability to take out layers and improve effectiveness. We believe in a flat organization." He adds that when new tasks or activities are started "the challenge is to avoid creating new layers. We have not created a new layer of man-

> Firms are using the freedoms which new technologies provide to take out layers of management.

agement in response to innovations and new developments." He is , in effect, implementing one of the oldest business maxims: "there are always savings to be made in management." He and other business leaders are adding the twist that removing layers provides immediate opportunities to link savings to improvements in productivity and responsiveness.

At the highly successful Scandinavian Airline Group, SAS, the dramatic turnround in its fortunes in the 1980s linked delayering with a renewed emphasis on getting closer to customers and focussing attention on their needs. A top SAS manager described the situation at the start of the turnround.

In those days, many employees felt that passengers were a disturbing element they had to contend with, rather than the ones who were in fact paying their salary. Taking control of a situation, and bypassing the regulations in order to please a customer, were not the things to do at SAS.

The freedom to take control, the ability to bypass regulation and the determination to please customers are key outcomes of the delayering efforts of effective companies.

Delayering and the creation of flatter organizations are not policies confined to large multinational corporations. The small British clothing company, Stirling plc, delayered its operations in an effort to improve margins, productivity and responsiveness to its key customers. Robert Coe, the company chairman who led the delayering effort, argued that creating a flatter organization was as important to Stirling as it would be to a giant corporation. "The gains were immediate and the only question was why we didn't do it earlier."

Taking out layers is only the start of creating a flatter organization. Flatter organizations work best when the capabilities and competencies of those in lower posts are expanded. Those leading the organization have wider responsibilities. Creating and communicating a vision for the future, which fits capabilities and scenarios, grows in importance; further, they have a primary responsibility for building the capabilities which give an edge in managing the future. Middle managers also have their roles changed fundamentally. It is probably no longer appropriate to use the term middle manager: these are really "heartland" managers since their task is to manage the heartland of the organization. They are responsible for delivering the culture, systems and ethos that deliver value, and manage the information systems and ensure effective feedback and control throughout the organization. Operations management center their work on skill delivery, team building, ensuring quality in everything from service to operation and delivering change.

The dynamic model (see Figure 12.1) illustrated highlights the dynamic nature of these roles in an organization striving to get closer to its role and purpose by becoming flatter. Visions and strategies are getting closer and the roles of senior managers and heartland managers are overlapping and converging. Developing people is less a specialist function and more a continuous responsibility, while delivering change is everyone's task.

Figure 12.1

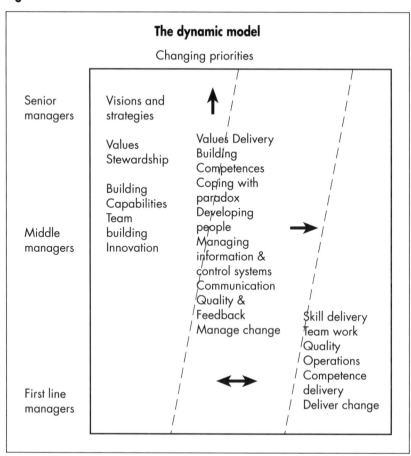

Organic and process based

Flatter structures free companies from the limitations imposed by hierarchies. This is a double edged sword: managers whose careers were built in the multilayered hierarchies of traditional companies feel uncomfortable without either the structure or sense of position provided by hierarchies. They lack the sense of how far they have come and how far they have to go in their career. Some companies have

Developing people is less a specialist function and more a continuous responsibility, while delivering change is everyone's task.

abandoned their efforts to build flatter organizations in the face of this disquiet. Relayering is occurring as organizations give up the struggle to delayer.

Part of the problem lies in the effort to delayer and build flatter structures, without other changes in the organization's structure. Enterprises that retain rigid, mechanistic systems of management, reward, remuneration, communication and control find it hard to operate these systems without multitiered structures. Firms that have delayered most effectively have changed the basis of their work and replaced mechanistic structures with more naturalistic, organic structures. The key feature of organic structures is that they are nonhierarchical in most of their activities. Teams come together to perform tasks. Lines of work, control and information follow natural not preconceived structures. Jack Welch of General Electric sees this aspect of delayering as so important that he is looking for ways to separate reward systems from hierarchy, and locate it in performance.

At Matsushita, the organic structure means that "hands off management is the rule." Says Tomio Koide of Matsushita Singapore, "Japan gives a sales and a profit target and the subsidiary must achieve them. That is the only basis. As long as these targets are achieved, local management has complete autonomy. " The analogy with the organism is taken even further. Mike Matsuoka of MELAC, Matsushita's European subsidiary adds " losses show bad health and invite many doctors from Japan who provide advice and support."

Larry Hunter of Wharton describes the modern "high performance workplace" as an organic structure "built upon broadened jobs and enhanced employee discretion." There is "high employee involvement and lowered status differences between managers and workers." The importance of teamwork recurs in studies of the most effective companies and the link is being broken between the formal structure and the real work of the business. At Pillsbury, James Behnke, Vice President for Growth and Technology, saw this breakdown of the formal structure and the blurring of the lines between roles, tasks and people as so vital that his business cards carried the legend "Senior Vice President, Blurring."

> *The importance of teamwork recurs in studies of the most effective companies and the link is being broken between the formal structure and the real work of the business.*

Cross functional

Innovation, change and the management of technology are areas in which the gains from breaking down barriers, blurring identities and building organic structures are most obvious. Innovation based growth such as James Behnke follows does not fit neatly into the confines of the specific disciplines of a specialized group within the management bureaucracy. Arthur Koestler's work on creativity described how most creative acts result from the ability to bisociate.

Bisociation involves taking two things that seem to be separate and bringing them together to create a new unity. Henry Ford took the modular or component based manufacture developed by Whitney and the continuous conveyor belt, first used extensively in the Liverpool docks, and produced the assembly line. Biro invented the ball point pen after he saw the potential for linking the properties of printers' ink and the use of the fountain pen. Velcro was developed by Georges de Mestral after he linked the technical properties of zippers and the physical properties of burrs.

Managerial bureaucracies with their emphasis on formal structures and lines of communication stand in the way of the creative interaction of functions and interaction. All too often the formal structure produces barriers to innovation that can be overcome only with difficulty. Even the pharmaceutical industry, despite its reputation for innovation, has faced these problems. Aspirin is perhaps the most successful drug in history. Its development by Bayer was almost stifled at birth because Heinrich Dreser, the head of Bayer's research lab, preferred his own development, heroin, which was "ten times more effective for dealing with coughs than codeine but with none of its side effects." The successful trials of Aspirin were, in contrast, dismissed as "the usual Berliner bragging, the product has no value." Fortunately for Bayer the logjam was broken. Almost 100 years later, Xerox had no such good fortune when developments from their Palo Alto laboratories were consistently blocked – only to be picked up by rivals.

In organic structures, the tunnel vision which characterized traditional management is replaced by task and purpose based relationships. Communication follows natural flows and people work together on a "need to" not a "must do" basis. It is no surprise that the process approach to reengineering follows the same principles. The successful transformation at Taco Bell was based on a recognition that structures, qualifications and specialization are only of value if they combine to meet customer needs. John Martin, the CEO of Taco Bell, summarized this with his criticism of the formal, structured approach.

We were a top-down "command and control" organization with multiple layers of management, each primarily concerned with bird dogging the layers below them ... [we had] handbooks for

**everything, including literally, handbooks to interpret other hand-
books ... I had a notion that our customers didn't give a hoot
about any of our elaborate systems.[4]**

Flexible

A cross functional organization creates the scope to build greater
flexibility into the enterprise. Change, development and responsiveness require the kind of flexibility shown by the most
successful businesses today. Richard Branson has built much of
Virgin's success to date on its flexibility or organizational flex. This
is not the flexibility that comes from lack of purpose, direction or
lack of an understanding of the firm's strengths. He knows what
Virgin is capable of achieving, and out of that adopts a flexible
approach to internal needs and outside opportunities. At Polaroid,
flexibility became an all encompassing philosophy as the corporation led its industry through new areas and new technologies. It
reflected the ethos and values of its founder, Dr Land. His succes-
sor, Bill McCune, described Land's approach: "Land thrives on
informality; thus, Polaroid has no organizational chart."

The successes of these entrepreneurial firms are being matched
by older established firms like Ford, Rover Group, Milliken
Industries, BASF and Nestlé. In the public sector, large organizations like the UK's Post Office and National Health Service are
moving from the highly formal and structured to the flexible,
with no loss of standards and greatly improved performance.

Collegiality

The shift to more flexible, cross functional, organic and process
oriented structures changes the nature of relationships which
determine the way the structure works. These changes, allied to
the creation of flatter organizations held together by networks,
is moving control systems towards more collegiate structure
and away from authoritarian approaches. Britain's *Management
Development to the Millennium* study summarized the effects of
these changes.

The vast majority of interviewees spoke of future management styles relying less and less on traditional command and control structures, and more and more on co-operative, collegial styles of management. Such an approach was variously described, but always centred around the idea that the manager of the millennium will have to influence rather than coerce ... This notion was best summarised by the interviewee who said "you can't tell people, you have to convince them." Another suggested that in the organisation of the millennium, "managers will have to influence people rather than organise them.

These fit in with the notion that the definition of management may need to change from "getting things done *through* others" to "getting things done *with* others." Collegiality imposes additional demands on the manager. Collegiate organizations are shaped more by consensus than instruction. This model fits well with the emphasis on debate and discussion which characterize Japanese firms, but is hard to fit alongside the "macho" management which managers in Anglo-Saxon economies love so much. Shared values and a common vision are important features of collegiate structures. Investment in value definition and maintenance is a priority.

The collegiate structures that emerge in the business and related communities are unlikely to share all the features of the collegiate structures that dominate in universities. The new kind of collegiality weds a sense of purpose and willingness to invest in trust and consensus with clear and accepted systems of authority and immediacy of purpose. The internecine rivalries and petty wrangles that bedevil university life may have a role in education but are counterproductive in the wider economic community.

Operations

The operations of the enterprise determine the ways in which a particular structure converts the organization's policies into action. Sometimes the line between operations and structures is as blurred as James Behnke wants every line within the business to be. There are, however, some aspects of the way corporations operate that show marked differences between the needs of a time of revolutionary change and the likely new environment, and the conditions seen prior to the revolution. These differences may reflect a dominant organizational culture, or mirror the needs of the types of organizations that do best during times of radical change.

Drive

Those firms that are performing best today seem to be infected with a sense of purpose and drive. In Britain, the retail group Associated Dairies (ASDA) was transformed during the early 1960s from one of the worst performing foods retailers to an exceptional performer. At the heart of this transformation was the hands on management style of a new generation of managers, led by Archie Norman, and the sense of purpose that he transmitted throughout the company. Jan Timmer led the same kind of transformation on an even greater scale at Philips, pushing constantly for change and driving the large and lumbering electronics giant out of the crisis which almost led to its bankruptcy. He worked hard to communicate a sense of purpose. As one of Holland's leading journalists said at the time: "He left no one in any doubt about the urgency of the situation at Philips." Timmer sums his approach up simply: "I tell managers, don't get in the way, don't create obstacles." At National Semiconductor, CEO Gilbert Amelio is driving the same kind of initiative throughout the corporation. The principle he uses is plain: "We are driving this company from being merely viable to being truly great."

This "hands on" drive is more closely linked with entrepreneurial concerns where the owner's sense of purpose is communicated throughout the enterprise. Ann Taylor of Ann Taylor Fashion takes the notion that step forward with her view that "It doesn't take a genius to build a business. It takes someone relentless enough to go at it again and again." This is similar to the drive shown by firms like Microsoft. Wallace and Erickson in their biography of Bill Gates[5] summarized his approach. "Gates pushed his people hard because he wanted them to be better. Each day, he said, they should come to work thinking 'I want to win.' ...The combination of ambition and wanting to win every single day is what Gates referred to as being 'hard core'."

> Initial drive is relatively easy. Almost every new broom expects to sweep clean.

Initial drive is relatively easy. Almost every new broom expects to sweep clean. Real success comes from rekindling drive after setbacks and disappointments or even creating a new sense of purpose after great success has already been achieved. This only happens when the sense of drive is communicated and retained by the entire management group. At National Semiconductor, Jim Burley, the Human Resources Director, says "it will be great when change gets to the point that it's not what Gil says but what we say."

Performance focus

Drive that makes a difference to corporate performance is not the ego driven drive of the media image, but purposeful, performance focussed drive. The focus on performance is perhaps the clearest difference between the really successful, the surviving and the rest. Hamel and Prahalad describe numerous examples of corporations that overtook seemingly larger and more powerful rivals. The key to many of these successes is the greater focus of the firm around its core capabilities, and its determination to convert these into major sources of competitive advantage. Jack Welch at General Electric came up with the simple notion that General Electric would only stay in markets in which it could be a number 1 or number 2 seller. He built this approach on the evidence that the product or brand leaders were in the best position to maximize the returns for their efforts. A business or a business leadership group that cannot articulate the fundamental rules that control or shape its company or industry cannot hope themselves to control or shape the company or industry.

In the absence of a performance focus, three sets of problems emerge. First, the firm gets distracted into a wide range of activities that are not part of its mission or role. The clearest signs of the decline of RJR Nabisco

The focus on performance is perhaps the clearest difference between the really successful, the surviving and the rest.

before its acquisition by KKR lay in the unsuccessful forays into new markets, the fleets of corporate jets and the massive sponsorship program. All distracted the firm from its primary areas of activity and its greatest opportunities for earning and returns. Second, the relationship between performance and reward weakens. Activities that make no material contribution to success get rewarded while crucial activities are starved of rewards and status. Third, lack of direction creates opportunities for rivals with a greater sense of purpose to overtake the company.

Leverage

The advantage created by a strong sense of focus is further reinforced when the organization concentrates maximum leverage behind its core capabilities and activities. Focus × Leverage is, perhaps, the greatest source of competitive advantage today. Mars levered its core competence in confectionery when it launched its range of ice cream based products. The multiplier effect of its investment was far greater than if it had diversified into a new area. Canon has adopted the same principle with its range of laser printer engines. It wed its technical expertise with the market power of its customers, to dominate this market. Microsoft uses its Windows program suite in the same way. The search for leverage is the key corollary in the effort to understand better the firm's sources of competitive advantage.

Value added

Japanese corporations like Toyota, Kao, Honda, Hitachi and NEC led the way in focussing attention on the scope for building success by adding value. The preoccupation with adding value is one of the most fundamental shifts in the thinking of management today. A value creation approach has been an integral feature of the success of corporations as diverse as Home Depot, Intel, Ericsson, Rover Group and BT.

The steps in creating a value driven organization are easier to describe than to implement. Crucial to the development of a value driven business are two basic assumptions. The first is that the firm and the business need some form of mental map of what leads to value creation in their organization. The second is that value creation starts, and gets its greatest returns, at the point of production or consumption, This means that those closest to the point of production and the market will have the greatest impact on value creation. At AT&T the emphasis on high performance is part of every manager's performance appraisal. Divisional managers must measure themselves against their ability to achieve high performance against economic, people and customer criteria. The EVA assessment examines their Economic Value Added while their PVA and CVA measure their People and Customer Value Added.

Beyond the mental model of what drives value in the organization, management requires some sense of how to turn this map into a program which can energize those who have the greatest impact on value creation. In delivering the newly energized organization, the task of management is to avoid building in systems and structures that complicate issues. The Keep It Simple Stupid (KISS) principle has particular relevance. The most effective way to push performance standards up while adding value, is to concentrate work around identified critical success factors. These critical success factors should be benchmarked against "best in class," "best overall," and "theoretical best" standards. This effort to drive up the ways value can be added links notions of focus with the sense of purpose that is so important today.

Time competitive

Among the most important contemporary benchmarks are those based on time. Stalk and Hout[6] describe how new information and control systems permit corporations to achieve dramatic breakthroughs in performance, and reduce costs, by seeking ways to transform the time relationships in their company and industry. Savings in time produce large savings in costs while increasing customer satisfaction. Time based management provides opportunities to build and retain major technological advantages over firms with slower turnaround or response rates.

At Honda, the focus on seeking ways to get a competitive edge through time based competition saw development cycle times cut by 50%, although the model range increased and costs dropped. Domino's Pizza in the USA won a similar competitive advantage with their delivery time guarantee. The recent softening of the guarantee has done little to reduce their competitive edge over their rivals in the fast food delivery market. Aprillia, the Italian motorcycle producer and design group, won their contract with BMW on the basis of their design and development promise. They exceeded their promise, delighted their customer and increased their margins.

Information technology

Information technology is at the heart of many of these changes in operations and the altered structures of organizations. The revolution in IT is integral to the transformation in practice that characterizes the new environment. The challenge facing organizations is to fully exploit the new technology, and move beyond the superficial use of the techniques and equipment. There is abundant evidence of superficial and unproductive use of the $900Bn a year that is invested in IT. Gary Reiner of General

Electric has gone as far as to say: "We have found that in many way technology impedes productivity." Donald Marchant of IMD links these failures to get real value out of IT from four dysfunctional uses:

- control fixation;
- behavioral regression;
- mindset paralysis;
- reactive approach.

Control fixation does not address real problems with real and relevant information, but keeps looking in greater detail at information that gave no guidance before. Behavioral regression is the phenomenon that occurs when managers distract themselves with totally irrelevant data instead of tackling the issue in hand. Mindset paralysis is linked with behavioral regression but reflects the inability of managers to change their thinking in the light of new conditions. A reactive approach to information is part of the behavioral approach of the crisis managers who want information before, during, and after they act, and then ignore the evidence. The combination of these dysfunctional uses of information erodes the gains that are possible from new information technology. They reflect the attitudes and behavior of old style separated members of the managerial bureaucracy, who have not shifted from their divided labor approach to the integrated and integrating possibilities of the new environment.

Information technology gains its maximum impact when the culture of the organization shifts to one in which the functional gains from IT can be maximized. This culture fully integrates the use of information technology into the key strategic areas of the organization, from sourcing products and services to operations, logistics, production and quality management systems and focusses these on the needs of customers. This type of boundaryless information system is already in use by firms like National Panasonic, that have redirected their marketing efforts around the attempt to mass customize their products. Marks and Spencer in Britain have adopted the same principle to break down the barriers between their operations, those of their suppliers and the needs of the market. In the process, companies moving in this direction have reintegrated their internal operations to reshape their management methods and organizational culture.

> *Information technology is the means by which the organization, its structure and operations are redirected more effectively than ever to serve the needs of its strategy.*

Strategy

Information technology is the means by which the organization, its structure and operations are redirected more effectively than ever to serve the needs of its strategy. In high performing firms, this redirection emphasizes the primary purpose of the firm as meeting customer needs, in an increasingly global and rapidly changing environment.

Customer driven

Few business activities more clearly reflect the changing nature of the business environment than marketing. The first industrial revolution was the era of the order taker or salesman. Scarcity was the dominant state and when supplies were scarce, the marketing function revolved around the order taker, who rationed supplies to match production capacity. When demand was scarce, the salesman won orders and production responded. The bureaucratization and separation of management work over the last century saw the salesman evolve into the marketing executive, and that role further divide and subdivide. Advertising and market research became specialisms, then subdivided themselves into media and non-media advertising, industrial and consumer markets. On it went, until mystery shopping and financial press relations were distinct and highly specialized sectors of a once unified category of management.

The marketing ethos was shaped by an attempt to achieve something called a "marketing orientation" in companies. The terms used highlight the passive and formalized nature of this approach, compared to the active and largely informal implications of building a customer driven business. These customer driven businesses are fiercely dedicated to identifying the needs of different types of customers, and to bending the organization and its operations to meet these needs. The thrust of the marketing oriented company was often to reinforce the role of the marketing function or department. The customer driven company may not need this specific activity. A commitment to meeting the customers' needs permeates all business activities: so why make it the specialist task of a specific department?

The leadership group in the business, regardless of the functional origins, led this drive to meet buyer needs. Their task is to devise a way to focus everyone in the firm around the task of meeting needs and there is no compromise to this.

Vision directed with shared values and culture

The sense of a shared vision characterizes many of the most successful corporations of today. The visions of firms achieving extraordinary growth are seldom the narrow financial visions of firms like Hanson, but the bigger and wider visions of the Microsofts, Toyotas and Grand Metropolitans of this world. Vision from the top is seldom enough for these high performers. The leadership vision is disseminated, made tangible, shared and eventually owned by the vast majority of people within the enterprise.

The sense of shared commitment remains one the major competitive advantages of Japanese companies. Initially, many commentators saw this as culturally specific, and linked with important aspects of Japanese society. The successful transfer of their operations offshore has undermined that theory. A trip to

259

Sunderland in England and discussions with Nissan workers highlights the skill with which the notion of a shared and owned vision has been translated across continents and between cultures. The transformation of British Airways under John King showed the same skill in creating a vision, and winning buy in from an established labor force.

The creation and communication of this vision is one of the most important and powerful ways to integrate and energize an organization in the public or private sector. The skill lies in articulating a vision which can be understood, owned and delivered. All three aspects of building a vision directed company converge around the idea of establishing values that all members of the organization can share. This poses special problems in areas of the public sector and among professional groups where loyalties are divided and

> *All industrial revolutions are driven by entrepreneurs who take risks, innovate and redraw the rules of competition and performance.*

members subscribe to different values. Here, two processes interact to encourage or prevent the sharing of values around a shared culture. The greatest barriers lie in formal or institutionalized divisions in the managerial labor pool. The development, training or learning undertaken by people within the organization can either reinforce these divides or break them down. The solution lies in building unitary cultures founded on continuous, personal and professional development.

Entrepreneurship and innovation

All industrial revolutions are driven by entrepreneurs who take risks, innovate and redraw the rules of competition and performance. The preoccupation in the past with the division of labor and specialization, tended to localize entrepreneurship in specific activities and business areas. It was a first generation pursuit which was soon overtaken by normal business. The accelerating pace of change indicates that these entrepreneurial skills of risk taking, innovation and the redrawing of rules are more important, on a continuing basis, for larger groups of the labor force. Firms will need to exploit the full entrepreneurial abilities and innovativeness of all those involved if they are to prosper. The five paths to entrepreneurial wealth and innovative success are:

- understanding the distinctive anthropology of the time;
- building a vision;
- focussing on enriching others;
- sharing a vision;
- capitalizing on the transmission of data and the use of IT.

Global perspective

Terms like the global marketplace or the global village give some indication of the sharp increase in world trade over the last 20 years and the extent to which distances have shrunk. Customers are increasingly aware of the global nature of the marketplace that supplies foods, textiles, vehicles, cosmetics, drinks, business and personal services from across the world. In the rich developed parts of the world, the

The local company can soon become the uncompetitive company.

global market is the local high street. The globalization of business extends beyond the search for new customers. The geographic mobility of manufacturing means that even relatively small firms are capable of setting up overseas production. This inevitably forces them to become involved in training, development and education of their workers and managers but the lessons they learn are fed back into their home operations.

Firms that are locked into a local or national market miss out on these opportunities to transfer technology and improve their performance. The local company can soon become the uncompetitive company. Sometimes the most valuable lessons derive from the lessons learned from the increased complexity of the global market-place that comes from the mixture of diversity, change and new linkages that characterize international or global business. The same added complexity goes some way to explain why so many early moves overseas end in failure or high cost, and why early returns often fall short of aspirations.

The potential gains far outweigh the costs for the firm that successfully breaks through the pain barrier of globalization. These gains include profits, market, technological and learning efficiencies. The risks of failing to build a global perspective are enormous. Not only is the firm giving a built in advantage to those that do move overseas as they are protected from you in their home market. The purely local firm cuts itself off from ideas and opportunities.

Stakeholder focussed

Globalization often highlights the interests of the different stakeholders that shape the organization. Shareholders meet the short-term costs while some employees might face the longer-term costs. A stakeholder focus to business decision is part of a wider shift in the priorities and focus of organizations emerging from the new economic circumstances. The preoccupation with the interests of shareholders fitted the needs of an environment in which capital was the main variable in the economist's three primary elements: land, labor and capital. Land and labor were largely homogeneous and immobile, while capital was heterogeneous and mobile.

The addition of technology as the fourth factor in the equation and the increasing heterogeneity of labor transforms the situation. In addition, the nature and role of capital markets has altered. The increased role of the state in supporting investment or managing markets makes it a major stakeholder in organizations. The state's involvement broadens the impact of other interests, notably the wider community, with its interest in issues like health, safety, and the environment. The heterogeneity and greater mobility of labor sharpens its roles as a stakeholder.

The complex and diverse nature of these stakeholder interests means that those enterprises that learn to manage their relationship with these stakeholders will have many advantages over those that fail to do so. Until now, Virgin has been especially effective at managing its links with these diverse groups. One element in its success against British Airways was the skill with which it sustained an effective stakeholder focus.

THE NEW UNIFIED ORGANIZATION

The major characteristics of the successful firm in the new economy can be tabulated. The ways these are combined in any one enterprise will vary between firms and over time. The essential skill of these organizations will be their ability to take in signals from the outside, adapt their behavior and build success. Ultimately, this relies on the ability to learn and the fit between the managers in these organizations and the environment in which they operate. "Tomorrow's interactions may depend more on shared understanding than on sharing the same office corridor," says (Nobel Laureate) Arno Penzras of Bell Labs.[7]

◆

People and enterprises that are able to look above the next horizon, learn from these insights and wed their competences to new demands gain a massive edge over their rivals.

◆

Chapter 13

♦

A KNOWLEDGE BASED INDUSTRIAL REVOLUTION

THE NATURE OF THE REVOLUTION

The great economic revolutions of the last two hundred years contain a number of defining characteristics. Among these defining characteristics is the nature of the source of energy that shaped the dominant production, logistics and operating systems. Coal played this role in the first industrial revolution and it was used to produce steam to drive the machines that remain the abiding images of the last century. Those companies that were first and/or best at exploiting this energy prospered. Watt, Stephenson, Arkwright, Vanderbilt, Cunard used coal to drive the machines that powered their factories, trains and ships.

Oil played a similar role in the 20th century. Black Gold took over from King Coal as the clearest symbol of this century. Oil or its control won or provoked wars, rivalries and wealth. At the end of World War I, the French leader Bérenger called oil "the blood of victory." In the business world not only did oil companies grow into some of the world's largest corporations but key industries like chemicals, engineering, vehicles and aerospace depended on oil.

It is now possible to see that the dominant energy source of this latest industrial revolution is knowledge. Knowledge and

265

its products are the new primary source of competitive advantage. Access to knowledge, the ability to distribute knowledge and the capacity to adapt to the implications of changing knowledge, in sum, the ability to learn, are the keys to success and prosperity for the individual, the enterprise and the community. Computers, information and the innovators associated with them dominate the front pages of business and news magazines in the way Henry Ford, J.P. Morgan and Charles Schwab once dominated thinking about business. Magazines like *Time* reflect this interest with cover stories like "Can Machines Think."[8] Learning, the development of learning individuals, enterprises and communities are at the heart of the new industrial revolution. In this environment the needs

The accelerated pace of change means that managers can only adjust by recognizing the nature of the changes affecting them, developing the skills and competences to manage change and prepare themselves for further, faster change.

of a new kind of worker and customer lie at the centre of attempts to get an edge, especially in the face of the paradoxes that permeate work.

Charles Handy[9] uses the Sigmoid or S shaped curve to point out shifts in the pace of change and the need to introduce fundamental changes in management practice or individual behavior to reflect changed circumstances. Handy's view is that one's working life moves from periods of relative stability to times of "sharp change" or "adjustment." This gains special importance during a knowledge based industrial revolution. The accelerated pace of change means that managers can only adjust by recognizing the nature of the changes affecting them, developing the skills and competences to manage change and prepare themselves for further, faster change. This process of adjustment is made easier (or harder) by the manager's ability to learn, i.e. modify behavior in the light of knowledge and experience.

This kind of learning does not occur in isolation or in simple one step processes. People learn better in a learning environment. This means that behavior changes in the organization or community in the light of knowledge. Simply acquiring information is not enough. The double cycle of learning occurs when knowledge is acquired then applied. Organizations that internalize this kind of thinking adapt their policies and practices in the light of their experiences and accumulated knowledge, and are able to break out of the straitjackets of custom and practice when necessary. People and enterprises that are able to look above the next horizon, learn from these insights and wed their competences to new demands gain a massive edge over their rivals.

These issues are vividly illustrated in the growth sectors of modern economies. Industries like computing, telecommunications, materials, the media and education have emerged to challenge established giants while new industries like biotechnology are evolving. These are information, knowledge and expertise rich industries where the ability to manage these resources determines success. Even those organizations that are firmly rooted in well established sectors of public and private enterprise get ahead by "learning to learn" and adding an information and knowledge edge to their business. The Simplot family based their prosperity on potatoes. Richard Simplot left school young and soon started his agricultural business. It grew because he recognized the value of using other people's expertise. An innovative freezing process was the cornerstone of the company's early success. Simplot followed this up by spotting the growth of McDonald's and convincing Ray Kroc of the value of frozen French fries. Simplot grew with McDonald's. Most recently Simplot has moved further into the information and technology sector by investing heavily in Micron Technology.

New generation entrepreneurs share some traditional characteristics of traditional entrepreneurs. Ted Turner of CNN spoke for generations of entrepreneurs when he said that his prime motivation lay in "finding out what you could accomplish if you really tried." His interest "was always in why people did the things that they did, and what causes people to rise to glorious heights." Like his heroes Turner "just wanted to be the best," and realized that information, news and knowledge would dominate future markets long before his rivals did.

I came up with the concept of a new channel even before my Superchannel [1977] was up on the satellite. Business is like a chess game and you have to look several moves ahead. Most people don't. They think one move at a time. But any good chess player knows when you're playing against a one-move opponent, you'll beat him every time.

By thinking ahead Turner spotted that the technology and the need had converged. The technology to deliver 24 hour television news existed because of the convergence of satellite, cable, computers and other communications technologies. The hunger for instant access news was emerging and Turner was determined to deliver. "I think the people of America need this in depth news service, and I'm willing to risk everything I have to provide that service" was Turner's view when he announced the launch of CNN in 1980. By 1995, 14 of the 15 richest people in North America had founded their fortunes in industries rooted firmly in the knowledge, information or communications industries (see Table 13.1).

The push of discovery, invention, innovation and change is only one aspect of the pressure on organizations to adapt. The life cycles of products and services are getting shorter: in communications, for example, radio and film took almost 70 years to move from an interesting innovation to a mature technology; television took only 30 years to change from a technical curiosity to a mass market phenomenon; but the personal computer took less than 10 years to complete the same evolution. Portable telephones took less than 4 years to move from being a technical

Table 13.1

America's Richest, 1995 (Forbes)			
Rank	Individual	Industry	Knowledge Information or Communication Corp. Y/N/DK
1	Bill Gates	Information Technology (Microsoft)	Y
2	Warren Buffen	Investment (Berkshire Hathaway)	Y
3	John Kluge	Media (Metromedia)	Y
4	Paul Allen	Information Technology (Microsoft)	Y
5	Sumner Redstone	Cinemas (Viacom)	DK
6	Richard De Vos and Jay Andel	Conglomerate (Amway)	N
7	Si and Donald Newhouse	Publishing	Y
8	Walton family	Retail (Wal-Mart)	N
9	Ronald Perelman	Media (New World Communications)	Y
10	Lawrence Ellison	Information Technology (Oracle)	Y
11	David Packard	Information Technology (Hewlett-Packard)	Y
12	Walter Annenberg	Publishing	Y
13	Rupert Murdoch	Publishing	Y
14	Mars Family	Foods and confectionery	N
15	Barbara Cox, Anthony and Ann Cox Chambers	Publishing	Y
16	Pritzler Family	Conglomerate	N
17	Steve Ballmer	Information Technology (Microsoft)	Y
18	Gordon Moore	Information Technology (Intel)	Y
19	Edgar Bronfman	Drinks (Seagram)	N
20	Kirk Kerkorian	Investment and media	Y

wonder to public nuisance. Products that once seemed like staples show all the characteristics of fashion items.

Herding cats

The pace of technological change and the ability of markets to absorb innovation means that industries, organizations and communities are in a constant state of flux. Periods of stability or consolidation are increasingly rare, if they exist at all. People and organizations that prosper are able to consolidate while changing. Stability is merely a platform for the next move forward. Organizations and management patterns are adapting to this new environment. New groups of workers with new values are growing in importance. The management of talent is a new priority. Conventional reward and control systems have little effect when others are seeking their services or if they work in a community whose internal values sustain them more than external demands. Managing talent has been compared to herding cats – willful creatures with no herd instinct.

In this environment learning organizations have a special prominence. They provide a creative environment in which talent works by giving the enterprise access to the knowledge and expertise that shapes the future.

Learning organizations have adapted their ethos, values and actions to the dynamics of the new industrial revolution. The key features of these learning organizations are emerging. They include:

- Openness and transparency in operations so that creative links are built across the venture.
- A minimum of bureaucracy and hierarchy enabling information and resource flows to move to a need basis.
- Team based systems that seek to tap into the total potential of all team members.
- An emphasis on collaboration inside and outside the organizations to gain the best returns for all those involved.
- People centred policies and operations.
- Change orientation and acceptance that change is endemic.

In sum the organization must learn to learn.

Dr Yoshio Maruta strives to build the highly successful Kao Corporation of Japan as a learning organization. In his words this means

the Kao organization is like the paperweight on my desk. It is flat. There is a small handle in the middle, just as we have very few

senior people. But all information is shared horizontally, not filtered vertically. Only then can you have equality and equality is the basis for trust and commitment. In today's business world, information is the only source of competitive advantage. The company that develops a monopoly on information, and has the ability to learn it continuously, is the company that will win regardless of its business.

Kao has used this approach to achieve record rates of growth and dominance in many of its markets.

Peter Senge[10] has done more to examine the distinctive nature and advantages of the learning organization than anyone. Senge points out that "the old days when a Henry Ford, Alfred Sloan or Tom Watson learned for the organization are gone. ... The old model, the top think and the local acts, must now give way to integration thinking and learning at all levels." Senge argues that the role of the leadership group has changed fundamentally in response to a range of new opportunities and threats that cannot be fitted within corporate "command economies." Notions of empowerment, building a corporate vision and creating a network based enterprise fit well with the notion of building learning organizations. The broad, integrating principles of building, releasing and engaging provide the framework around which the learning organization is built (see Table 13.2).

Notions of empowerment, building a corporate vision and creating a network based enterprise fit well with the notion of building learning organizations.

KNOWLEDGE AND LEARNING

The last few years have seen a ferment of ideas as firms look for ways to get an edge or to simply survive in this increasingly

Table 13.2

The Learning Triad		
Building a learning culture	*Releasing the talents of the workforce*	*Engaging everyone in the change*
Encourage individual vision	Think	Focus on relationships not elements
Communicate compulsively	Distinguish between analysis and advocacy	Avoid blame
Make visions live, change and respond	Self analyse	Do not get blinded by detail
Break down barriers	Avoid defensive routine	Seek out leverage
Concentrate on positives		Distinguish symptoms from causes

turbulent and unpredictable world. For many managers, it seems that proposals for improving performance such as Total Quality Management, continuous improvement, time based competition, outsourcing, business process reengineering, focus on core competences or capabilities, value based management and others are more confusing than constructive. This sense of confusion is increased as first one idea then another is proposed, then debunked. The current turmoil over delayering vividly illustrates the problems faced by managers.

The arguments for delayering are, nevertheless, persuasive: it reduces costs, improves communication, speeds decision making and links performance with response. The track record of delayering at General Electric, ABB and many other famous companies is well known and fits in with the notion that "there are always savings to be made in management." Despite that, there is growing evidence of disillusionment: results do not match the claims; staff morale collapses; complaints and criticisms grow alongside genuine problems of designing reward and remuneration systems to reflect the new conditions. Reports increase that early delayerers are reintroducing layers.

The layers provide a comfort factor for managers that is hard to replace easily or quickly. David Harvey of Business Intelligence points out that "the trouble is, there is no ready replacement for the traditional [hierarchical] pay scheme."

Problems will remain for those firms and individuals that fail to see the three unifying themes behind these ideas. First, acceptance that change is continuous, so continuous adaptation to change is the essential precondition for survival and prosperity. Second, that the key to adaptation lies in people and their ability to learn to adapt. Peter Drucker summed this up in his comment that "knowledge flows through technology but resides in people." Third, that the changes are fundamental and require a fundamental rethink in organizational thinking, methods and approaches to work. At Glaxo Pharmaceuticals delayering and a wide ranging review of business process meant that reward systems were redesigned. The goal is to draw out the best use of personal competencies in response to corporate, individual and team outputs and against market rates. Sir Richard Sykes the CEO of Glaxo has no inhibitions about radical change.

The goal is to draw out the best use of personal competencies in response to corporate, individual and team outputs and against market rates.

The environment changes. We have to change. How do you think we are here today. We are here through natural selection, through evolution, through change, it has to go on through every aspect of life.

KEEPING FIT

Deep rooted reviews of approaches and ways of managing are an intrinsic feature of the current shift in systems and ideas; turbulence is an intrinsic feature of the scale of change occurring today. Managers and organization that cannot cope with ambiguity or expect outcomes to be predictable and easy to manage will struggle, become stressed and unable to handle difficult situations. Organizations now face the corporate equivalent of the Yerkes Dobson Law about stress, that simply stated means that the relationship between stress and performance is a bell shaped curve (see Figure 13.1). The greater the stress, the more performance improves until it collapses!

Figure 13.1

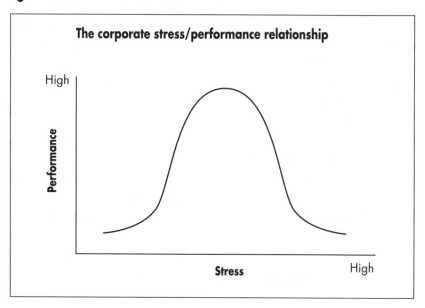

Understanding and managing the relationship between the stress the organization faces and the effect on performance is a crucial part of the armory of leaders. The corporate culture plays an important part in determining the ability of the enterprise to cope with stress but also affects the way the enterprise manages stress to maximize performance and avoid the collapse in performance that is an inevitable feature of too much organizational stress.

The FIT corporation links Feedback, Information and Training to manage the relationship between stress and performance.

Like all fitness training it starts with a clear understanding of the organization's starting point. This is closely linked to the prevailing organizational culture. At firms like Johnson & Johnson there is a determined effort to achieve a "triple A" standard in organizational culture management. This is founded on the effort to understand, articulate and act in terms of the desired culture. Some organizations and groups seem to thrive on a high stress level: investment bankers and surgical teams operate on levels on stress and tension that others would reject. Even here, however, there are limits as the recent problems at Woolwich Building Society, Barings, KKR and Saatchi and Saatchi illustrate.

Knowledge and information are important defenses against the corporate stress levels that undermine corporate performance. The creation of a learning environment is especially important when new knowledge is emerging that can undermine the expertise held by people within the firm. It is, however, in-sufficient to simply acquire knowledge. Cambridge University, for example, has had more Nobel Prize winners in the sciences than have most nations. For most of the last half century UK investment in research and development has significantly exceeded that of its major rivals, but Germany and Japan have won major, innovation based market advantage while spending relatively small sums on research and development. Their successes turned on the ways knowledge was sought out and employed. The creation of opportunities for people to use their knowledge and learning provides the best route to justifying further knowledge acquisition. The local and organizational culture provides the best cues to the ways knowledge is used and the effectiveness of the transfer of ideas, understanding and information from one

> *Knowledge and information are important defenses against corporate stress levels that undermine corporate performance.*

275

context to another. This exchange is crucial to the technology transfer process in the contemporary environment.

The key to personal prosperity for many lies in becoming one of a new breed of knowledge workers. Successful learning organizations will be made up of these knowledge workers who take pride in their knowledge, expertise or competence, and in its development and enhancement. Knowledge workers gain their economic value, freedom and power because they:

- own the means of production;
- manage their own control systems;
- supervise themselves;
- manage their own networks;
- are able to break down barriers and create new opportunities for themselves and their businesses.

They are especially important in new, small or growing businesses where innovation and opportunism wedded to entrepreneurship are the keys to competitive success.

THE MYTHS AND REALITIES OF LEARNING ORGANIZATIONS

The popularity of the concept of the learning organization over the last few years has spawned a series of myths that can stand in the way of attempts to build and sustain learning organizations in any context. The most common myth is that the creation of a learning organization is based purely on a set of core organizational beliefs and assumptions. In this context, the learning organization is an act of faith requiring limited investment, support systems or structure. Alongside this is the notion that organizations can be transformed into learning organizations by imposition. This is especially common in those enterprises in the private and public sector that have traditionally dealt in knowledge, learning and expertise, like publishers, media companies, IT firms and universities. They assume that because they deal with "learning" they are, by definition, learning organizations.

In reality, each of these myths must be challenged. The creation or articulation of a set of core organizational beliefs and values is the starting point for the construction of a learning organization. It will only work and be maintained if a sustained effort is undertaken to understand and adapt the venture's culture and operating systems. These must be tuned to support the goals of building a learning organization. Operating, reward and development systems must underpin the mission of building a learning organization, since traditional reward and punishment systems may not be wholly compatible with these goals. Organizational control systems need to evolve in ways that reflect the new mission and purpose. Building a learning organization is not a peripheral activity to support other tasks or functions: it is a redefinition of the entire venture.

> *The creation or articulation of a set of core organizational beliefs and values is the starting point for the construction of a learning organization.*

David Garvin, in the *Harvard Business Review*,[11] draws together the key features of this redefinition. He defines a learning organization as "an organization skilled at acquiring and transferring knowledge and at modifying its behavior to reflect new knowledge and insights." Eckhard Pfeiffer had to achieve all these at Compaq Computers when he took over after Rod Canion's sacking. He had to lead a root and branch review of the group's strategies while solving a host of immediate problems. Corporate morale was hit by the first layoffs in the company's history. Additional threats included an over-priced product range and aggressive new competitors like Dell. According to Pfeiffer, everyone seemed "confused, in doubt, lost." Dealers were struggling to shift products while Compaq's famous "can do" philosophy was hit by a series of poor performances. "Intense communication" was the key to the successful turnaround achieved by Pfeiffer while constant efforts were made to ensure that everyone in the firm and in its supplier and dealer networks was kept informed of developments at Compaq. The more they understood the strategies being adopted the easier it was for them to influence, contribute to and own the turnaround.

Culture and behavior cannot be imposed on the organization. Information, education, development and voluntary internalization of the new culture are essential to the successful creation of learning organizations. Later, Pfeiffer concluded that their weekly meetings were "in hindsight, never enough." Senge[12] emphasizes the importance of co-creation in shifting thinking, changing culture and building the values and attitudes of a learning organization into the enterprise. This involves shared visions and negotiated outcomes.

> *The more they understood the strategies being adopted the easier it was for them to understand, contribute to and own the turnaround.*

Ultimately, the members of the learning organization negotiate outcomes based on their learning needs and the fit between their learning and market or operational expectations. This pragmatic dimension to the development of the learning organization gets lost in much of the development literature. Learning organizations will prosper only if they are more effective in the new economic environment. Central to this shift are the five core skills of learning organizations:

- Systematic problem solving.
- Experimentation.
- Learning from experience and history.
- Learning from others.
- Transferring knowledge through the organization.

Systematic problem solving concentrates managers' attention on the patterns which shape issues rather than on the issues themselves. It is designed to link three distinct aspects of learning: recognition of the need to learn from past experience, awareness of pattern so that problems are prevented; and the accumulation of expertise. Experimentation is the creation of low risk learning environments in which variables are controlled and the implications of outcomes dissected, analyzed and built into the experience of the organization. Arie de Geus, planning director of Shell and pioneer of portfolio planning, firmly diagnosed the longevity of some companies as a result of their ability to conduct and learn from "experiments at the margin." These tests of the firm, its ideas and capabilities add to its competence and knowledge at low cost and little risk.

> *Systematic problem solving concentrates managers' attention on the patterns which shape issues rather than on the issues themselves.*

Learning from history and experience goes beyond the ritual recognition of success that organizations perform so well. It means examining the implications of failure and accumulating a genuine body of internal knowledge. Learning from others is increasingly important as industries and markets converge. Benchmarking, competitor analysis and environmental scanning are just some of the techniques used by organizations to maximize the gains they can make from the successes and failures of others. Localized, poorly disseminated knowledge is the bane of many organizations both large and small. Some people control the flow of knowledge to protect their own position, while others fail to appreciate to value of transferring knowledge to others.

The combination of these approaches can produce a revolution in thinking and attitudes in a firm. Sir Graham Day saw a revolution in thinking at Rover while he was Chairman.

During the mid 1980s a number of us, particularly in manufacturing business, somewhat belatedly became aware that our international competitiveness was being negatively impacted by the static knowledge and skills of our people at all levels. It was a small but critical step to translate this understanding into programmes to lift the knowledge and skills on a continuing basis. ... Rover's need to establish what we now term a learning organisation, came from the imperative to secure the company's survival. Now it contributes to Rover's increasing competitiveness and value as a business.

Even after the acquisition of Rover by BMW the transformation continues. Employees are associates and continuous development is an integral feature of the organization's development and that of its people.

The same environment imposes new demands on organizations. An environment in which all or most ventures are, or aspire to be learning organizations poses an immediate challenge and fundamental questions about traditional centres of learning or those parts of the enterprise with specific remits for training and development. These can respond by trying to sustain or defend their current position or by adapting to the new environment. There is growing evidence that the former position is increasingly difficult to sustain. In part, this difficulty reflects the dangerous assumption that a centre of learning is automatically a learning organization. Many providers of training, development or research fail to meet the primary conditions for the creation of learning organizations. Their work is often highly compartmentalized with little exchange or openness. Values are often imposed instead of being negotiated. Systems of support and development frequently lack good links with either organizational or personal development. More worrying, different forms and types of learning are devalued. Weak institutional links with the wider community may worsen this situation.

These traditional centres of knowledge and training need new partnerships with business and other parts of the public sector.

The new partners can work together to build up the five component technologies of learning organizations identified by Senge:[13]

- Systems thinking.
- Personal mastery of personal competencies.
- Mental models.
- Shared vision(s).
- Team learning.

As described earlier, systems thinking enables managers to identify repetitive patterns of behavior that are associated with positive and negative outcomes. Understanding the pattern provides not only an early warning but also a chance to appreciate the underlying causes of success and failure. The commitment to personal mastery of work is a repudiation of the atomized and fragmented approach to work associated with the old style division of labor. The focus lies on seeking ways to gain value for the individual by a personal investment in the role or task. Business managers have a poor record, compared to their peers in areas like sports, in personal investment in building their mastery of their work.

CONFIDENT HUMILITY

Companies like BP, Levi Strauss and 3M have made a massive corporate commitment to giving all their people the chance to master their role, task and work. BP expresses this as belief "in continually developing a style and climate that liberates the talent and enthusiasm of all our people." This view is echoed by Levi Strauss. Its corporate commitment is to be "a company that all our people are proud of and committed to, where all employees have an opportunity to contribute, learn grow and advance." While at 3M the philosophy is summed up as "if you ain't getting better, you're getting worse."

This type of thinking does not emerge easily or intuitively for most people. Learning is best performed within structured frameworks. Senge calls these structures the mental models that managers shape and refine to break free of the superficial while retaining intuition and creativity. Ken Ohmae[14] describes one aspect of this when he explores the mind of the strategist.

Strategists do not reject analysis. Indeed they can hardly do without it. But they use it only to stimulate the creative process, to test the ideas that emerge, to work out their strategic implication, or to ensure successful execution of high potential "wild" ideas that might otherwise never be implemented properly. Great strategies, like great works of art or great scientific discoveries, call for technical mastery in the working out but originate in insights that are beyond the reach of conscious analysis.

This blend of technical mastery of the role, task and underlying competencies and original insights is an increasingly important part of the mental modelling of effective managers in successful organizations. The work and balance involved was well summarized by Edison when he said that all great discoveries were 90% perspiration and 10% inspiration. It is the way the perspiration is organized that makes the difference between the persistently successful and the persistently unsuccessful.

The fundamental task of organizations is to bring together groups of individuals so that their combined efforts can achieve more than their separate efforts. The creation of shared vision translates this fundamental organizational principle into the individual and personal world of learning and thinking. The respondents to the *Management Development to the Millennium* project placed increasing emphasis on this capacity to build shared vision and convert personal learning into organizational learning. Managers have special responsibilities to create a climate in which this occurs because they can persuade others to

> *It is the way the perspiration is organized that makes the difference between the persistently successful and the persistently unsuccessful.*

buy into sharing and mutual support through effective communication, increasing people's sense of worth and ensuring they have empathy with others.

Team learning is an integral feature of the success of Japanese business, and involves the two key practices of dialog and discussion. True dialog breaks down the barriers between participants and focusses attention on their ability to contribution rather than on their formal role. Discussion and its corollary, the ability to produce negotiated outcomes, develop this notion of contribution and partnership and highlight the capacity to listen, hear and respond. Listening is not sufficient if the views and insights of others are not recognized or appreciated. Hearing takes the process further because the ideas of others enter the consciousness of those taking part. The hardest element is response because that might mean conceding a long held view and accepting the ideas of others. Mike Walsh of Union Pacific underlines the confident humility that is an essential corollary of this perspective. In Walsh's view "my biggest challenge is to be worthy of the staff. The staff in this and most other companies are capable of a great deal more responsibility than most managers have a clue."

BOUNDARY DEFINITION

Significant changes in this environment require not only the strategic and operational policies outlined above but a redefinition of external and internal boundaries. The emergence of learning organizations in the private and public sector provides opportunities for intermediaries like universities, government agencies, professional advisors to initiate and shape new, strategic partnerships. A true alliance of interest exists, since these intermediaries can operate at the strategic interface between the partnership groups. Their distinct role and capability provides a platform for building true and open partnership with individual enterprises, their staff or groups of firms. This relationship must move beyond the client – supplier relationship that has dominated so many links in the past.

A learning organization from within the commercial sector will shift its relationship with its partners from an exploitative link to a strategic partnership. Despite the successes of firms like Marks and Spencer and Motorola, few UK or US firms have established the kind of bonding with providers and middlemen that places these links at the center of their corporate strategy. Exchanges of people, ideas, investments or developments are typically limited and local. The fully integrated learning organization remains an aspiration rather than an example. The integration of learning organizations into learning communities is even more rare.

Redefining external boundaries is only one aspect of the process of redefinition. It is equally important to redefine the boundaries between disciplines and activities. The cutting edge of most innovative activity lies either at the boundary of a discipline or at the interface with other disciplines. The ability to work with colleagues from different backgrounds and different expertise is an integral feature of the learning organization. Shifting this focus probably poses the greatest single challenge to contemporary thinking. The primacy of the tightly focussed specialism, profession or position in the hierarchy is reinforced by most of the reward and control systems in modern organizations. Jack Welch, President of GE, talks of challenging this position by "cutting back on useless titles ... rewarding people based on what they do ... rather than what they control." Challenging this requires a major shift in the organization and its control systems.

Hope springs eternal

The changing environment, described above, creates massive opportunities for organizations and major new demands on managers. Creating a new partnership between learning and application will enhance many kinds of organizations, especially those willing to transform their thinking and their mindsets. The opportunities created by the new industrial revolution must be grasped strategically and developmentally. Strategically because they are part of a shift in the role and focus of the enterprise; developmentally because they build on existing competences and capabilities of the firm to create, in Hamel's term, "competences for the future."

> The opportunities created by the new industrial revolution must be grasped strategically and developmentally.

Imposition of arbitrary solutions will reduce the potential gains, since progress requires a realization of the importance of change as something to be accepted not opposed. It will not be comfortable, but it is necessary, if the long-term gains for the community, individuals and enterprises are to emerge. Effective change is based on interaction as well as action. Lord Sheppard, the architect of Grand Met's transformation from a minor hotel group to a major food corporation, says "We can be fast because we have very short lines of communication; there is a two way dialogue with almost daily exchanges to hone the process." This is reminiscent of the approach of top sports teams and great scientific collaborations.

This approach is especially important in areas like innovation and technology transfer. Effective technology transfer occurs where the nature of the organization is understood, the links are developed over time and true partnerships created. The asset base exists albeit in a more limited form than policy makers believe. The task is to build learning organizations and communities that allow the assets to be realized while re-investments are made to cope with yet more change and development; it can only be achieved if this kind of thinking is understood, accepted and internalized by those individuals who shape these responses together with managers and their colleagues inside and outside the enterprise. New managers are needed for the new environment: they changed during the industrial revolutions of the late 18th and late 19th centuries and will change once again during the revolution of the late 20th century.

◆

We are reaching the point where
the nature of management is
changing to reflect a
fundamental shift in the nature of
the modern economy.

◆

Chapter 14

◆

MANAGERS AS YOU HAVE NEVER KNOWN THEM

MYTHS AND EXPECTATIONS

There is a comfortable myth among managers and writers about management that the world can change but management will remain the same. The central definitions and preoccupations of management have hardly changed since they were first articulated at the turn of this century. Compare the writings of Samuel Smiles, Frederick Taylor, C. Northcote Parkinson and Henry Fayol with current writers like John Harvey-Jones, Tom Peters, Peter Drucker and Kenneth Blanchard. The earlier works may be more florid and the more recent more verbose, but the similarities seem far greater than the differences.

In a sense this degree of consistency is reassuring. Over 100 years ago Douglas McCallum was advising managers not to "embarrass principal officers, nor lessen their influence with their subordinates." In the 1980s, Mark McCormack could still advise people not to "go one by one with the boss" because even "if you win the battle you're going to lose the war. And the more right you are, the more damage it will probably do in the long run." The degree of consistency is reassuring – up to a point. The same economic paradigm ought to produce broadly similar principles for effective management. Some changes are evident lately. There is more emphasis on innovation, globalization and attention to the core competences of the organizations; the need to review assumptions and learning to learn has won greater prominence; the extent of change has grown as the pace of change has increased.

We are reaching the point where the nature of management is changing to reflect a fundamental shift in the nature of the modern economy. Donald McCallum and Mark McCormack might agree that if you lessen the influence of bosses over their subordinates, you and the company will lose out in the long run, but it is not clear that this deferential, hierarchical thinking meets today's needs. It does not seem to fit into the ideas of Jack Welch at General Electric, Richard Branson at Virgin or Eiji Toyoda at Toyota where performance is more important than deference. The strategies of many of the most successful corporations of today seem to center on breaking down barriers between managers and their

> *Collaboration is more important than control.*

colleagues. They are designed to enable power to reside where it has most operational value rather than where it supports the status quo. Collaboration is more important than control.

These internal changes reflect wider external changes in the economic and social environment. The technologies, markets, social relations and cultural assumptions that underpin management behavior are altering rapidly. Managers and management practice are not immune from these shifts. The image, role, preoccupations and practices of managers are experiencing a revolution that mirrors the economic revolution in the wider environment. A casual examination of the media image of the manager of just a few years ago highlights the difference. Jack Lemmon in the film *The Apartment* pursues his buttoned up road from the 17th to the 29th floor (key to the executive toilet included) by pandering to the needs of his bosses. In the advertising industry of the 1960s and 1970s, Dick York in the TV series

Bewitched could portray a deferential, suited executive. Today's images emphasize enterprise not deference and are probably ahead of reality in symbolizing a heterogeneous workplace with concerns beyond the bottom line.

Traditional, deferential managers find it hard to cope with "casual dress" Fridays, delayering or reengineering. The rules that surround their way of managing have changed, and according to Robin Linnecar of KPMG "the tools for managing in this age don't exist." In part, the difficulties reflect conscious decisions by organizations to change structures without thinking through the management implications. Organizational control structures based on incremental promotion up an elaborate hierarchy cannot work when the hierarchy is being whittled away. Loyalty based controls soon wither in the face of large scale redundancies. Remuneration based controls have always been vulnerable to competitive deals that win the most talented away. Power and authority based controls are less effective when power and authority are replaced by consensus and support.

Changes in the rules coincide with shifts in the nature of the managerial labor pool. Increased diversity in the managerial labor pool leads to different assumptions and ambitions and there is just as much diversity among female managers as among male. Within the female managerial laborforce there is, however, evidence of greater emphasis on consensus based management, wider social networking, more tolerance of difference, greater willingness to adopt radical solutions and less acceptance of confrontational or authoritarian management styles. In the future it will be easier to imagine an organization with a wholly female management group than a totally male management group.

> *Organizational control structures based on incremental promotion up an elaborate hierarchy cannot work when the hierarchy is being whittled away.*

Technological and market changes provoke and demand these and other changes. For the last century technical competence among managers was largely confined to their functional specialism, marketing, finance, human resources, operations and so on. Managers are increasingly expected to wed this competence to an understanding of other functions. Ernest Saunders of Guinness is probably the last business leader who could seriously argue that, because he had a marketing background, he did not understand the finances of the Guinness Group while he was Chief Executive. Information technology is so pervasive that managers without any real understanding of how to use computers and get the best from them are at a growing disadvantage. The move towards devolved authority and small operating units means that general management skills are an increasingly important part of the portfolio of even the most specialist manager. These public changes are the most obvious ones in the nature of management. Deeper modifications in the ways managers do their work and play their part in organizational development are occurring at the same time.

THE DISAPPEARING MANAGER

In the mid 1980s a series of research studies in the UK produced estimates of the likely size of the managerial labor pool in the year 2000. It was projected that organizations would require almost 3 million managers, only a slight increase, to meet their needs. This excluded small firms (those with fewer than 100 employees) and the self employed. Ten years later a comparable study by the UK's Institute of Managers, using the same dataset, estimated that fewer than 2 million managers would be needed to meet the same set of needs. Some more recent estimates suggest that even this figure is generous.

Evidence of sharp contractions in the size of the managerial labor pool is emerging from across the developed world. Large corporations, public agencies and voluntary bodies are taking out layers in the management hierarchies, extending the span of control of existing managers and reducing the numbers of specialists. The century long expansion of the managerial labor pool seems to have halted. Some voices are questioning the extent of the contraction. There is evidence that many managers from the private sector are relocating to the public and voluntary sector, thereby adding a stronger management dimension to their work, or displacing administrators. This is likely to be a temporary phenomenon as the technical changes described earlier are unlikely to leave the public and voluntary sector "over managed" for long.

The sharp contraction in the managerial labor pool has hit some groups within management harder than others. The hardest hit are older, male, middle managers with limited "private" expertise. The least affected are younger managers with significant private expertise. Private expertise is a specialist skill or competence that is vested in the personal rather than the firm. Those managers with the greatest entrepreneurial skills or strongest links with markets or operations have survived longer than those without these skills or networks. The success of the former managers goes deeper than their ability to act independently or work with customers. They often have the capacity to adjust to a fundamental shift in the nature of management.

MINDSETS FOR THE MILLENNIUM

Functional separated and functionally specialized managers will struggle to compete in the emerging environment and in the most effective organizations. A different mindset is required which reflects the needs of organizations.

Some features of this mindset are emerging, notably the ways managers will learn to deal with the different challenges of their internal and external environment. The ability to handle and manage change is especially important. Handling change is made harder for managers by a fundamental change in the relationship between control and ambiguity in their work (see Figure 14.1).

Figure 14.1

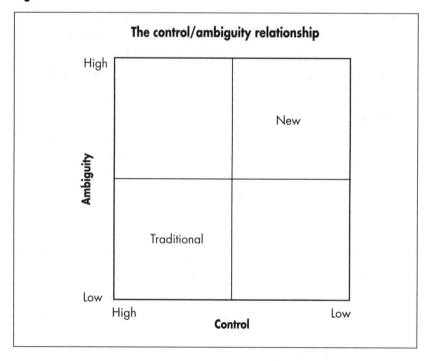

The control/ambiguity relationship

Traditional management operates in an environment of low ambiguity and high control: the low ambiguity reflects the clarity that exists about the responsibilities of managers. Their position in the firm is well understood. They work in a relatively well understood structure. Managers have considerable control over their subordinates and the work undertaken. It is often assumed that senior management will avoid any actions that undermine the authority of middle management. People understand that even if they win the "battle" they will lose the "war."

This situation has been transformed over recent years. The control functions of managers have declined in importance.

Often this results from a deliberate attempt to liberate the potential of all members of the workforce. The manager's control is often a barrier to creativity and open communication. Some of the most successful business leaders pride themselves on the ability to break down traditional lines of authority. They refuse to be restricted by bureaucracy and their position. Managers are expected to deliver results without recourse to power or the exercise of management control. This leads to increased ambiguity about the manager's role and work. Managing ambiguity is a prime management task.

Employability

This repositioning of the control/ambiguity relationship requires a managerial mindset which links skills in empowerment with a proactive approach to business development. Successful managers have developed strategies to encourage people to internalize

> *Managing ambiguity is a prime management task.*

control instead of responding to external controls. Empowerment strategies are part of this: they develop the capacity of people to act for themselves, while framing communication policies that get the best from everyone. Lack of direct control and high levels of ambiguity enable managers to build more creative environments with the associated risks. Resilience and flexibility are the hallmarks of the effective manager in this environment as they take an increasingly proactive approach to handling organizational issues.

The development role of managers shifts significantly in the new environment. Until recently, the main role of the line manager was to enable people to undertake skill or role development and free their subordinates to take relevant opportunities. This has shifted to a more proactive role in the most successful businesses. Enabling is replaced by encouraging as firms help people to achieve their full potential (see Figure 14.2). In firms like Ford this extends beyond work related activities to extensive personal development. In effect they are preparing themselves and others for the new environment in which personal development and competence development go together. These firms accept that they may not be able to guarantee lifetime employment but they can provide lifetime employability.

The task of managers is not merely to free their subordinates but to act as mentors before, during and after their training or development. This brings additional value to work related training as these trainees are helped to apply the results of their work. Its long-term value lies in shifting the focus of training from external inputs to internal outputs. It is part of the shift towards self managed learning that is another feature of learning organizations. The learner is the central character in any move towards self managed learning. He or she takes personal responsibility

Figure 14.2

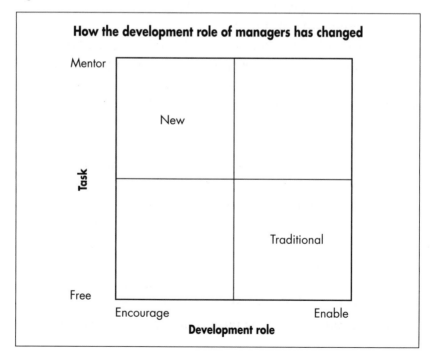

for their development. Some firms are looking to the employees to set up learning contracts with their line managers.

Managers who wish to maximize their contribution to this process require a combination of organizational sensitivity and whole environment thinking. Organizational sensitivity requires an understanding of the formal and informal systems and forces that shape the enter-prise and the ways people work within it. An appreciation of the culture and the core compe-tences of the venture and the degree of flex that can be achieved within the existing structure are equally important. Managers wishing to get the most from their colleagues and

> *Organizational sensitivity requires an understanding of the formal and informal systems and forces that shape the enterprise and the ways people work within it.*

Figure 14.3

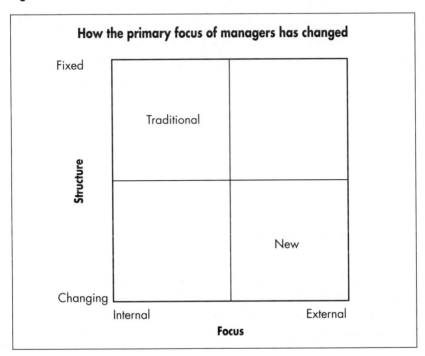

How the primary focus of managers has changed

- Structure: Fixed / Changing
- Traditional (top-left), New (bottom-right)
- Focus: Internal / External

subordinates through coaching and mentoring need access to skills which underpin these roles in any organization, plus their distinctive features within a specific context.

Trust is an essential feature of coaching and mentoring. The best coaches understand the capabilities of their colleagues and the ways to get the best from others at key moments. This cannot be achieved overnight as it requires close observation of successes and failures and a willingness to be tested to the limit. A high level of rapport is important so that trust is built on real understanding not false assumptions. Sports literature indicates that trust, respect and shared objectives are more important that affection or ability. Great coaches get mediocre talents to out-perform greater talents when it matters. Mentoring shows many similar features but is typically more individual, two directional and open ended. Mentors help their subordinates to find their own way around issues and problems. Mentors probe and prompt to help them perform, rather than indicate or pro-vide solutions. This feature of mentoring is especially important in dealing with high levels of ambiguity.

The shift in the role of managers is part of a wider change in the primary focus of their work (see Figure 14.3). Traditionally, many managers could focus their attention mainly on the rela-tively stable internal workings of the organization. Others were responsible for interacting with, interpreting and responding to the external environment. This was as true for customer rela-tions as for liaison with the local community. Now there is a wider appreciation of the more diverse roles managers play in a fluid environment. The challenge of meeting customer needs cannot be restricted to those with a specific sales or marketing role. Everyone in the enterprise is expected to focus their atten-tion on market needs. There is growing recognition of the value of employee volunteering and other tasks in the wider commu-nity. Shareholders and other stakeholders impose increasingly well articulated demands on all members of the enterprise.

Managers require a mindset able to accommodate these major shifts. Successful managers have learned to push the limits of these agendas by extending their work beyond the formal requirements imposed by their job or task description to a much wider contribution. Committed managers shape and redefine their role to meet the needs of the market, the enterprise and their colleagues. High levels of energy and a clear action orientation symbolize the new managerial labor force. Their commitment partly explains their greater willingness to take risks to push the organization forward.

MANAGERS, ENTREPRENEURS AND LEADERS

Management literature abounds in attempts to distinguish between managers, entrepreneurs and leaders. These distinctions were an important feature of the professionalization and codification of management work but have limited value during the type of economic and environmental change taking place today. Turbulence calls for managers who can identify opportunities inside and outside the organizations. The same managers are expected to grasp these opportunities and use them to build up the capabilities of and returns to the business. Efforts to break organizations down into smaller operating units reinforce the importance of the entrepreneurial manager. The same pressures call for a stronger leadership dimension to management. Effective leaders transform the capabilities of those with whom they work; they bring an additional dimension which moves the organization beyond itself.

Turbulence calls for managers who can identify opportunities inside and outside the organizations. The same managers are expected to grasp these opportunities and use them to build up the capabilities of and returns to the business.

Breaking down the barriers between the roles of manager,

entrepreneur and leader can involve a major culture shift in many organizations. There is widespread suspicion of entrepreneurs because they question assumptions, challenge autonomy and seek freedom of action. Each of these characteristics creates problems for large, well established bureaucracies with their embedded systems and established authority structures. Their strength and persistence for most of their history has relied on the willingness of those involved in the enterprise to accept certain shared assumptions that might extend from beliefs about the ways people organize themselves to the nature of the marketplace.

> *Effective leaders transform the capabilities of those with whom they work; they bring an additional dimension which moves the organization beyond itself.*

The ability to challenge these assumptions is an essential feature of the organization's response to new conditions. The struggle to incorporate ideas of personal enterprise into the bureaucratic mindset has led to notions like intrapreneuring, new enterprise management and corporate venturing. They encapsulate the need of ambitious organizations to merge the notions of management – with its emphasis on working with others – with the creativity, risk taking and sense of personal responsibility which are integral to entrepreneurship. The leadership role adds a further dimension to the new management paradigm: it highlights the wider responsibilities of managers to their colleagues, those with stakes in the firm and the wider community.

Reinventing management

The reinvention of management is the first stage in the move to the new management paradigm. The pressure for reinvention not only reflects corporate imperatives, it is a key factor in business response to wider concerns expressed about the kind of society in which business thrives, and the role of business in society. Innovation, creativity, wealth creation, the effective use of resources and the ability to generate returns to investors are established business imperatives. But they were framed in a context in which natural resources seemed relatively unlimited and scarcity was the dominant economic preoccupation. People were confident of their ability to predict the consequences of their actions. Few of these assumptions are sustainable today.

Every serious business leader is aware of the limits to the natural resources available to us. Coal, the energy source of the first industrial revolution, may exist in abundance but the most optimistic projections of oil reserves forecast serious shortages if present consumption patterns persist. The recent sharp rises in raw materials prices as Western economies pick up after the recession of the early 1990s highlight the sensitivity link between raw materials and economic performance. Crises in the beef, agricultural foodstuffs, metals and pharmaceutical industries are closely associated with attempts to squeeze more output from finite resources.

There is evidence that a mixture of science and economic development can eliminate some of the worst features of industrialization. It is equally clear that novel science, pressure for innovation and shorter lead times take firms into new territory where the long-term outcomes are unclear or unknown. The thalidomide crisis of the late 1970s is no longer a one-off event. The unforeseen and negative medium to long-

Crises in the beef, agricultural foodstuffs, metals and pharmaceutical industries are closely associated with attempts to squeeze more output from finite resources.

term consequences of new food products for cattle in Britain, hormone treatments for livestock in the USA, chemical treatment plants in Japan and many other developments pose major dilemmas for responsible managers introducing new technologies and products and processes without any clear picture of their long-term environmental impact. Old style confidence in likely outcomes is not sustainable.

The reinvention of management is a business and social imperative. The business case rests on the massive changes in the commercial world. These cannot be separated from wider issues of the nature and pattern of social, environmental and economic development. Some of the most successful of today's companies deliberately respond to these concerns and this response is not confined to firms like Body Shop with an overt environmental mission. Shell rethought its approach to the disposal of North Sea Oil installations in the light of environmental concerns. Society's concerns are easily transformed into business concerns: the Exxon Valdez oil disaster eventually cost Exxon over $15Bn. The bulk of these losses were in reduced sales and a drop in Exxon's share price.

Different names, different faces, different genders

Reinvention goes beyond the way managers perform their work. The composition of the managerial labor pool is affected by concerns about the white, male, Judeo-Christian dominance of management and management thinking in Western industrial society. Barriers to the entry of female managers are slowly being eroded in organizations that recognize the long-term problems these obstructions cause: they cut firms off from a major source of talent which means firms are also missing out on the different perspectives that a nonsexist workplace provides. Less progress has been made in creating opportunities for ethnic minorities and the disadvantaged. A managerial labor pool that fails to reflect the diversity of the environments in which it operates is unlikely to understand those environments. Companies, public agencies and authorities find it easier to understand the needs of the increasingly diverse and articulate markets when they have genuine insight into those needs. The German word *Verstehen* was used by

Max Weber to communicate the kind of intuitive understanding or insight that comes from membership of a group.

The bureaucratization of management, the division of managerial labor, specialization and hyperspecialization do not sit comfortably with these changes. The reintegration of management work so that executives focus on the unity of their work and the wholeness of the environment is an integral part of the reinvention of management. It is a prerequisite for the strategic and operational changes occurring in organizations. Reengineering efforts will be ineffective in organizations where managers cannot look at the total business process and adopt radical, real world solutions. Managers who are locked into their role in the bureaucracy or focus too narrowly on their specialism cannot play their full part in reengineering the business. Similar difficulties exist with efforts to allocate resources around those core capabilities that fit the enterprise for competitive advantage today or in the future.

Functional specialisms or the effort to defend positions inhibit the "whole business view" that is a feature of these efforts. Hamel[15] points out that

Companies, public agencies and authorities find it easier to understand the needs of the increasingly diverse and articulate markets when they have genuine insight into those needs.

The reintegration of management work so that executives focus on the unity of their work and the wholeness of the environment is an integral part of the reinvention of management. It is a prerequisite for the strategic and operational changes occurring in organizations.

given that it may take five, ten, or more years to build world leadership in a core competence area, consistency of effort is the key. Consistency depends first of all on a deep consensus about which

competencies to build and support, and second on the stability of the management teams charged with competence development. ... Without such a consensus, a company may well fragment its competence-building efforts, as various business units pursue their independent competence-building agenda.

Fragmentation of effort, lack of consensus and division are associated with separated management. They provide major barriers to the consensus which is necessary for corporate renewal. The differences in approach are vividly illustrated in three key areas of work:

- quality improvement;
- innovation; and
- service improvement.

Successful quality improvement initiatives rely on total company commitment based on a strong sense of individual ownership. The clearest difference between Japan's Deming based approach to quality and Western approaches lies along the divide between integration and separation. In Japan quality programs are based on an integrated, corporate commitment that contrasts sharply with Western functional systems based on external control and supervision.

> *The least effective programs vest power in a specific area, fail to get cross functional commitment and exclude suppliers and customers.*

Similar divisions occur with innovation. The most effective innovation programs integrate the different activities of the enterprise and draw in buyers and suppliers. The least effective programs vest power in a specific area, fail to get cross functional commitment and exclude suppliers and customers.

The service revolution of the last decade saw similar patterns occurring. Commitment to, say, service guarantees depends on the firm's ability to get the best from their people, marketing and operations in combination, not as separated activities. Christopher Hart highlights this in his descriptions of service breakthroughs.[16]

> **Breakthrough service does not mean you must become a high cost producer. Manpower's procedures are not radically more expensive than its competitors; they're simply better. ... A company that inadequately screens and trains temporary worker recruits, establishes no detailed customer specifications, and fails to check worker performance loses customers.**

HEARTLAND MANAGERS

It is noticeable that much writing about management is dominated by an analysis of the roles of senior and operational management. The role of top managers as providers of vision and direction is well documented. Comparable attention is given to the importance of operations management in delivering policy, but, in contrast, the role of middle managers has received scant regard. In part this reflects the discomfort writers and commentators feel when talking about middle management's role. Often it seems that there is an implicit hostility to the middle management function. Delayering programs are targetted to eliminate tiers of middle managers. The empowerment of operations managers or workers is explicitly directed to reduce the power of middle managers. These approaches often fail to appreciate the massive contribution that middle managers can make in delivering policies, implementing change and improving performance.

Part of the problem lies with the very term "middle manager." It conjures up images of bureaucracy and hierarchy. For some the link between middle aged spread and the growth of corporate fat is easily made. It is more useful to view middle management as "heartland management." Heartland managers are responsible for value delivery and the creation of a culture in which the search for added value is total company commitment. The same managers are vested with the task of building competences and ensuring that the capabilities of the enterprise match the needs of their markets. They face the greatest challenge in resolving the paradoxes created in a turbulent economic environment. Resolving these paradoxes depends on their skills in developing and getting the best from the people in the organizations. Many firms have found that transferring authority for education, training and development to heartland managers improves both the relevance of this work and the effectiveness with which it is applied.

Head office functions are under close scrutiny in many organizations. The people or human resource roles have been transformed as responsibility for people development moves from the center to local management. Central functions operate more as brokers than deliverers. Heartland managers can direct development work more accurately to support change and performance improvement. They largely control the feedback systems which allow local experience to be converted to corporate insight. The effectiveness of an organization's management information and control systems largely turns on the quality and capability of middle management.

> *The effectiveness of an organization's management information and control systems largely turns on the quality and capability of middle management.*

The long-term contribution of heartland management turns on their ability to incorporate their traditional organizing and controlling roles into this "heartland," with its value delivery and development role. It means transferring much of their responsibility for organizing to operations managers. Self control by involved workers is cheaper and more effective than externally imposed control.

Value building and delivery will increase in importance, while sharing the people development work is a priority. The increased importance of information systems and technologies requires middle or heartland managers who are able to interact successfully with technocrats while ensuring that the technology is driven by business goals.

The shift to the manager/leader/entrepreneur is especially noticeable in the work of middle or heartland management. The increased ambiguity and limited control they exercise means that they are obliged to use enterprise and intuition more often than rules and structures. The development of this type of manager requires a greater commitment to sustained on the job training and development with a new focus on networking. These networks provide access to new information sources especially about external performance. The search for benchmarking opportunities is part of a wider search for new criteria against which performance can be measured and enhanced.

Focus

The weakness of many benchmarking approaches lies in the lack of focus and direction in the benchmarking. The proliferation of opportunities during an economic revolution means that those firms that concentrate resources against major opportunities outperform those that squander resources across a number of opportunities. Treacy and Wiersema highlight the importance of focus in the marketing success of firms as diverse as PepsiCo and Harley-Davidson. Focus means that the firm can build up a body of market knowledge far greater than that of its unfocussed rivals. At the same time the focussed company can refine its use of

> *The search for benchmarking opportunities is part of a wider search for new criteria against which performance can be measured and enhanced.*

307

resources to win better quality inputs at lower costs. Focus can enhance the firm's reputation so that it can gain maximum leverage from the resources it employs. The focus of Harley-Davidson means that it has

Focus means that the firm can build up a body of market knowledge far greater than that of its unfocussed rivals.

already received orders for its 100th anniversary edition: the bike will not be available for sale until 2003. Focus for Mars means that it can launch the most successful new range of ice creams in 20 years on to the UK market.

The perceived danger of focus lies in the apparent narrowing of the organization's options. The most common worry is what if the market changes and we are locked in the wrong area? Effectively managed, focus does not need to be restrictive. Marks and Spencer is a highly focussed company, its focus being on quality supplier and customer relations. It means that it seldom enters into short-term, opportunistic purchasing relationships. There is little point in sending the Marks and Spencer clothing buyers details of an overproduction of plain T-shirts. They will not be interested because they seek suppliers who can meet their quality, price and design standards in the long term.

This type of focus relies heavily on managers with in-depth knowledge of the organization and its capabilities. It allows the organization to operate the type of "tight–loose" structure identified by Peters and Waterman[17] as a characteristic of the best firms. The subsequent criticism of their work has not devalued the argument for management structures that are able to tightly define strategy while giving managers loose guidelines so that they can implement policies in the light of their local knowledge. Operational freedom of this kind is hard to execute effectively with narrowly focussed, separated managers but works well with managers who have the breadth of knowledge and experience to fit capabilities to conditions.

ADVENTURERS AND MERCHANTS

The new generations of managers will need to incorporate traditional management skills with the capacity to combine adventure and merchanting. Some are best described as adventure capitalists because they do not rely on convention for their success. They recognize that business and public management during an economic revolution provide opportunities for new adventures in shaping and directing organizations. They do not rely on convention to protect them but challenge convention to create new opportunities. Charles Lazarus of Toys "R" Us broke convention himself when he changed the shape of toy shopping. He encourages his managers to question approaches and seek new ways to sustain the adventure of building business. At Home Depot, Bernard Marcus has followed the same route and Richard Branson of Virgin and Anita Roddick of Body Shop subscribe to a broadly similar liberating or adventure capitalism. At Florida Light and Power the same philosophy is applied to a major utility while Hewlett-Packard continues its decades' long growth based on the same view of the business world.

Adventure capitalists do not rely on conventional thinking or approaches for their growth. They recognize that wealth creation during an economic revolution relies on a new approach to the business rules of engagement. At Sun Microsystems rules are deliberately challenged in its technologies and approach to the market. This is made easier by a powerful and sustained commitment to liberating managers to take the best route forward rather than either the easiest or the best trodden way. Firms like Sun break down barriers between the technological, marketing and people functions in creating a management culture which is willing to continuously recreate itself to match market needs. At Johnson & Johnson the corporate culture was deliberately recreated to espouse this approach. Its recent sales and profit are closely identified with this transformation in its management culture and thinking.

Enabling is a key concern for adventure capitalists. They recognize that their greatest contribution often lies in the four aspects of enabling that most affect business development. The first aspect is the role that leaders can play in enabling others to maximize their contribution to the success of the enterprise. This means that they look for ways to prepare the ground, provide support and make it easier for others to achieve their potential. They "get their jollies," or the greatest satisfaction, from the successes of others. The second element in this enabling approach is a focus on enabling technologies. Most substantial organizational shifts are predicated by shifts in the enabling technologies. It was the advent of Ro-Ro shipping that allowed Japanese car makers to shift their product across the world. Many enabling technologies are closely associated with the third dimension of enabling: the process that makes it easier for customers to reach suppliers.

Market enabling technologies either reduce the cost of search for buyers or the costs of supply for producers. The supermarket or the shopping mall are among the most obvious of these developments. Dramatic shifts and improvements in logistics are making it easier to bundle, unpack and rebundle combinations of goods and services in ways that meet customer needs in innovative ways. The next shift in delayering seems certain to take the process out of the company and into the networks of relationships between customers and suppliers. The fourth aspect of enabling underpins each of the other three. It is the effort to enable all those in the organization to develop their full potential so that they can contribute to the maximum. At Britain's highly successful Unipart business, John Neill has created the Unipart University to extend this mission across the aspirations of the workforce.

Adventure capitalists in large organizations want to transform their businesses from the inside. In growing companies transformation is equally important. They may not want to build the same type of vast organization but they expect to share the sense of vision and reach of large enterprises. They will fill the gaps left by large organizations because they can match the global reach of large organizations while retaining their own attention to detail and flexibility. They expect to lead, wheel and deal alongside their larger rivals. Much of their edge is gained from the seemingly inevitable tendency of large organizations to underestimate their capability: it is hard to imagine a small enterprise that does not owe some of its success to the habit of giant rivals to underestimate them. IBM underestimated the potential of Bill Gates and Microsoft to challenge their power. Lord King once commented about Richard Branson that "if they'd worn suits, I'd never have underestimated them." Charles Schwab's discount brokerage house succeeds because the traditional brokers underestimated the ability of a West Coast discounter with a small technical sales staff to break into their market.

The dominant characteristic of these adventure capitalists is their ambition. They do not search for opportunities to consolidate. They have very high comfort thresholds. The comfort threshold is the level of success or achievement at which you are comfortable. Adventure capitalists never stop trying to grow because they know that when you stop growing you start declining. They strive for exceptional success[18] usually based on winning an implementation edge[19]. The implementation edge comes from devising ways to get ahead through actions that add value. This calls for a mixture of operational intimacy, width of vision and confidence.

THE CURIOUS MANAGER

Operational intimacy describes the new relationships that managers need with their organization, its competences, competitive capabilities and markets. It is built on a constant questioning of these competences and capabilities in order to understand them better and be able to deploy them to greater effect. Taking things for granted is perhaps the most dangerous position in the new environment. Customer intimacy is the corollary of operational intimacy. It describes the close understanding and rapport which suppliers establish with their users.

Width of vision highlights the importance of search and enquiry for management success. Those enterprises that fail to look beyond their own environment for new ideas, insights and lessons are doomed to failure in an increasingly diverse and complex environment. It is no coincidence that the first and second industrial revolutions were shaped by those countries, firms and entrepreneurs that sought the best ideas, regardless of their origins. The curious manager who seeks ideas and lessons on how to manage, how to orga-nize and how to meet customer needs will be the successful manager. Post World War II Japanese and German compa-nies deliberately adopted the best ideas from around the world and linked them to the best of their existing knowl-edge. The Japanese use of Deming's ideas on quality and the German use of the Allied Commission's proposals on trade union reform sharply con-trasted with the complacency of UK corporations. The resulting successes in quality and trades union relations in those two countries sharply contrast with the UK experience.

> *Width of vision highlights the importance of search and enquiry for management success. Those enterprises that fail to look beyond their own environment for new ideas, insights and lessons are doomed to failure in an increasingly diverse and complex environment.*

Confidence is an important feature of managerial success. Basil Liddell Hart, the British military historian, concluded in his analysis of success and failure that "helplessness induces hope-lessness, and history attests that loss of hope and not loss of lives is what decides the issues of war." The same pattern can be seen in business rivalries. Those managers and organizations that see themselves as helpless in the face of internal or external pressure soon lose any faith in their ability to affect events positively. This hopelessness is soon communicated across the enterprise and inhibits innovation, introduces barriers to change and undermines the organization's ability to change. Creating a sense of confidence and self belief is the greatest challenge facing organizations during an industrial revolution.

Those managers and organizations that see themselves as helpless in the face of internal or external pressure soon lose any faith in their ability to affect events positively.

◆

"Any color so long as it's black" was a powerful maxim for the first quarter of the century but it was overwhelmed by variety and diversity.

◆

Chapter 15

◆

FUTURE IMPERFECT

It is always dangerous to try to forecast the outcomes of a revolution. Turbulence, rivalry, innovation and luck can all have a marked effect on the likely results and it is easy to confuse short-term advantage with long-term success. Henry Ford seemed to have set his seal on the last industrial revolution with his determination to maximize output of a standard product. "Any color so long as it's black" was a powerful maxim for the first quarter of this century but it was overwhelmed by variety and diversity. Market segmentation and branding were more important sources of success.

Despite these worries about the dangers of prediction, some themes seem to be emerging from the confusion and debate about the new industrial revolution. The most immediate is the importance of action. The eventual outcome of the revolution will be shaped by managers and leaders who act and experiment. Their successes and failures will shape the pattern of organizational development. The most successful organizations are those that have built into their operations the capacity to act, absorb success (and failure), learn and move on. Charles Wang's "relaxed, kind of drive" describes those organizations

> The eventual outcome of the revolution will be shaped by managers and leaders who act and experiment.

that combine a drive to success with the ability to support the risks and concerns of those units and managers that provide their cutting edge. The blame culture that pervades some organizations is perhaps an equally clear indicator of prospective failure.

BUILDING BLOCKS AND BIOLOGY

The determined effort to move an organization forward and build success requires an understanding of the enterprise's capabilities and competences which are held in turn together by the organization's architecture. A clear understanding of the current and future capabilities of the organization probably calls for an effort to define and understand its genetic code. This genetic code describes the ways the different building blocks that make up the enterprise act together to determine how the whole organization will work. Existing capabilities are part of this genetic code and some of them are clearly vital to the current viability of the business. Potential capabilities are those that can be grafted on (sometimes with negative effects) to match market needs. Some existing capabilities can be changed into endowments which generate returns with relatively little further investment. Other existing capabilities may stand in the way of change.

The ways in which these capabilities combine with competitive competence affect the ways in which the firm meets market needs and copes with rivalry. Those that create a competitive advantage are especially important. Management's task is to understand the

> *This genetic code describes the ways the different building blocks that make up the enterprise act together to determine how the whole organization will work.*

genetic code of the organization and adapt their policies to gain maximum advantage from this code. Just as in biology the genetic code of the enterprise can only be worked out by a mixture of experimentation and close scrutiny. It seems likely that those organizations and managers that will prosper during and after the revolution are those that can encompass experimentation and are willing to review and explore their capabilities in the light of these outcomes.

The genetic code of the organization describes its key characteristics not only in terms of the features that are unique to it but those that it shares with others and those that shape its responses to the external environment. Clues to the fit between environment and performance are especially important as specific enterprises may be particularly well suited to one environment but may fail when transferred to another. James Moore[20] places these issues into a wider ecosystem context and gives important insights into the risks and opportunities from diversification and business development: diversify into an environment which does not match the genetic code of the organization and the costs and risks are high; miss a chance to move into an environment in which the enterprise can prosper and the lost opportunities are equally expensive.

CONSTANT REGENERATION

This process of experimentation and development is an integral feature of the constant regeneration of the enterprise in the face of external challenge. Success is based on an ability to constantly regenerate the organization and follow the routes to wealth and success creation. Five paths to wealth and success have been identified:

- the ability to understand and adapt to the distinctive anthropology of the time;
- the ability to build a vision in tune with this anthropology;
- the creation of visions that enrich others;
- the successful transmission of data and the use of IT; and
- the skill in transforming the organization so it reaches the future ahead of competition.

The distinctive anthropology of the time is made up of the mix of culture, values and attitudes which shape the expectations and aspirations of people. This will determine the incentives that will shape internal performance and the needs that shape market response. The distinctive anthropology of the time is the specific mix of these factors which shape a particular community and its responses. The second element in success, the ability to build a vision that is in tune with this anthropology, involves combining the most valuable visions in terms of the environment with a delivery system. The delivery system is the distinct combination of goods and services that the organization delivers. A competitive advantage is earned when these are delivered in ways that are superior to rivals. The creation of visions that enrich others sharing the vision is the third element in the success. In an information rich environment such as exists today, the successful transmission of data and use of IT provides the fourth success factor. These are hard to separate from the fifth variable, which is having the skills to transform the enterprise so that the organization can get to the future first.

Those organizations and managers that get to the future first have some common features: they do not rely on convention. They see that conventional thinking is centered on the past and usually reflects the capabilities of currently dominant organizations. There is evidence that high growth organizations keep their eyes on enabling technologies. They recognize the importance of enabling technologies in creating opportunities to extensive business development. A global perspective is increasingly important as the cost of access to markets drops and information becomes widely available.

The most successful concerns wed an entrepreneurial approach to the ability to spot large gaps in business and deploy the resources to exploit these opportunities. Incremental developments have less value in revolutionary change. The fluidity of the environment places a premium on the ability of managers and leaders to lead, wheel and deal and, in the process, redefine the environment to maximize their opportunities. The sharp increase in competitiveness at times of rapid change calls for an increase in competitive drive across the enterprise. The central irony of this type of change lies in the need to innovate and change with little knowledge of likely outcomes. The ultimate paradox is that we must act now but we do not know the result of our actions.

THE ROLE OF TRUST

In these circumstances trust plays an important part in business success. Trust based organizations are more able to introduce change, win more cooperation from employees and are more likely to meet customer needs. Change is easier to introduce because people recognize the efforts of business leaders to minimize any negative effects from change and only introduce those changes which add value to the organization. People cooperate because they endorse

The fluidity of the environment places a premium on the ability of managers and leaders to lead, wheel and deal and in the process redefine the environment to maximize their opportunities.

the policies and values of those managing the venture. Respect for employees is the best way to encourage them to respect and support customers. You can hardly expect your employees to delight your customers if you do not delight them.

Alliance or partnership based organizations rely heavily on trust. Strategic alliances are playing an increasingly important part in the long-term developments of organizations in the public and private sectors. Managers across these organizations will play a vital part in framing these alliances and delivering their negotiated outcomes. Trust based relations inside and outside the business are important in giving individuals the confidence to frame these alliances and ensuring that the partnerships develop within a healthy overall framework.

The building blocks of trust are common to both individual and organizational trust. The four key features are:

- recognition of the legitimacy of the aspirations of all parties;
- shared language and assumptions;
- openness and candor;
- negotiated outcomes.

Those enterprises that fail to develop internal and external trust will play an increasingly high price as change and diversity increase during the new industrial revolution. Low trust organizations will face very high costs in managing the high talent, knowledge worker or high freedom enterprises that seem set to dominate the new economic environment.

An ethical edge will be an important aspect of the new trust businesses. There is already evidence that social esteem and the perceived ethical stance of organizations affects their recruitment, marketing and financing. Significant numbers of talented workers will choose to work for organizations which take an affirmative approach to ethics, environmental and social responsibility. This is part of the process of reintegrating management work. The bureaucratization of management with its associated division of tasks and roles created an environment in which ethical neutrality could be assumed. Events of the last few years have destroyed the limited legitimacy that existed for this position. The unified approach to management contains an assumption that the

The bureaucratization of management with its associated division of tasks and roles created an environment in which ethical neutrality could be assumed. Events of the last few years have destroyed the limited legitimacy that existed for this position.

"whole manager" will take over the whole of their roles and responsibilities.

Management during and beyond the revolution will retain key elements of older systems of management and yet it is inevitable that fundamental changes will occur. Some features of this change can already be identified. These include the ability to manage paradox, the capability to absorb change and a willingness to seek to understand the fit between the organization and its environment. The managerial labor pool of successful communities and enterprises will adapt to reflect the environment in which they operate. This will be diverse, challenging and complex.

The managerial labor force in Western industrial societies will need to break free from its dominance by white male assumptions and ways of working. Increasing diversity will provide a platform for organizations to face up to the challenges of new rivals, new ideas and new conditions. It is very hard for those communities locked into established

> The managerial labor pool of successful communities and enterprises will adapt to reflect the environment in which they operate.

patterns of success to sustain their success. The UK conspicuously failed to sustain its competitive edge from the first industrial revolution to the second and there is evidence that the USA faces the same difficulties today. There is both hope and threat for all. Those organizations and societies that prospered most were not those that entered the revolution with the greatest assets. The greatest successes were those that adapted and responded most effectively to the new environment, regardless of their previous endowments.

NOTES

◆

Preface

[1] Johnson, H.T. (1992) *Relevance regained: from top-down control to bottom-up empowerment*. New York: The Free Press.

[2] Ford, H., with Samuel Crowther (1926) *Today and tomorrow*. New York: Doubleday.

[3] Ford, H. *ibid*.

[4] Goss, T., Pascale, R. and Athos, A. (1993) "The Reinvention Roller Coaster: Risking the Present for a Powerful Future," *Harvard Business Review*, November – December.

[5] Iansiti, M. (1993) "Real World R&D: Jumping the Product Generation Gap," *Harvard Business Review*, May – June.

[6] Drucker, P. (1984) *Towards the new economics*. London: Heinmann.

[7] Ormerod, P. (1994) *The death of economics*. London: Faber & Faber.

[8] Locke, R. (1996) *The collapse of the American management mystique*. Oxford: Oxford University Press.

[9] Fukuyama, F. (1995) *Trust*. New York: The Free Press.

[10] Sampson, A. (1995) *Company Man*. London: HarperCollins.

Part I: DIFFERENT DAYS, DIFFERENT WAYS
1 The Third Industrial Revolution

[11] Schama, S. (1989) *Citizens*. New York: Alfred A. Knopf, Inc.

[12] Burrough, B. and Helyar, J. (1990) *Barbarians at the gate*. London: Arrow.

[13] Scully, J. (1987). *Odyssey: From Pepsi to Apple*. New York: Harper Collins.

[14] Sampson, A. (1995) *Company man*. London: Harper Collins.

[15] Locke, R. (1996) *The collapse of the American management mystique*. Oxford: Oxford University Press.

[16] Litterer, J. A. (1961) "Systematic Management: The Search for Order and Integration", *Business History Review*, Spring.

[17] Simon, H. (1996) *Hidden champions*. Boston, Mass.: Harvard Business School Press.

[18] Kuhn, T. S. (1970) *The structure of scientific revolutions*. Chicago: University of Chicago Press.

[19] Gill, J. and Whittle, S. (1993) "Management by Panacea: Accounting for Transience," *Journal of Management Science*, 30 no.2, March.

[20] Chandler, A. A. (1977) *The Visible Hand: The Managerial Revolution in American Business*. Cambridge, Mass.: Harvard University Press.

21 Abegglen, J. C. and Stalk, G. (1985) *Kaisha: the Japanese corporation*. New York: Basic Books.

22 Locke, R. *ibid.*

23 Quoted in Simon, H. (1996) *Hidden champions*. Boston, Mass.: Harvard Business School Press.

24 McCormack, M. (1991) *The 110% solution*. New York: Villard Books.

25 Blanchard, K. and Johnson, S. (1982) *The one minute manager*. New York: HarperCollins.

26 Byham, W. C. and Cox, J. (1989) *Zapp!* London: Century Hutchinson.

27 Peters, T. (1987) *Thriving on chaos*. New York: Alfred A. Knopf, Inc.

28 Pirsig, R. M. (1981) *Zen and the art of motorcycle maintenance*. New York: William Morrow & Co., Inc.

29 McCormack, M. (1984) *What they don't teach you at Harvard Business School*. New York: Bookwise Inc.

30 Parkinson, C. Northcote (1957) *Parkinson's Law*. London: Penguin.

31 Fishman, C. (1996) "Whole Foods Teams," *Fast Company*, April–May.

2 Reformers and Revolutionaries

32 Hamel, G. and Prahalad, C. K. (1994) *Competing for the Future*. Boston, Mass.: Harvard Business School Press p. 5.

33 *Fortune*, 27 June, 1994, p. 18ff.

34 Andrews, K. R. "The Concept of Corporate Strategy" in Mintzberg, H., Quinn, J. and Ghoshal, S. (eds) (1995) *The strategy process*. New York: Prentice-Hall.

35 Ray, M. and Rinzler, A. (1993) *The new paradigm for business*. Los Angeles: Pedigree Books.

36 Smith, R. E. (1983) *Japanese society: tradition, self and the social order*. Cambridge: Cambridge University Press.

37 Bartlett, C. and Ghoshal, S. (1995) "Changing the Role of Top Management: Beyond Systems to People," *Harvard Business Review*, May–June.

38 Porter, M. (1980) *Competitive strategy*. New York: The Free Press.

39 Peters, T. (1987) *Thriving on chaos*. New York: Alfred A. Knopf, Inc.

3 Structures and Strategies for Survival and Prosperity

40 Gordon, D. M. "Chickens Home to Roost: From Prosperity to Stagnation in the Postwar US Economy" in Bernstein S. and Adler K.(eds) (1994) *Understanding American economic decline*. Cambridge, Cambridge University Press.

41 Mant, A, (1977) *The rise and fall of the British manager*. London: Macmillan.

42 Bartlett, C. and Ghoshal, S. (1995) "Changing the Role of Top Management: Beyond Systems to People," *Harvard Business Review*, May–June.

43 Bartlett, C. *ibid.*

44 Hammer, M. and Champy, J. (1993) *Reengineering the corporation*. New York: HarperCollins.

45 Sloan, A. P., jnr (1963) *My years with General Motors*. New York: Doubleday.

46 Hakim, C. (1979) "Occupational Segregation," Department of Employment, Research Paper no. 9, London.

47 Carter, S. and Cannon, T. (1992) *Women as entrepreneurs*. London: Academic Press.

48 Economist Intelligence Unit (1994) *The successful corporation of the year 2000*. London: Economist Publications.

49 Hammer, M. and Champy, J. (1993) *Reengineering the corporation*. New York: HarperCollins.

50 Hamel G. and Prahalad, C. K. (1994) *Competing for the Future*. Boston, Mass.: Harvard Business School Press p. 22.

51 Kanter, R. M. (1988) *The change masters*. London: Routledge.

52 Webber, A. M. (1995) "What's so New about the New Economy?," *Harvard Business Review*, January–February.

53 Treacy, M. and Wiersema, F. (1993) "Customer Intimacy and Other Value Disciplines," *Harvard Business Review*, January–February.

4 To Know is to Succeed

54 Mills, D. and Friesen, G. B. "Empowerment" in Crainer, S. (ed.) (1995) *The Financial Times handbook of management*. London: Pitman.

55 Zuboff, S. (1988) *The age of the smart machine*. New York: Basic Books.

56 Handy, C. (1995) *The Empty Raincoat*. London: Arrow Books.

57 Womack, J. P., Jones, D. T. and Roos, D. (1990) *The machine that changed the world*. New York: Rawson Associates.

58 Womack, J. P. *et al. ibid.*

59 Kilduff, M. (1993) "Deconstructing Organisations," *Academy of Management Review*. 18, no.1, January.

60 Pettigrew, A. and Whipp, R. (1993) *Managing change for competitive success*. Oxford: Blackwell.

61 Machiavelli, N. *The Prince.*

62 *Fortune*, 7 May, 1993, p. 30ff.

63 Kagona, T. *et al.* "Mechanistic vs Organic Management Systems: A Comparative Study of Adaptive Patterns of US and Japanese Firms" in Locke, R. (1996) *The collapse of the American management mystique*. Oxford: Oxford University Press.

64 Reich, R. B. (1994) *The work of nations: preparing ourselves for 21st century capitalism*. New York: Doubleday.

65 *Fortune*, 20 February, 1995, p. 32.

66 *Fortune*, 28 November, 1994, p. 22.

67 Webber, A. M. (1993) "What's so New about the New Economy?," *Harvard Business Review*, January–February, p. 24ff.

[68] Leontief, W. (1971) "Theoretical Assumptions and Unobserved Facts," *American Economic Review* LXI, p. 1ff.

[69] Sargent, T. and Wallace, N. (1975) "Rational Expectations, The Optimal Monetary Instrument and the Optimal Money Supply Rule," *Journal of Political Economy*, April.

[70] Sargent, T. (1987) "Rational Expectations" in *The new Palgrave dictionary of economics*, London: Macmillan.

[71] Schwab, K. and Smadja, C. (1994) "Power and Policy: The New World Economic Order," *Harvard Business Review*, November–December.

[72] Bower, J. L. (1995) "Disruptive Technologies: Catching the Wave," *Harvard Business Review*, January–February.

[73] Drucker, P. (1994) *Towards the new economics*. London: Heinemann.

[74] Fukuyama, F. (1995) *Trust*. New York: The Free Press.

[75] Drucker, P. (1994) *Towards the new economics*. London: Heinemann.

5 Learning the Lessons

[76] Chandler, Alfred D., jnr (1990) *Scale and scope: the dynamics of industrial capitalism*. Cambridge, Mass.: Harvard University Press.

[77] Taylor, F. W. (1911) *Scientific management*. New York: Harper.

[78] *Fortune*, 29 May, 1995, p. 71.

[79] White, R., Hodgson, P. and Crainer, S. (1996) *The future of leadership*. London: Pitman.

[80] Zuboff, S. (1988) *The age of the smart machine*. New York: Basic Books.

[81] *Fortune*, 8 March, 1993, p. 53.

[82] Miller, D. (1994) "What Happens After Success: The Perils of Excellence," *Journal of Management Science*, May.

[83] Hammer, M. & Champy, J. (1993) *Reengineering the Corporation*. New York: HarperCollins.

[84] *Fortune*, 5 September, 1994, p. 58.

[85] Kay, J. (1993) *Foundations of Corporate Success*, p.vi. Oxford: Oxford University Press.

Part II: ENTERING THE PARADOX

[1] Fukuyama, F. (1995) *Trust*. New York: The Free Press.

6 The Nature of Paradox

[2] Hamel, G. and Prahalad, C. K. (1994) *Competing for the Future*. Boston, Mass.: Harvard Business School Press.

[3] Handy, C. (1995) *The empty raincoat*. New York: Arrow Books.

4 Mintzberg, H. (1987) "Crafting Strategy," *Harvard Business Review*, July–August.

5 Hague, Sir Douglas (1991) *Beyond universities*. London: Institute for Economic Affairs.

6 Chamberlin, E. H. (1943) *Theory of monopolistic competition*. Cambridge, Mass.: Harvard University Press.

7 Robinson, E. A. G. (1941) *Monopoly*. London: Nisbet.

8 Stalk, G., jnr and Hout, T. (1990) *Competing against time*. New York: The Free Press.

7 Rewards and Standards

9 Hamel, G. and Prahalad, C. K., (1994) *Competing for the Future*. Boston, Mass.: Harvard Business School Press.

9 Goodbye to All This

10 Zemke, R. (1989) *The service edge*. Minneapolis: New American Books.

11 Hamel, G. and Prahalad, C.K. (1994) *Competing for the Future* Boston, Mass.: Harvard Business School Press.

10 Global Action

12 Ohmae, K. (1995) *The evolving global economy*. Boston, Mass.: Harvard Business School Press.

13 Reich, Robert B. (1990) "Who is Us?," *Harvard Business Review*, January–February.

14 Reich, Robert B. (1991) "Who is Them?," *Harvard Business Review*, March–April.

15 Fukuyama, F. (1995) *Trust*. New York: The Free Press.

16 Peters, T. "The Boundaries of Business: Partners – The Rhetoric and The Reality" in Ohmae, K. (1995) *The evolving global economy*. Boston, Mass.: Harvard Business School Press.

11 Adventures in Wonderland

17 Peters, T. and Waterman, R. (1982) *In search of excellence*. New York: HarperCollins.

18 Treacy, M. and Wiersema, F. (1996) *The Discipline of Market Leaders*. New York: Addison Wesley.

19 Treacy, M. and Wiersema, F. *ibid*.

[20] Prahalad, C. K. and Hamel, G. (1990) "The Core Competence of the Corporation," *Harvard Business Review*, May–June.

[21] Kay, J. (1995) *Foundations of corporate success*. Oxford: Oxford University Press.

[22] Porter, M. (1987) "From Competitive Strategy to Corporate Strategy," *Harvard Business Review*, May – June.

Part III: THE MILLENIUM MANAGER
12 The Changing Face of Organizations

[1] Womack, J.P., Jones, D.T. and Roos, D. (1990) *The machine that changed the world*. New York: Rawson Associates.

[2] Economist Intelligence Unit (1994) *The successful corporation of the year 2000*. London: Economist Publications.

[3] Institute of Management (1994) *Management development to the millennium*. London: Institute of Management.

[4] Hammer, M. and Champy, J. (1993) *Reengineering the corporation*. New York: HarperCollins.

[5] Wallace, J. and Erickson, J. (1992) *Hard drive*. New York: Wiley.

[6] Stalk, G., jnr and Hout, T. (1990) *Competing against time*. New York: The Free Press.

[7] *Fortune*, 12 June, 1995, p. 62.

13 A Knowledge Based Industrial Revolution

[8] *Time*, 1 April, 1996.

[9] Handy, C. (1994) *The empty raincoat*. New York: Random House.

[10] Senge, P. (1990) "The Leader's New Work: Building Learning Organisations," *Sloan Management Review*, 7, Autumn.

[11] Garvin, D. (1993) "Building a Learning Organization," *Harvard Business Review*, July –August.

[12] Senge, P. (1995) *The fifth discipline: the art and practice of the learning organisation*. London: Doubleday.

[13] Senge, P. (1990) "The Leader's New Work: Building Learning Organisations," *Sloan Management Review*, 7, Autumn.

[14] Ohmae, K. (1982) *The mind of the strategist*. New York: McGraw-Hill, Inc.

14 Managers as You Have Never Known Them

[15] Hamel, G. and Prahalad, C.K. (1994) *Competing for the future*. Boston, Mass.: Harvard Business School Press.

[16] Hart, C.W.L. (1988) "The Power of Unconditional Service Guarantees," *Harvard Business Review*, July–August.

[17] Peters, T. and Waterman, R. (1982) *In search of excellence.* New York: HarperCollins.

[18] Starbuck, W. H. (1993) "Keeping a Butterfly and an Elephant in a House of Cards: The Element of Exceptional Success," *Journal of Managerial Science,* November.

[19] Bergquist, W. (1993) *The postmodern organization: mastering the art of irreversible change.* New York: Jossey-Bass.

15 Future Imperfect

[20] Moore, J.F. (1996) *The death of competition.* New York: HarperBusiness.

INDEX

◆